An
Overgoverned
Society

W. Allen Wallis

The University of Rochester

THE FREE PRESS
A Division of Macmillan Publishing Co., Inc.
NEW YORK

COLLIER MACMILLAN PUBLISHERS
LONDON

The Free Press
A Division of Macmillan Publishing Co., Inc.
866 Third Avenue, New York, N.Y. 10022

Collier Macmillan Canada, Ltd.

Library of Congress Catalog Card Number: 76-14390

Printed in the United States of America

printing number

2   3   4   5   6   7   8   9   10

Library of Congress Cataloging in Publication Data

Wallis, Wilson Allen.
  An overgoverned society.

  Includes index.
  1. United States--Economic policy--Addresses, essays,
lectures. 2. Industry and state--United States--Ad-
dresses, essays, lectures. 3. Price regulation--United
States--Addresses, essays, lectures. 4. Welfare state--
Addresses, essays, lectures. I. Title.
HC106.5.W314   330.9'73'0925   76-14390
ISBN 0-02-933710-0

Copyright Acknowledgments

Dunlop, Prentice–Hall, 1962. [This book is out of print. All rights are held by the American Assembly, Columbia University.] (See pp. 197–208.)

"Neomercantilism and the Unmet Social Need-ers" appeared in The New Argument in Economics: The Private vs. the Public Sector, edited by Helmut Schoeck and James W. Wiggins, Van Nostrand. Reprinted courtesy of The Institute for Humane Studies, Inc., Menlo Park, California. (See pp. 233–241.)

"Political Entrepreneurship and the Welfare Explosion" appeared as "Causes of the Welfare Explosion" in Welfare Programs: An Economic Appraisal, by James Tobin and W. Allen Wallis. Reprinted with permission of The American Enterprise Institute for Public Policy Research. (See pp. 242–258.)

"Demagogues and Loopholes," which appeared as "Demagoguery Clouds Tax Debate," reprinted courtesy of The Rochester Democrat and Chronicle. (See pp. 262–264.)

Contents

Preface *ix*

I POLICY *1*

   1. FDR as a Prophet *3* / 2. The Faltering Economy *11*
   3. What Can We Do About It? *25* / 4. The Rule of Law *32*
   5. The Open Society *35* / 6. Abolish the Draft *43* / 7. The Rise
   and Fall of the Price of Steel *52* / 8. Ends and Means at
   Watergate *60* / 9. Power to the People *68* / 10. Doctors
   and Lawyers *71*

II GOALS *75*

   11. What Do We Really Want from Our Economy? *77*
   12. Challenges to the American Economy *83* / 13. Business and
   Government *87* / 14. Economics of Ignorance, and Vice Versa *94*

III PRICES *105*

   15. The Price System *107* / 16. Wages, Productivity, and Prices *111*
   17. Price Stability *120* / 18. Price Control *127* / 19. How To
   Ration Consumers' Goods and Control Their Prices *131*
   20. Guidelines *145* / 21. The Nixon Economic Decrees *163*
   22. Foul-up by Consensus *172*

IV GROWTH *173*

   23. Economic Growth *175* / 24. American Economic Power *191*
   25. Automation and Unemployment *197* / 26. Economic Statistics
   and Economic Policy *209* / 27. Taxes *218* / 28. Fiscal Policy *224*

V WELFARE *231*

   29. Neomercantilism and the Unmet Social Need-ers *233*
   30. Political Entrepreneurship and the Welfare Explosion *242*
   31. Social Security *259* / 32. Demagogues and Loopholes *262*
   33. The Pace of Change *265* / 34. Modern Communication *267*

Notes *269*
Index *277*

For more than two generations an increasingly coercive organization of society has coincided with an increasing disorder. It is time to inquire why, with so much more authority, there is so much less stability. . . .

Why should it be that, in a time when men are making the prodigious claim that they can plan and direct society, they are so profoundly impressed with the unmanageability of human affairs? . . .

The attempt to regulate deliberately the transactions of a people multiplies the number of separate, self-conscious appetites and resistances. To establish order among these highly energized fragments, which are like atoms set in violent motion by being heated, a still more elaborate organization is required—but this more elaborate organization can be operated only if there is more intelligence, more insight, more discipline, more disinterestedness, than exists in any ordinary company of men. This is the sickness of an overgoverned society, and at this point the people must seek relief through greater freedom if they are not to suffer greater disasters. . . .

The predominant teachings of this age are that there are no limits to man's capacity to govern others and that, therefore, no limitations ought to be imposed upon government. The older faith, born of long ages of suffering under man's dominion over man, was that the exercise of unlimited power by men with limited minds and self-regarding prejudices is soon oppressive, reactionary, and corrupt. The older faith taught that the very condition of progress was the limitation of power to the capacity and the virtue of rulers.

For the time being this tested wisdom is submerged under a world-wide movement which has at every vital point the support of vested interests and the afflatus of popular hopes. . . .

The fact that the whole generation is acting on these hopes does not mean that the liberal philosophy is dead, as the collectivists and authoritarians assert. On the contrary, it may be that they have taught a heresy and doomed this generation to reaction. So men may have to pass through a terrible ordeal before they find again the central truths they have forgotten. But they will find them again, as they have so often found them again in other ages of reaction, if only the ideas that have misled them are challenged and resisted.

–Walter Lippmann, THE GOOD SOCIETY
(written 1933 to 1937)

Preface

THESE THIRTY-FOUR ESSAYS span the third of a century from 1942 to 1976. A unifying theme may be found in the passages written by Walter Lippmann some forty years ago that are quoted on the facing page. Something of that theme is implicit in the earliest essay, though it was written twenty-five years before I first read Lippmann's *The Good Society*; and the theme is explicit in several of the latest essays. Implicitly and explicitly, it runs through most of the others.

Eleven of these essays (2, 11, 16, 19, 22, 23, 25, 26, 29, 30, 32) were written to be published; of these, five (2, 16, 23, 26, 30) were delivered as speeches in advance of, or instead of, publication. Three (14, 17, 24) are edited transcripts of speeches. The other twenty were written to be delivered as speeches, though several were published later.

The only changes of substance in this collection were made to reduce repetition. Otherwise, except for the deletion or substitution of a word or phrase here or there and the elimination of material that was particular to a place or occasion, the essays have not been altered. I was tempted, of course, to bring facts up to date and to eliminate speculations that now seem impercipient. Had I started down that path, however, the end could only have been complete revision. Since the points that seem of interest and importance do not depend on up-to-the-minute facts and figures, no revising beyond that mentioned has been done.

My outlook, like that of so many of my fellow graduate students at the University of Chicago in the 1930's, was shaped far more by the late Frank Hyneman Knight (1885–1972) than by any other influence or set of influences. This is far from saying, however, that Professor Knight's views were the same as mine—or, for that matter, the same as those of any of his other students. Indeed, as George J. Stigler has said, "Knight's immense influence did not generate imitative discipleships, partly because he applied to himself the suspicion of authority."

–W. Allen Wallis, *The University of Rochester*
March 31, 1976

I

Policy

I

FDR as a Prophet

A PROPHECY BY Franklin Delano Roosevelt struck me forcibly when I heard him make it in January 1936. I have been reminded of it many times during the intervening years as I have observed it coming true to an extent that would astonish even the prophet himself.

FDR's prophecy was this: "... we have built up new instruments of public power ... such power would provide shackles for the liberties of our people."

That prophecy has materialized to a degree that scarcely anyone foresaw in 1936. Notice I do not say that no one foresaw it. One reason the prophecy struck me so forcibly when I first heard it was that it exactly fitted in with what I had learned as a graduate student in economics at the University of Chicago from 1933 to 1935, from such faculty members as Henry Simons and Lloyd Mints and above all Frank Knight, and from such fellow graduate students as Milton Friedman, Homer Jones, and George Stigler.

Before I discuss the prophecy, I want to quote it again. What I have quoted here consists of phrases from two sentences. They give a central thought of the two sentences, but to avoid charges that I may have twisted the meaning by taking phrases out of context, I will give the two sentences in full: "In 34 months we have built up new instruments of public power in the hands of the people's government. This power is wholesome and proper, but in the hands of political puppets of an economic autocracy, such power would provide shackles for the liberties of our people."

Presented before The Milwaukee Society in Milwaukee on 13 January 1975.

The prophecy was made when the 1936 election was on the horizon. It amounted to saying that the powers of the government had been built up in such a way that there was no choice but to re-elect FDR, since others might misuse the power. That, if true, would have meant that the people had already had their liberty to elect someone else shackled. It meant, as Al Smith put it at the time, "If you are going to have an autocrat take me." Smith added, "We don't want any autocrats. . . . We wouldn't even take a good one."

Smith, I note nostalgically, proceeded to advocate several platform planks on which FDR had been elected in 1932—reduction of federal expenditures by 25 per cent, balancing the budget every year, handling unemployment and old-age insurance through the states, and "removal of Government from all fields of private enterprise." The Democratic platform of 1932, as quoted by Al Smith, makes Barry Goldwater look like a wild-eyed communist. This is a point to keep in mind when you see people rewriting history to say that the outcome of the 1932 election represented a "rejection of the old order" and a "deliberate turn to the left and government intervention." On the contrary, the platform attacked President Hoover for the Reconstruction Finance Corporation, the Farm Board, public works programs, excessive cost of government, and deficit spending. Those are the things the voters sought to turn away from, if the rhetoric of the campaign means anything—but, of course, campaign platforms, promises, and rhetoric never mean much and probably have little influence on elections.

In the years since FDR made his remarkably prescient prognostication, American life has changed drastically. We talk a lot about changes in technology, in farming, in urbanization, in standards of living, in health, in education, in communication, and so on. But surely none of these changes is as great as the changes that have come about in the relation between people and government.

When FDR made his prediction, there were innumerable areas of private life into which the Federal government did not intrude, because it was prohibited by the Constitution, and many other areas were left to the states, again because of the Constitution.

In 1935, for example, when the administration was drafting the first social security legislation, there were the gravest doubts within the administration itself that the law could be written in such a way as to be acceptable constitutionally. Frances Perkins, Secretary of Labor, who was in charge of drafting the legislation, tells in her memoirs that she got a tip on how to write the bill so that the Supreme Court would uphold it. Where did she get the tip? Straight from the horse's mouth, from a justice of the Supreme Court, Justice Stone.

Today, in contrast, it is hard to think of any area of private affairs in which the Federal government is reluctant to intervene. There are a few areas where the courts still constrain the government, but these are almost exclusively the domains that are important to the academic-journalistic complex—namely, where their personal and rather commercial interests in free speech are threatened, or where election or law enforcement procedures seem disadvantageous to those who are vaguely described as "disadvantaged." And the courts themselves have thrown off virtually all self-restraint; it is almost inconceivable that a judge today would refuse to intervene in a situation because it is outside the jurisdiction of the courts.

Recently Alexander Solzhenitsyn was quoted as making a statement about the Russian government that is too nearly true of ours, that it dislikes any relations between individuals which it does not supervise. It is not, of course, "the government" as an entity that wants to supervise in this country. Rather, for almost any relations between individuals there is some group which has a special interest in supervising, and the influence of special interests in our system of government is so strong that generally they get their way. (By "special interests" I refer not only to commercial and economic interests but to such organizations as the Sierra Club, Common Cause, Ralph Nader and his multifarious franchised activities, organized religion, higher education, and so forth.)

We assure ourselves and our children that ours is a government of laws, not men. Well, sometime stop and check up on the "laws" that are regulating you, and see whether this is true. You will soon be making out your Federal income tax return. For the most part, you will have to work with an intricate body of rules and regulations handed down by various Internal Revenue employees, Tax Court officials, and Federal judges.

The tax law that Congress enacted made some general statements, but to apply these to the infinite variety of individuals and circumstances requires elaborate interpretations. If you or your business has anything but the simplest kind of return, there is a chance that it may be reviewed. A review involves sitting down across the table from a man—not a law. And the review includes a lot of horse-trading: "I'll give you this if you'll give me that"; "if you hold out on this point I can make it more expensive for you than it's worth."

The taxpayer always fears that it may not be wise to press too hard, because if he annoys the Internal Revenue man he can find himself in worse trouble, not only for himself but for others connected with him. Besides, he fears that if he wins this time they will really be "laying" for him next time. Whether these fears are often realized is beside the point; the point is that what is feared is men and human emotions, not laws.

The ordinary taxpayer is almost without effective recourse from the decisions an IRS agent makes, because of the costs in time, in legal fees, and in the psychological strain that arises because, fortunately, most people still respect (or fear?) the government enough so that it is by no means a matter of indifference to them to be at odds with it, even if they win eventually. Indeed, publicity may cause damage that never will be corrected by exoneration, however complete.

What I have said about the tax laws, namely, that the regulations governing you with the force of law are mostly the edicts of officials, applies in almost every field. The Occupational Safety and Health Act is an excellent example—or should I say "horrible" example?—of government by men rather than by law. The Environmental Protection Act is another. As for automobile safety, let me remind you that Congress was never hebephrenic enough to legislate those squawk-and-balk interlock devices on cars, nor the $100 bumpers, either.

Although Congress passes the basic laws on which the mountains of regulations rest, it would be naive to think that Congress gives every law thorough scrutiny. Look at the 1969 tax law and then tell me whether you believe that *your* Congressman studied all of it. Do you think he even read all of it? Do you suppose any single Congressman, even Wilbur Mills himself, studied every bit of it?

How many other equally voluminous bills were enacted at the same session of Congress, and do you suppose that all of them were carefully studied in full? Did your Congressman scrutinize the appropriations for Health, Education, and Welfare, or for the Defense Department?

If you know how Congress works—or at least how it has worked in the past—you realize that there has to be, and is, division of labor. Committees and subcommittees control most of the legislation. Within the committees and subcommittees the staff are sometimes more influential, at least on the bulk of the legislation, than the members themselves. And in the crucial all-night session at which a final bill is actually worded, the staff often is supplemented by outsiders with special interests in the bill.

All of these developments confirm the wisdom of the Founding Fathers in limiting narrowly the powers of the Federal government. They did this only partly from antipathy to governmental control of private affairs. To be sure, such antipathy was strong at the time, because of direct experience in the preceding hundred years. But an equally powerful reason for restricting the power of the Federal government was the realization that the form of government they wanted —a democratic government—cannot endure if it intervenes extensively into the affairs of the people. Democratic processes—representative processes, if you prefer—simply cannot handle complex, highly technical matters satisfactorily.

A democratic government cannot design efficient automobiles, it cannot design a sound energy policy, it cannot eliminate prejudice and discrimination, it cannot manage transportation, it cannot assure the soundness of investments or the accuracy of information about them, it cannot guarantee the effectiveness and safety of medicines— it cannot, in short, do most of the things that our government undertakes to do.

(This is not the occasion to prove the point, but it is important at least to assert that all of these problems can be handled far better without a direct governmental role. Scarcely anyone understands this any longer, but it is an exceedingly important truth.)

Congress, perhaps partly in recognition of its own incapacity to do all the things it undertakes to do, has come increasingly during the past 40 years not to legislate itself but to delegate to thousands of employees the right to make what are effectively laws, and the right to enforce them.

Another important fact about representative government that the Founding Fathers recognized is that direct election by the people is likely not to produce the most competent representatives to carry on the people's business, and furthermore is likely to promote demagoguery.

Thus, in the Federalist papers one of the features described with pride, as an argument for accepting the proposed constitution, was that the people could not get directly at the government. Only the House of Representatives was to be elected directly by the voters. Senators were to be elected by state legislatures; the President and the Vice President were to be elected by a special electoral college; and judges were to be appointed by the President and Senate.

Perhaps in an unconscious response to the weakness of government by representatives elected directly by the people, there is currently a strong movement toward government by the judiciary, which is now the only part of the Federal government that still is not elected by the people. Whatever the reason, the fact is that a great deal of administrative business is now done by the courts.

It has been recognized for 50 years or more that the courts revise the Constitution through their interpretations and reinterpretations, and it has been recognized for perhaps 25 years that in effect the courts legislate in innumerable matters, including apportionment of Congress, legislatures, and school districts, and criminal law and the operation of prisons, but it has not been widely recognized that currently the courts are assuming many functions that formerly were regarded as executive responsibilities.

Much of this shift into direct administration has resulted from the "Litigation Explosion" of recent years, in which almost anyone who is displeased with an administrative procedure or conclusion, whether he is much affected personally or not, can sue and seek to have the court at least upset the administrative result and perhaps issue an administrative ruling of its own. Thinking up possible lawsuits and recruiting people in whose names they might be prosecuted on a contingency basis is one of the true growth industries of this decade.

An even more dangerous threat to the liberties of our people that has arisen from the new instruments of public power that FDR boasted about comes from the widespread loss of confidence in the government. Public opinion polls show that all branches of government are held in low repute, except the military. (There may be an ominous foreshadowing here of where the people will turn if the loss of confidence in government goes much further; but one note of optimism I can leave with you is that personally I am confident that a South American pattern will not develop here.)

Loss of confidence in government is easily explained by looking at the government's record in almost everything it promises, from delivering the mail to assuring adequate supplies of energy. But it may be due in large part, as Warren Nutter pointed out in a brilliant article in the *Wall Street Journal* recently, to the welfare state having passed the stage where more people gain than lose by it, and reached a stage where for most people the costs exceed the benefits. "There are, after all," Nutter wrote, "two natural equilibriums for the welfare state: one in which the majority benefits at the expense of the minority, and the other in which the minority benefits at the expense of the majority. Once the welfare state reaches a certain relative size, the first is ruled out by the facts of life, and the second by the nature of democracy. That leaves only the borderline situation in which half try to gain from the other half. That circumstance . . . so weakens government as to imperil democracy itself."

This brings to mind a famous letter written by Edmund Burke in 1791: "Men are qualified for civil liberty," he said, "in exact proportion to their disposition to put moral chains on their own appetites; in proportion as their love of justice is above their rapacity."

Going beyond the dangers to liberty that FDR recognized in the new institutions that he created, then, there may be an even more ominous danger in the forces of rapacity that these institutions have channeled into government. Rapacity is always present, of course, but it is most menacing when there are governmental institutions whose control can satisfy rapacious appetites through the use of raw power.

The circulars announcing this talk said that I would include a discussion of "affirmative action" in educational institutions. To comply with government regulations on labeling, I will have to say something about that, although I have talked long enough already. You remember the ruling by the Federal Trade Commission that if a package is labeled "chicken salad" it must contain at least some chicken. That led someone to inquire about cottage cheese, and someone else to ask for a ruling on Danish pastry.

Because the hour is so late, I will say only that affirmative action is a system of quotas for various ethnic groups, depending on which ones have been able to muster enough political attention, and for women. The purpose of the act, mitigating unjustified discrimination, cannot be given a meaningful operational definition and cannot possibly be achieved by government. Those who administer the act deny indignantly that what they call "goals" are quotas, but to my mind these denials only illustrate the intellectual degradation and mendacity to which otherwise honorable men sink when they engage in coercive activity on behalf of special groups, carried on under an Orwellian banner of justice, equity, fairness, morality, and virtue. The administration of the act has been marked by deception, by actions that verge on extortion or blackmail, and by extensive political intervention. In short, it is a perfect fulfillment of FDR's brilliant prophecy of 1936, that he had launched us on a path that would shackle the liberties of the people—all in a good and virtuous cause, of course.

To recapitulate, like a good college professor, what do I think I have told you?

My major theme has been that government power, however worthy the objectives for which it is established, inevitably forges fetters for freedom. My second point is that our government in 1975 restricts freedom in innumerable ways. With more time, I would have argued also that these restrictions on freedom are almost never necessary to accomplish the objectives from which they arise, and in fact usually are counterproductive.

A third point is that a government that attempts to control as many and as complex affairs as ours now does cannot succeed by democratic or representative methods. With more time, I would have argued that it cannot succeed by authoritarian methods either, though it may be able to create an appearance of success. A fourth point is that representative government is likely to fail when representatives are chosen through direct election by the people. The people, even more than their elected representatives, are unable to grasp the complexities and technicalities with which modern governments deal, so they become easy prey to demagogues. A fifth point is that we have in fact moved a long way toward a government of men rather than laws, for most regulations that we consider laws are in fact edicts of appointed officials, and many executive functions are carried out by judges.

A sixth point is that the creation of instruments of government power channels forces of selfishness or arrogance into politics and makes the struggle for political power a ruthless, life-or-death—or, at least, jail-or-be-jailed—matter that disrupts the social fabric.

A seventh point, due to Warren Nutter, is that our welfare state is approaching the point where at least half the people pay out more to support benefits to others than they receive as benefits for themselves. This means that half the people tend to be disaffected with government, so it threatens the very existence of free democratic institutions.

In short, as Lord Acton said 88 years ago, "Power tends to corrupt and absolute power corrupts absolutely."

2

The Faltering Economy

THE TITLE OF THIS LECTURE was assigned to me, not chosen by me. It reminds me vaguely, for reasons that I cannot quite capture, of the lectures and symposia that used to be popular under titles like "The Challenge of the Future," "Whither Mankind?" or "Was Civilization a Success?" Those lectures would have been enlightening if, instead of Eleanor Roosevelt, U Thant, or Buckminster Fuller, they had been given by Mark Twain, W. C. Fields, or Art Buchwald. Perhaps you will think the same of this lecture.[1]

Since the title was assigned, it occurred to me that I ought to look up the word "faltering" in the dictionary. What I found is certainly appropriate to the economy today: "To move unsteadily or waveringly. To stumble; tremble, totter; be unstable. To hesitate; to speak brokenly or weakly; to stammer. To hesitate in purpose or action; to waver, flinch, give way, fail. To utter with hesitation, or in a broken, trembling, or weak manner."

My research in the unabridged dictionary illustrated again the fact that pursuit of even the most trivial point can lead to a liberal education, for I discovered a completely different meaning of "falter," one which the program committee surely did not have in mind, namely "to hummel." "Hummel," it turns out, means "to separate from the awns." And an awn, it turns out, is "'one of the slender bristles, known collectively as the beard, which terminate the lemmas or scales of the spikelet in barley, oats, some varieties of wheat, and other grasses." Along the same path, which I will leave you to

Presented at the University of Chicago on 15 April 1975.

follow for yourselves in *Webster*, the intriguing information turned
up that in some lizards and snakes the copulatory organs are double;
and this has some relation to a vulgar description of what, as I shall
indicate, is making the economy falter. The wonder is not that the
economy is faltering but, in view of what politics is doing to it, that
it is not flat on its back.

In discussing the faltering economy, I will first mention the recent past. Then I will describe briefly the current state of affairs.
Mostly, I will talk about the future.

The Recent Past

In September 1974 I was rash enough to discuss publicly the prospects for the economy. As you will guess from my mentioning that,
what has happened since has confirmed and even exceeded my worst
fears.

My general theme was that there is no way to check inflation
without a period of rising unemployment, that rising unemployment
sets off frantic public spending, and that public spending stimulates
inflation. My conclusion—caricaturing it a little—was, therefore,
that attempting to check inflation will in fact aggravate inflation.

I must try to protect myself against being caricatured by others. I
do not say that price stability is incompatible with full employment.
The trade-off is not between inflation and unemployment, or between price stability and full employment, but between the rate of
change in inflation and the level of employment. It would be carrying coals to Newcastle to argue that point here at the University of
Chicago, for no one has done more to make it clear than Milton
Friedman.

Also, I do not suggest that we let people starve, or suffer serious
deprivation, in order to stabilize prices. But it must be recognized
that unemployment figures cannot be read directly as figures on economic hardship.

At the level of unemployment that prevailed last September,
about 5.8 percent, less than half of the unemployed had lost jobs.
The majority were new entrants to the labor force, voluntary quits,
or re-entrants. Less than half had dependents. Furthermore, the average duration of unemployment was under three months. Usually,
however, the higher the rate of unemployment, the higher the propor-

tion of the unemployed who have actually lost jobs, the higher the proportion on whom others are dependent, and the higher the average duration of unemployment; so when unemployment is half as much again, or 8.7 percent, hardship is more than half as much again.

Beyond factors such as these that make it invalid to translate unemployment directly into hardship is the fact that many unemployed suffer little reduction in disposable income. Unemployment benefits are tax exempt, and reduction in income taxes and social security taxes may go a long way toward making up the gap between lost earnings and unemployment benefits, especially when benefits are added for dependents, when the worker lives in states like Massachusetts, New York, and California with high state income tax rates, and when the spouse's earnings have put the family well above the minimum tax brackets. Indeed, in some cases, after-tax income is actually higher when a worker is unemployed than when he is employed.

Martin Feldstein, Professor of Economics at Harvard, in a lecture at the University of Rochester in 1974, used the following example: Consider a worker who earns $500 per month, who has two children, whose wife earns $350 per month, and who lives in Massachusetts. If he is unemployed for two months, he loses $1,000 in earnings, but he saves $162 of Federal income tax, $58 of social security tax, and $50 of state income tax, a total saving of $270, leaving a deficit of $730. (Actually, the deficit will be less, since he will save something on transportation and other costs of working.) He will receive unemployment compensation of half his previous earnings, or $500 for the two months, plus $6 per week for each child, or $104, a total of $604. This leaves only $126 of the gap unfilled. In other words, he receives only $15 a week less when unemployed than when employed. At that rate, he can afford to look long and discriminatingly for a new job. It would be financially advantageous, for example, to spend as much as 10 weeks extra hunting a job if thereby he could increase his pay by even as little as 5 percent. If it were the wife of this example who became unemployed for two months, the family's net income would fall by less than $60, so she receives only 25 cents per hour less if she is unemployed than if she works.

In interpreting unemployment figures, allowance has to be made also for increases due to factors other than measures taken to control inflation. Specifically, an increasing proportion of the labor force in the youngest age groups causes a rise in unemployment, simply because these groups include many new entrants and do much shifting of jobs, and historically have had high rates of unemployment. Also, increases in the minimum wage rate cause increases in unemployment, especially among the young and among blacks, Puerto Ricans, and certain other "minorities."

Nevertheless, increases in the crude unemployment figures receive major emphasis, with no interpretation (in fact, often with misinterpretation) in the news. This generates receptivity by the electorate to increased government spending of all kinds. This receptivity is exploited by all who wish to tap the Federal treasury.

A final misunderstanding against which I want to protect myself is the notion that government expenditures, or even deficits, in and of themselves necessarily cause inflation. The impact of deficits on inflation depends on how the deficits are financed. Historically, they have been financed largely by creating new money, and it is this new money that is inflationary. (Obviously even this is an oversimplification, for when the economy is operating below capacity it would be possible, at least in theory, to inject just the right amount of money with just the right timing to bring the economy back to full employment without inflation. Suffice it to say that in practical politics this is not possible, and even if it were politically possible it probably cannot be done with present techniques of applied economics.)

The best record of any major country in fighting inflation in the past decade was the record of the United States in the period from 1969 to 1972. The rate of inflation was cut nearly in half without unemployment rising to levels that caused hardship. The price control decree of August 1971 undoubtedly resulted from political hysteria. With a near unanimous consensus in favor of price and wage controls and with an election pending, price controls were imposed, the money supply was expanded, and during 1972 there was an appearance of price stability with rising employment. But since 1972 we have had inflation at a rate never equaled in this country in times of peace,[2] and above the average rate in times of war. In only one month in 1973 and 1974 did the Consumer Price Index rise at a rate below 5 percent per year, and in only one other month did the rate fall below 7½ percent per year. The increase from December 1973 to December 1974 was 12 percent.

Finally, in reviewing recent events, it should be noted that the behavior of the money supply has been erratic. The long-run trend is fairly clear, namely a steadily increasing rate of growth. The money stock rose an average of

2 percent per year from 1952 to 1962,
4 percent per year from 1962 to 1966,
6 percent per year from 1966 to 1971, and
7 percent per year from 1971 to mid-1974.

Whereas in the three quarters preceding the middle of 1974 the rate of growth exceeded 7 percent per year, in the three quarters since mid-1974 the rate has averaged only 3.5 percent per year.

History shows that it is not possible to tell what history shows about the future—certainly not by looking at the most recent decade. That is fortunate, for the record of the past decade suggests—and not only the record but an analysis of the processes that have produced that record—that with respect to inflation the United States in the future is likely to resemble, say, South America.

The Current Situation

The money supply was essentially stable from July 1974 until January 1975, although it probably has experienced healthy growth in the past few months. The rate of inflation seems to be abating, having averaged about 6 percent in the first quarter of 1975, as judged by the Consumer Price Index. That is an unfavorable rate of inflation, but it compares favorably with the 12 percent increase from December 1973 to December 1974.

Wages are still rising and are at an all-time high. Productivity, which had been falling for some time, seems to have turned up. Unemployment was 8.2 percent (seasonally adjusted) in February and apparently rising, and the rate for male heads of households was approaching 5 percent.

Corporate profits in 1974 were higher than in 1973, but the increase was largely due to inventory profits and in any case was scarcely more than the increase in prices.

In general, the physical volume of activity has been declining since the latter part of 1973, some activities having turned down early in that year and most by the end of the year. Most dollar volumes, however, continued to rise through 1974; some, in fact, like personal incomes and Gross National Product, were still rising in the latest figures that I have seen. This simply means, obviously, that declines in physical volume have been more than offset by increases in prices.[3]

Perhaps the strongest growth in the whole economy currently is in transfer payments by the government, that is, payments to individuals that are not payments for goods or services. Currently transfer payments are at an annual rate of $165 billion per year, or $770 per capita of total population.

In fact, government expenditures—all expenditures, not just transfers; and all governments, not just the Federal—are now more than half as large as the whole private economy. It is estimated that, for the 1976 fiscal year, government expenditures will be about 57 percent of total private expenditures.

When we examine the current faltering of the economy—and the facts that I have briefly summarized establish clearly that "faltering" is at least as favorable a term as can be applied accurately to the economy today—and when we look to the future of the economy, the massive and rapidly growing role of government must be the major focus of our attention. Government expenditures are increasingly inadequate as an index of the role of government in the economy, and particularly inadequate as a prognosticator of future faltering, staggering, or partial paralysis that may afflict the economy, because direct intervention by the government in management and control is now substantial, growing rapidly, and perhaps already more significant than government finance.

The Future

It is natural and almost universal to assume that in another six to eighteen months the economy will be back to "normal." While I assume that, too, I also have just a shadow of doubt. Once before within my adult life we had government intervention in the economy on a massive scale in an attempt to bring about recovery. That was in 1933 to 1936. You will remember that the economy simply did not recover. Until the Second World War there was no year in which the average rate of unemployment fell as low as 14 percent.[4] It was war, not government measures against recession, that finally revived the economy. Our current foreign policy does have certain resemblances to the foreign policies of England and France forty years ago, so perhaps a major war within the next five years cannot be ruled out as definitely as now appears to be the case. That is a horrible thought, in relation to which effects on the economy are inconsequential; and besides, I expect that the effects on the economy of another major war would be the opposite of the effects of the Second World War.

If we put such thoughts aside, put aside also the recession of the past year or two, and take a long view of the future of our economy, what we see is an enormous, vigorous, and innovative giant being entangled in a net, and gradually nibbled away by minnows. Gulliver and the Lilliputians.

I am referring to regulatory commissions, tax laws and regulations, pollution regulations, safety regulations, product liability regulations, nondiscrimination laws and regulations, licensing requirements, collective bargaining laws and regulations, reporting requirements, and so on. Each of these, even the worst, is trivial in comparison with the size and vigor of the American economy. But so are bacteria trivial in comparison with the size of an elephant that they can kill, not by butchering it but by impairing one after another of the organs whose functions are essential to its health and life.

Because we take these multifarious interventions for granted, and because we assume that even though they may be obnoxious they are petty, we fail to note their magnitude and aggregate effects. If you ever studied integral calculus, you undoubtedly recall that an infinite number of infinitesimals can amount to a finite quantity, sometimes a large one.

Recently I heard the head of a large business say that his business spent $1.5 million last year collecting data, recording and summarizing it, and reporting it to the Federal government—all on one item, showing that they are not discriminating in employment. This company, because of the nature of its business and its location, happens to have disproportionately large numbers of women and "minorities" among its employees; so it has had no additional expense as a result of filing the reports. The $1.5 million is simply the cost of reporting. Since the company has about $8 billion of annual revenue, the $1.5 million is hardly perceptible. Indeed, the company may even benefit, since its smaller competitors have proportionately larger costs in doing similar reporting, and undoubtedly some of them will report figures that cause even higher costs to be imposed on them.

The $1.5 million spent for the data and reports is, however, only the tip of the iceberg. Inevitably the effects of this kind of record gathering perfuse the organization. A bureaucratic atmosphere grows up, an attitude that what we do and how we do it is not what matters, just how meticulously we record our activities. Furthermore, the process unquestionably leads to hiring or promoting incompetents in order to make the records look good. The incompetents, in turn, not only waste their salaries but may do actual damage whose value exceeds any work they accomplish. In addition, the appointment or promotion of people on criteria other than performance has a demoralizing effect on any organization.

The program that the president of the company mentioned is in fact only one of scores that plague the same company. He noticed this one simply because it is new. The others he takes for granted, like blizzards, power failures, strikes, changes in consumer tastes, lawsuits, and innovations by his competitors. Recently his company published an advertisement announcing that "The Future Is Yours if You Do Business with Us." As a result, the company received a formal demand from a government agency that it submit research findings, verified data, and legal proof that the claim can be substantiated beyond a reasonable doubt. The president of the company got so much fun out of telling this story that he never stopped to count the stockholders' dollars that were used up in reassuring the government. The odds are that the government agency was not as silly as the request made it sound, and was not really serious about anything except protecting itself from one of the self-styled "public interest" law firms, which might more accurately be called champerty corporations, that routinely demand that the government agency require proof of any declarative sentence.

Last summer the head of a metallurgical firm, the largest in the world in its field, said that 20 percent of his firm's capital investments in 1974 would yield no return to the company. Whether they yielded a return to someone else, or at least to some fish in a river or deer in a forest, is not clear; but whatever the social returns were, it is certain that they were not properly balanced against the costs, and that there was an expenditure of resources not matched by goods and services of equal value.

We are all familiar with the fact that automobiles are being engineered in Washington, and many of us have noticed that it is not done better in Washington than in Detroit. But few people seem to give any thought to the economic consequences, and even those who do seem not to think in terms of social costs. Consider the bumpers now required on all cars that are supposed to prevent damage in a crash from the front or rear at five miles per hour or less. Suppose that these bumpers add $100 to the cost of a car. (Actually, they add more than $100.) How much damage would the bumpers have to prevent each year to justify the expenditure of $100 per car? In a normal year (though, as I indicated earlier, 1975 is a below-normal year, especially for motor vehicles) about 15 million vehicles are sold in the United States. At $100 per vehicle that comes to $1.5 billion per year. As a footnote, I may add that the best estimates are that the actual savings are negative, because it costs more to repair the damage to the bumper systems from crashes above five miles per hour or from the sides than is saved by eliminating damage from front or back collisions below five miles per hour, and also because the added weight adds to operating costs.

To get some idea of the pervasiveness of government intervention of this kind in the economy, I asked an associate, Mr. Kenneth F. Wood, to clip such items from the newspapers during February and March, 1975. Here is a sample of the kinds of things revealed by the clippings. No doubt there will be at least one person here who feels, with regard to any one of these items, that it is a good thing. I suggest, however, that the total pattern is such as to outweigh by far any favorable effects.

One clipping reports that the Federal Communications Commission wants to limit to three hours the amount of network programming that a local station can show between the hours of 7 and 11 P.M., but to exempt certain types of programs.

The Department of Health, Education, and Welfare is reported to be requiring the University of California at Berkeley to replace 178 white males with 97 women, 20 blacks, 42 Asians, 10 Chicanos, 0 American Indians, and 9 others. This is to be done within 30 years.

Another item mentions the effect of the minimum wage rate of $2 in causing unemployment, especially among the young and blacks, and above all among young blacks.

The U.S. Customs Service imposes huge fines on businesses, and says that it needs to do this in order to negotiate more effectively with the businesses on what fines they will actually pay.

An article on the effects of prohibiting the use of DDT mentions a great increase in the prevalence of malaria in Ceylon and of a harmful moth in the forests of the Pacific Northwest.

The possibility that wage and price controls will be reinstituted has led some businesses to increase prices when they did not feel that such increases were advantageous in prevailing circumstances.

The regulation of retirement benefits and investment procedures will raise pension costs of the Consolidated Edison Company by 14 percent.

The controller of the currency warned banks not to take large deposits from people who might try to eliminate Jews from the boards of the banks.

The food stamp program, currently running at about $4 billion per year, is expected to be $5 billion in the next fiscal year. It is estimated that 60 million people will be eligible in fiscal 1977, although only 15 million are now receiving the stamps.

The Governor of New York complained that New Yorkers are not getting all the food stamps they could, set up a toll-free telephone line to call for advice on how to get them, and set a goal of an additional $100 million a year in food stamps.

Government allocations of capital have created a variety of vested interests. Federally guaranteed loans now amount to $200 billion, and in addition there are $50 billion of direct loans outstanding.

A number of local governments have banned the use of phosphates in detergents.

Licensing boards are expanding the number of occupations that must be licensed, and also the number of types of business that must be licensed the way liquor stores and taxis are now.

The Federal government increased the support price for milk, leading to a 2 percent rise in retail prices. This was done after the President vetoed an even larger increase that had been passed by Congress.

In March the government changed the effective date for automobile pollution standards from the 1977 models to the 1978 models. One reason was that the devices the government plans to require seem to boost the amount of another pollutant. This change was made after two years of warnings to the government, and after far greater costs have been incurred than would have been if 1978 had been the original target date. Indeed, no sensible person attempting a basic technological innovation sets a date and introduces the product on that date whether or not it works reliably and whatever it costs.

There is a shortage of natural gas in New England and surplus gas in Alaska, but the only ships capable of carrying it are registered under foreign flags, and foreign-flag ships are not allowed to carry goods between United States ports.

Several states have introduced controls over all land near seashores. These amount to the state's taking joint ownership of the property without compensation.

A number of cities have passed laws prohibiting growth, or at least limiting the number of new buildings that can be built.

The government is appropriating large and growing subsidies to maintain passenger service on the railroads. The resulting costs per passenger mile are such that most passengers, if offered the choice, probably would prefer to pocket the subsidy and find some other way to travel.

The Securities and Exchange Commission is attempting to form a single central market for securities, covering the entire country.

The Securities and Exchange Commission plans to require a great deal of additional detail in the quarterly reports of corporations, and to require some degree of auditing of these quarterly reports.

The Environmental Protection Agency is proposing rules to make jet airplanes quieter, at a cost estimated at $880 million.

An editorial in *Science* two weeks ago (written, incidentally, by a long-term government employee) says, "Government may imagine that it is neutral toward the rate and quality of technological risk-taking, but it is not. . . . Regulatory policies . . . rarely consider impacts on innovation. . . . Changes in tax treatment of industrial research and development, if approached narrowly, can choke off outlays for innovation."

So much for the clippings. Here are a few more examples:

The Food and Drug Administration's regulations, together with certain acts of Congress, have changed the U.S. from a leader to a substantial laggard in developing new medicines. The therapeutic areas in which this U.S. drug lag is most pronounced are cardiovascular, diuretic, respiratory, antibacterial, and gastrointestinal. In appearing before a Senate committee last fall, Dr. William Wardell of the University of Rochester Medical School testified as follows:

> To take some obvious examples, the U.S. was at least the 30th country to approve the anticancer drug adriamycin; the 41st country to approve the antimania drug lithium carbonate; the 51st country to approve the antituberculous drug rifampin; the 64th country to approve the antiallergic drug cromolyn; and the 106th country to approve the antibacterial drug co-trimoxazole.
>
> Even when a drug is finally admitted to the U.S., the indications for its use are often ridiculously restricted and out-of-date. For example, the U.S. has more restrictions on the use of co-trimoxazole than any other of the 107 countries in which the drug is currently marketed. Here, it is still only approved for the short-term treatment of chronic urinary tract infections. More important medically are situations in which this drug may be life-saving, in some of which no other effective therapy is available. Such situations were recognized as early as 1962, but are still essentially un-

known (and certainly unapproved) uses in the U.S., some 12 years
later.

Perhaps the most astonishing recent example of the unrealistic
gap between regulatory philosophy and medical practice is that of
propranolol. It is hard to believe that an advisory committee was
still debating the approval of this drug for angina at a time when
a physician's *failure* to use this drug (e.g., as a trial in most patients prior to coronary artery surgery) would be regarded as substantially suboptimal medical practice. The regulatory fate of this
drug, for an indication (angina) in which it has long been a ther-
apy of choice, bodes ill for its regulatory chances in an equally important indication, hypertension. In this latter respect, American
regulatory philosophy is already a decade behind medical practice.

The so-called energy crisis is a product of government policies.
Governments have prevented drilling offshore, they have impeded or
prevented the construction of nuclear power plants, they have
sharply reduced the mining of coal, they have regulated natural gas
prices in ways that have retarded exploration and encouraged wasteful use, the Alaska pipeline has been delayed for 5 years while a billion dollars' worth of equipment lay idle, and so forth. These facts
are widely known, though rarely mentioned in the hunt for a scape-
goat. But what is not widely known is the extent to which the oil
industry is being managed by the government.

Charles DiBona, formerly with the University of Rochester, is
now Executive Vice President of the American Petroleum Institute.
In a recent conversation he remarked that the oil industry in the
United States is subject to the most detailed and total control of any
industry in the country. "More than 60 federal agencies and regulatory bodies exercise authority over the oil industry, and 157 federal
groups are 'interested' in it." I asked Mr. DiBona to send me a description of these controls that I could include in this lecture. What
he sent is longer than the whole lecture, but I will quote just enough
to give the flavor:

> When the Cost of Living Council and the Economic Stabilization
> Act passed into history on April 30, 1974, the control of the petro-
> leum industry continued under the Emergency Petroleum Alloca-
> tion Act of 1973. As each new control developed cracks and prob-
> lems, a new and more elaborate control was created. The present
> rules make the petroleum industry the most fully and elaborately
> controlled industry in the country (perhaps the world).

At present, the Federal Energy Administration:

1. controls the price of about 60 per cent of the crude oil produced in the U.S.
2. specifies who can buy the crude oil or requires the owner of crude oil to purchase an authorization from his competitor in order to use his own oil
3. has the power to specify refinery yields
4. controls the price of each product at the refinery through a complex set of rules which take an historical price (May 1973) and allow "pass-through" of certain but not all increases in input costs. It can also "tilt" the cost pass-through toward specific products (FEA apparently plans to use this power to force the recent tariff increase to have approximately the same effect as a gasoline excise tax).
5. specifies that a refiner must continue to sell to all customers who were supplied in 1972. If a refiner is making more products than he made in 1972, customers of record have first rights to the increased products available. FEA has second rights to reassign such increases. If FEA refuses to assign new products, the company may try to locate a new customer.
6. specifies on a similar basis the allocation of products through the marketing and distribution system, and controls the jobber-dealer mark-up.

"There are no end of examples of misallocation," DiBona wrote. "For example: In the winter of 1973–74 there were long lines for gasoline in Boston and New York but none in upstate Vermont. That reason was that in the winter of 1972–73 skiing conditions were good. In the winter of 1973–74 skiing conditions were terrible and few skiers went to Vermont—but the gasoline went."

My point now is not whether the regulation of the oil industry is "fair," "just," or "equitable," but that it reduces the output of the economy. It destroys labor, natural resources, and capital which could have contributed to the health, welfare, and happiness of the people.

The final example I shall discuss, to support my thesis that the number of impediments to the economy is now so great that economic progress is jeopardized, is the litigation explosion. The champerty corporations to which I referred earlier, which call themselves "public interest" law firms, are only a small part of this explosion.

In the past decade, the legal expenses of the typical corporation have risen about twice as much as its sales revenues. Legal costs often are around a quarter to three quarters of 1 percent of sales.

There has been a striking growth in the number of lawsuits filed in the Federal District Courts. For the five years 1968–73, the number of environmental suits rose at a compound rate of 45 percent per year, or by a factor of 6.4 for the 5 years. Securities regulation cases grew 24 percent per year, by a factor of 2.9. Antitrust cases, 11 percent per year, a factor of 1.7. Labor law cases, 7 percent, a factor of 1.4. Patents, copyrights, and trademarks, 2 percent, a factor of 1.1. Fair employment practice cases, of which there were over 1,000 in 1973, were not even recognized as a separate category in 1968, but all civil rights cases (most of which probably do not involve businesses) grew at an average annual rate of 36 percent, or a factor of 4.7 over the 5 years.

These lawsuits are just the tip of the iceberg. The real business of most lawyers, of course, is to *prevent* lawsuits. So corporations are swarming with lawyers, who read or even write the outgoing mail, package labels, advertisements, instruction manuals, public speeches, press releases, and employment manuals, and in fact monitor nearly every detail of corporate practice. And the costs of these lawyers probably are the lesser part of the total costs incurred from delay, waste motion, and bureaucratization. They generate an attitude that production, service, and quality are less important than procedures, legalisms, and protecting your flanks.

To summarize then, my general view of the future, if not pessimistic, is not optimistic. I do not think we are going to hell on a bobsled, just in a handbasket. An economy as vigorous and resourceful as ours can take a tremendous amount of plugging its springs and obstructing its channels before it becomes stagnant. I am confident that, barring the possibility of the country's being conquered militarily, this will not become a poor nation in my lifetime; I think that it probably will not in my children's lifetimes; and I hope that it will not in my grandchildren's lifetimes. But we cannot overlook the fact that enormously wasteful policies are being imposed on the economy through political actions, and that there is a rapid acceleration in the number and extent of these political actions. Most of the effects are nearly infinitesimal, but the numbers are becoming infinite.

As I said at the beginning, it is a remarkable tribute to the strength and resiliency of our economy that, despite a rain of political blows, the economy is only faltering.

3

What Can We Do About It?

ABOUT WHAT? About the tide in public affairs that is moving in the wrong direction, and moving in the wrong direction at a rapid and accelerating pace.

What concerns us is a powerful movement away from limited government and individual freedom, and toward pervasive government and collective control of all activities. It is a shift away from a rule of law, toward a rule of officials: a shift from laws passed by elected legislatures and enforced in courts under the constitutional and common law guarantees that we call "due process," toward regulations, orders, and directives issued by appointed government employees and enforced by them. It is a shift away from judging conduct by criteria of propriety, prudence, and intent, toward judging conduct by consequences, even when the consequences were beyond the knowledge or control of the person judged. It is a shift away from trust in good faith, competence, and responsibility, toward reliance on detailed prescriptions by government and documentation by individuals of their actions, intentions, and motives.

In short, the problem is what Walter Lippmann called "the sickness of an overgoverned society," and the question is, what can we do to cure that sickness? Indeed, the immediate objective is not even to cure the sickness, but simply to slow its advance.

The particular manifestations of the sickness of overgovernment that concern us here are those relating to the economy. The damp-

Presented before the Business Council in Hot Springs, Virginia, on 9 May 1975.

ening of enterprise, innovation, initiative, and industriousness that already has occurred is causing substantial losses in human health, happiness, freedom, and well-being, although the full effects have not yet been felt. The prospects for even more governmentally imposed waste, inefficiency, rigidity, irresponsibility, and authoritarianism raise the possibility that before the end of the century this country may experience widespread and persistent deficiencies of the goods and services by which our health, happiness, culture, and spiritual values are supported.

Furthermore, in a nation that has come to believe that political processes can generate and distribute goods and services, disappointment of economic expectations may have disruptive political and social consequences.

To be concerned about the long-run consequences for business and the economy of the present course of public policy is by no means to be concerned with crass, materialistic, and selfish values. On the contrary, the ability to produce increasing amounts of goods and services with decreasing amounts of toil and effort is the foundation of our progress in culture, education, religion, ethics, and health.

Several times in the past I have participated in discussions by groups of businessmen deeply concerned to know "what can be done about it." In no case has anything emerged from the discussion that seemed to me realistic.

The last such occasion was typical. It involved about two dozen heads of businesses, a senator, a couple of representatives, a governor, one or two journalists, and three or four professors. After preliminary discussion about the importance and urgency of the problem, and about the special responsibility of businessmen for tackling it, the talk quickly focused on two nitty-gritty, nuts-and-bolts, down-to-earth, hard-headed, practical objectives. The first objective was to teach some simple economics to congressmen. The second was to get businessmen to do better on television and in other public relations. I will comment on each of these, just enough to suggest why I dismiss them as of no consequence.

As for teaching economics to congressmen, let me quote William Riker, Chairman of the University of Rochester's Department of Political Science: "Economists," Riker said—and he could equally well have said "businessmen"—"are ... inclined to discuss the actions of legislators as if the legislators' goals were to do what is economically best for the country. This seems to me to be foolish and false."

Now, please don't dismiss Riker's view as simply sarcastic. Riker explained:

> In the same way that economists assume that producers and consumers are maximizers of expected utility, so I assume are legislators. . . . Consumers . . . seek to maximize the utility of a market basket of goods and services within the constraint of a given budget, and producers . . . seek to maximize income from production. . . . Legislators seek mainly to maximize their chances of remaining in office. And this may lead them to do things that are quite out of harmony with economic imperatives.[1]

Some will react to this statement as cynical, or as casting aspersions on the courage, integrity, and patriotism of legislators; but that is a naive reaction. The legislator who does not get re-elected certainly will not do any good in the legislature and, in fact, probably will be replaced by someone "worse." Furthermore, actions that may contribute to a legislator's defeat only rarely affect the decision of a legislature made up of hundreds of members, so the legislator loses much and the public gains nothing if he votes for the public interest against the views of any appreciable group of his constituents. In short, ignorance of economics is rarely the explanation of a legislator's actions.

As for training executives in television and other techniques of public relations, the fact is that a businessman finds himself in much the same position as a legislator if he tries to go against public opinion. He may jeopardize his stockholders' interests if he supports an unpopular cause, even one that if it prevailed would be advantageous to all stockholders of all companies collectively. His positions on public issues may, if unpopular, react adversely on his sales to consumers, on his labor relations, and—most important—on his relations with scores of governmental authorities. For that reason, corporate advertising and other public relations activities seldom deal with issues of public policy, and when they do deal with them usually they try to identify the company with whatever is popular at the moment, even if it is purifying air and water in expensive but useless ways; subordinating the interests of human beings to those of birds, fish, and animals; or training the untrainable and hiring the incompetent. It can well be argued that responsible management of the stockholders' interests requires this, or at least that vigorous bucking of public opinion would be irresponsible, however wrong and damaging may be the public opinion that is bucked.

If we cannot handle the problem by teaching congressmen about economics or by teaching executives about television, what can we do about it?

The first thing we must do is try to diagnose the cause of the sickness. The sickness is rooted in public opinion. Elected officials have little leeway to defy public opinion, unless they can count on vindication before the next election. The prevailing opinion in this country today accepts collectivism and distrusts individualism.

To say that the current trend of public policy is deeply rooted in public opinion is to raise the question of how public opinion got the way it is. If we could answer that we could perhaps suggest how it might be shifted.

Between the beginning and the end of the nineteenth century a great transformation occurred among the leaders of American political and social opinion, and during the second quarter of the twentieth century this became a transformation not just in opinion but in law and practice. It was a transformation in views about how social progress and social justice can best be assured. The earlier view had a profound distrust of coercion of some men by others, so it regarded progress and liberalism as almost synonymous with limiting the power of government. The modern view has implicit faith in the omniscience, omnipotence, and beneficence of government, so it regards progress and liberalism as almost synonymous with expanding the power of government.

We cannot give a definitive explanation of changes in public opinion, any more than we can explain changes in styles and tastes, in customs and manners, or in language. But there are some things that can be said.

One of the most important things to be said is that public opinion on basic issues shifts slowly, but a change once in motion has great momentum and continues for long periods, impervious to facts and events that might be expected to stop it. For example, the body of opinion about foreign policy and national defense that is characterized loosely by the terms "isolationism" and "pacifism" has been growing throughout this century. The Second World War severely discredited and checked—even reversed—this body of opinion, and for perhaps twenty years it seemed to be repudiated. Yet today this body of opinion appears to have come to the fore again, and stands about where it would have if the twenty-year hiatus had not occurred.

Something similar has happened to the body of opinion about business and economics usually dubbed "interventionism" or (inaccurately) "socialism." That body of opinion has been gathering strength in this country since the beginning of the century, in other words for three generations, in England for four generations, and in Europe for at least five generations. The performance of the economy throughout this century (except during the Great Depression of the 1930's, which was caused by government actions),[2] whether that performance is judged by improvements in quantity, quality, distribution, equity, or conditions of work, thoroughly repudiates that body of opinion, yet today it is flourishing more strongly than ever before and, indeed, appears to be on the verge of total victory.

This is not to say that such tides of opinion never reverse. They certainly do; in England and America the nineteenth century was, as I indicated, an example, and so was the eighteenth century. At any time there are counter currents in existence, and anyone hoping to reverse the general tide should seek out and nourish promising counter currents.

Where are the most promising counter currents to be found? I believe that almost exclusively they are to be found in what one of my colleagues at Rochester calls "the academic-journalistic complex." That is, they are to be found not among the makers and doers but among the intellectuals: the people who get their data secondhand and their experience vicariously, and who write and talk; the college professors, schoolteachers, ministers, commentators, columnists, novelists, dramatists—even poets and lyricists. These are, of course, also the chief carriers of the prevailing tides of opinion. These are the people who disseminate ideas. They select from all the ideas those that are to be passed on to a wider public with approval, those to be denounced and discredited, and those to be ignored. They do this, with few exceptions, honestly and conscientiously according to their own best judgments—and their judgments are an outgrowth of what they believe to be facts and sound analyses.

The intellectuals that I am talking about are not creators of ideas nor are they themselves capable of penetrating or profound analyses of ideas; rather, they are what Friedrich Hayek calls "intellectual middlemen." They are influenced by the ideas and analyses of scholars and researchers. Their views will change gradually if they are exposed to a flow of ideas and analyses that discredit the views they hold and substantiate others, provided those ideas and analyses can withstand intensive professional scrutiny and can be verified.

People who believe in a free society, in limited government, in individualism, in private property, in free enterprise, and in a market economy are, with a few notable exceptions, remarkably indiscriminate in their support of intellectual activities, including universities, research organizations, and public information programs. They are at least as likely to support activities that are part of the problem as to support those that can do something about it. To some extent this is because they do not understand how public opinion is formed. To some extent it is because they are interested only in quick results —meaning before the next election—when they should think in terms of generations. To some extent they simply lack the sophistication to know which of the counter currents have the qualities that will make an impact on honest intellectuals.

Let me be specific by mentioning a few examples of what seem to me effective and promising sources of counter currents to the prevailing tide of opinion.

The National Bureau of Economic Research, now fifty-five years old, is the fountainhead of most of our factual knowledge about the economy. National income, gross national product, productivity, income distributions, savings and wealth, financial flows, the quantity of money, and business indicators are among the economic measures that we owe to the Bureau. The Bureau is supported by foundations and hundreds of businesses, yet my impression is that its annual budget is much smaller than that of, say, the Brookings Institution.

The University of Chicago's Economics Department and Business School, which are about eighty years old, are by far the largest source of college professors who support free enterprise and a market economy. Lawrence Laughlin, Jacob Viner, Frank Knight, Henry Simons, Milton Friedman, James Lorie, George Stigler, George Shultz, Yale Brozen, and Walter Fackler are some of the best-known names associated with economics and business at Chicago. Yet my impression is that private and corporate support of these units at Chicago is far less than for the corresponding units at, say, Harvard.

Among other organizations that could be mentioned and subjected to similar comparisons are the Tax Foundation, the University of Virginia's Thomas Jefferson Center, the Hoover Research Institute, the UCLA Economics Department, the American Enterprise Institute for Public Policy Research, the University of Rochester's Economics and Political Science Departments and its Graduate School of Management, the University of Miami's Center of Law and Economics, and others. None of these is adequately financed.

None represents exclusively a free market viewpoint, or any other one viewpoint. Indeed, their influence among intellectuals depends more on their objectivity, competence, and tolerance than would be the case if they were more in conformity with the prevailing orthodoxy.

To summarize briefly what I think we can do about it:

We can recognize that public opinion, not ignorant or malevolent legislators, is the root of the problem. We can try to understand the processes by which public opinion is formed. We can support objective research, scholarship, and education of high quality that have the capability of challenging prevailing opinion and nourishing counter currents of opinion among the intellectuals.

We can recognize that in any serious effort to do something about it time must be measured not by the two-year intervals between elections but by the twenty-five-year intervals between generations.

Finally, we can discriminate in financial support between organizations, institutions, and individuals that are part of the problem and those that have a potential for doing something about it.

4

The Rule of Law

THE MEANING ATTACHED TO THE PHRASE "rule of law" is coming to be in practice the opposite of what traditionally we have understood by it. Traditionally, the ideal of the rule of law has been that all men were equal before the law, regardless of rank, position, race, religion, income, occupation, or any other characteristic; the law was blind. The ideal of the rule of law has precluded retroactive legislation, and it has precluded laws intended to burden or benefit some people differently from others in the same circumstances.

The term "rule of law" now is coming to mean that all activities and relations between people should be regulated by law. It is argued that in an interdependent society any action of an individual and any transaction between individuals necessarily affects other members of the society, so it is intolerable that there should be any activities or transactions that are not regulated by law. Since human beings cannot exist except in a society, and a society is by definition interdependent, it follows that "whatever is not compulsory should be prohibited." This is coming to be the new meaning of "the rule of law"; instead of protecting freedom, the new rule of law annihilates freedom.

Possibly, as lawyers, you welcome this reversal of the concept of the rule of law, for it is creating a huge market for lawyers. But I do you the honor of presuming that you do not welcome it, that it distresses you as much as it does me.

Presented at the University of San Diego Law School on 15 January 1976.

Can we cure what Walter Lippmann called "the sickness of an overgoverned society," or at least slow its advance? Public opinion polls, the pronouncements of new governors from California to New York, editorials in traditionally liberal newspapers, and many other signs suggest that there is a deep and pervasive mood in the land that yearns for relief from the sickness of overgovernment that is manifested in the perverted meaning of the rule of law.

But what of the political institutions through which such relief would have to come? Are they capable of bringing it about, even if a considerable majority of the people want it? I have grave doubts that our political institutions have that capability. The reason for my doubts is that our system of government is one in which minorities rule. It is possible for any individual to gain enormously if he can harness the coercive powers of government for his particular advantage, perhaps through funds to support his industry or profession, perhaps through giving him cheap loans, perhaps through increasing some welfare program such as Social Security, perhaps through protecting him from competition, perhaps through tax advantages.

If even a small percentage of the voters in a congressional or legislative district share a common interest that can be served through the coercive powers of the government, and if they will vote for or against a candidate almost solely on the basis of his stand on the issue of overriding importance to them, most candidates will have to support this interest or be replaced by someone who will. Most congressmen could not win if, for example, a bloc much above five percent of their supporters were to shift to their opponents.

When a legislature made up of members elected under these conditions convenes, it is probable that no single law could get a majority vote. As the legislators get down to work, groups in favor of one measure or another will attempt to find other groups with whom they can form coalitions, each group agreeing to support the other group's pet measure in return for support of its own pet measure. As the legislative season progresses, gradually some measures will command majorities and be enacted. Professor William Riker, of the University of Rochester's Political Science Department, has pointed out that, at the end of such a legislative session, it is quite likely that almost every legislator and most of the public would prefer that all the legislation of that session be wiped off the books. This is because the cumulative effects of the many measures benefiting others probably will offset the effects of the few measures benefiting any one person. Yet our political processes are such that at each session a good many laws inevitably will be passed.

The only effective protection against this, if representative government is to be preserved, is a series of self-denying ordinances, by which it is agreed that certain areas simply are not subject to legislative action. For, as Walter Lippmann said, the attempt to legislate in these areas "multiplies the number of separate self-conscious appetites," thus leading to an unstable and ultimately self-defeating situation.

Such self-denying ordinances are, of course, exactly what the founding fathers attempted to achieve when they wrote the Constitution of the United States. They specified certain powers for the Federal government, and prohibited it from doing anything else. But with the passage of time a series of measures, each seeming good and proper at the moment, have eroded the proscriptions until today it is difficult to name an area which the Federal government does not regulate.

Perhaps I *seem* to be saying that our sickness of over-government cannot be cured. Perhaps I *am* saying that. But if I am, I am saying it as a challenge to your generation. When I was your age, I really believed that the impossible merely takes a little longer. I hope that Lippmann was wrong when he wrote that "men may have to pass through a terrible ordeal before they find again the central truths they have forgotten." But I have no doubt that he was right when he said that "they will find them again, as they have so often found them again in other ages of reaction."

5

The Open Society

THREATS TO THE OPEN SOCIETY concern universities as much as any institution in the modern world. The very heart of the purpose of a university lies in openness. It is open to free inquiry, discussion, and criticism. It is open to all participants, subject only to their intellectual qualifications and their respect for its openness. The opinions and facts that its participants produce are open for the whole world to know.

By the phrase "Open Society," I suppose we all have pretty much the same thing in mind. In explaining it we get involved with terms like freedom, pluralism, voluntarism, opportunity, individualism, equality, justice, and—if we do not restrain ourselves—peace, progress, patriotism, prosperity, and purity.

My advice is not to pursue the task of defining the "Open Society." If we do, we may find that we do not know what we are talking about, or—worse!—that we are talking about a variety of contradictory things.

The phrase "Open Society" conjures up in my literal mind a picture of a society in which something is open. But just what is open in the Open Society? Not the door to get in, if we want to be able to apply the term to the United States since the First World War.

Once, of course, we were an Open Society in that sense. In the ten years before the First World War, for example, ten million peo-

Presented to the Annual Conference of the Public Relations Society of America in Philadelphia on 13 November 1967.

ple came through our open door. This was a 12½ percent increase in population in a decade from immigration alone. It was a movement of people that dwarfed the more spectacular transplantations brought about later by the great People's Tyrants of the twentieth century. To preserve openness of entry would be indeed a challenge. In fact, we are half a century too late.

No, the openness of our society is not open access to it. The openness must be within our society. But openness to what? Obviously the governorship of Pennsylvania, the chairmanship of General Motors, the presidency of the University of Rochester, and the heavyweight championship of the world are not open to everyone in the United States. In fact, only the heavyweight championship is open to anyone at this moment. The other jobs are filled.

Furthermore, when those jobs become vacant, they will not be equally open to everyone in the country. A list of a dozen would probably be sufficient to include all possibilities for the next chairman of General Motors, or at the outside a list of a hundred. The lists for the next governor of this state and the next president of my university would be longer, but would not include more than a small fraction of 1 percent of the population.

You will recognize immediately that while these facts are true, they say nothing about the openness or lack of it in our society. You may want to suggest that if, for example, every child born this year has an equally good chance to become heavyweight boxing champion, or to become chairman of General Motors, then the society is an open one. But surely it is going too far to require this as a condition of openness. Some of the children born this year will be girls; they are shut out of both the chairmanship and the championship.

Some of the boys born this year will grow up too small for one job, too stupid for the other. Must an Open Society find some way to offset these handicaps, and revise the Marquis of Queensbury rules so that the runt and the giant have equal chances of becoming champion?

To revise boxing rules to bring about this equality would require more ingenuity than I can muster. But let me assume that new rules are devised that offset the runt's disadvantage and the giant's advantage, so that, when the two pair off for the championship, the odds quoted in Las Vegas will be the same on each contestant.

Even this would not be sufficient to open up completely the path to the heavyweight championship. Although no one would any longer be excluded for purely physical limitations, there would still be some shut out by lack of motivation. They might have the size, stamina, and dexterity to become champion, but just not want to. Maybe they are lazy or too easily satisfied, and settle for becoming janitors, policemen, shop foremen, public relations men, or university presidents when, with proper motivation, they could have had as good a chance as anyone of becoming heavyweight boxing champion.

This lack of motivation would itself be a manifestation of lack of openness in our society. After all, this kind of motivation probably is acquired largely through family and neighborhood influences. Not all families and neighborhoods are alike. Children do not move freely among families, for our society is not at all open in that respect—families are not nearly as open to the free mobility of children as to the free mobility of husbands and wives. Furthermore, similar families tend to cluster in neighborhoods, and even when families move, they are likely to move to neighborhoods not a lot different from those they left.

Even if we were able to devise rules that would offset differences in motivation as well as in physique, so that any two boys born this year have the same chance of becoming champion, would we really have reached the Open Society? What about third parties? Boxing fans might feel that they had nothing like as open an opportunity for good entertainment under the new rules as under the old. Or, if we carry through the story for General Motors instead of boxing, imagining a set of conditions under which any two boys born in the same year have the same chance of becoming chairman of General Motors, regardless of intelligence, character, personality, and motivation, we might find automobile buyers disappointed by the results.

Does the Open Society aim only at seeing that all advantages are equally open to all, or does it also seek to increase the total amount of advantage—total welfare—as much as possible? If it aims at both objectives—and of course we all know that in fact it does aim at *both* a high level of welfare *and* an equitable distribution of welfare —then what about choices that involve more of one and less of the other? Obviously, carrying equality so far that everyone has an equal chance of becoming chairman of General Motors would involve too great a loss of employment opportunities for others, and too great a loss in goods and services for consumers. But where do we draw the line? What about arrangements that make it only a little more advantageous to be chairman of General Motors than to be— as was the brother of a recent GM chairman—a contented carpenter

at GM? Are the lines better drawn and the compromises better designed in an Open Society than in a restrictive one? I think they
are and you think they are. But what is our evidence?

Any serious effort to diminish the rate at which our society is
losing its openness must reckon with issues like these. It is no use
simply describing the glories of openness and pretending that proposals for closure and restrictiveness are wholly misguided. Closures
and restrictions, in my observation, usually are misguided, but seldom wholly so. What their sponsors claim for them would have some
merit, so to that extent they are not wholly misguided. What they
actually do, however, may fail to achieve much of what the sponsors
expect, or may bring about unanticipated bad effects, or both.

What I am trying to imply is that there must be real study and
analysis underlying efforts to keep our society open. In particular, in
confronting challenges to the Open Society, it is necessary to have
a good comprehension of the nature of those challenges and the
merit in them, as well as a good comprehension of the way an Open
Society functions and the dangers in closure. This requires, I fear,
considerably better teaching of the social sciences in our colleges
than we are likely to have soon and, basically, considerably more
and better knowledge in the social sciences.

Anyone seeking to cope with the tide of opinion that is running
increasingly against openness in our society needs to know something
about that tide. From time to time I urge people to read a certain
book on this subject. The book I recommend was first published in
1905, but be sure to get the second edition, published in 1914. The
title is *The Relation between Law and Public Opinion in England
during the Nineteenth Century*. The author is A. V. Dicey—Albert
Venn Dicey.

The most fascinating part of Dicey's book is a 72-page "Introduction to the Second Edition" written in 1914. If I had composed this
keynote address by simply choosing sections of that "Introduction"
and reducing the style to my own level, I am confident that you
would have credited me with deep insight into current opinion and
would have appreciated what you would interpret as many allusions
to contemporary events.

By 1900, Dicey tells us,

> The current of opinion had for between thirty and forty years
> been gradually running with more and more force in the direction
> of collectivism. . . . It . . . was in 1900 apparent to any impartial
> observer that the feelings or the opinions which had given strength
> to collectivism would continue to tell . . . strongly upon the legis-

lation of the twentieth century. . . . The main current of legislative opinion from the beginning of the twentieth century has run vehemently toward collectivism.

By "collectivism," Dicey means "the school of opinion . . . which favours the intervention of the State, even at some sacrifice of individual freedom, for the purpose of conferring benefit upon the mass of the people."

Some of the most significant material in the "Introduction" to Dicey's second edition is his analysis of the causes that have led to the acceptance of collectivist ideas. He gives six major groups of causes.

First, he mentions "the existence of patent facts which impress upon ordinary [people] the interdependence of private and public interest," because of which

> . . . the whole course of trade tends rapidly to place the conduct of business in the hands of corporate or quasi-corporate bodies. . . . The companies, moreover, carry on a business the successful management whereof assuredly affects the prosperity, and even the safety, of the [country]. . . . A modern strike again . . . turns out more often than not to involve social or public interests. . . .
>
> The advance, again, of human knowledge has intensified the general conviction that even the apparently innocent action of an individual may injuriously affect the welfare of a whole community. . . . Almost every addition . . . to . . . science, adds to the close sense of the interdependence of all human interests. The discovery, for instance, that the health of a nation depends . . . on the general observation of certain rules of health not only increases this sense of interdependence but also suggests that the fancies, the scruples, or the conscientious objections of individuals, or, to put the matter shortly, individual liberty, must be curtailed when opposed to the interest of the public.

The second reason cited by Dicey for the rise of collectivism is "the declining influence of other movements." He mentions the hopes once held for constitutional changes, for example republics or constitutional monarchies, and the disappointment in them. Parallels in this country would be the great hopes once attached to the initiative, referendum, and recall, or to the direct primary, or to women's suffrage, or to proportional representation, or to the Civil Service System.

Nationalism was from the Napoleonic wars until the First World War a basis for many extravagant hopes that were ultimately disappointed. The creation of the German Empire, for example, did not fulfill the hopes for it. On the contrary, it "imposed upon the world the all but unbearable burden of huge standing armies [and] involved the dismemberment of France. We can at any rate now see that national independence is nothing like a cure for all the evils under which a country may suffer."

"Where, again," Dicey asks, "can we find the generous enthusiasm [of 30 to 40 years ago] for raising backward races of the world, such as the negroes of America, to a position of freedom and equality . . . ? We may trust that this decline in public virtue is a merely transitory phenomenon."

Religion is another movement to whose decline Dicey attributes the rise of collectivism:

Preachers . . . of today have lost to some extent the belief . . . that human beings individually, or society as a whole, can be reformed by . . . teaching . . . religious truth. . . . Good and religious men now attach less importance to the teaching of religious dogma than to efforts which may place the poor in a position of at any rate comparative ease and comfort. . . . This . . . change gives to the preachers of today a new interest in social reform; and [it] opens the minds of such men to the importance of social improvement. But, to speak quite fairly, this change produces some less laudable results. It disposes zealous reformers . . . to overrate the benefits to be gained from energetic and authoritative socialism. The fervent though disinterested dogmatism of the pulpit may, moreover, in regard to social problems, be as rash and misleading as the rhetoric of the [political] platform. It is specially apt to introduce into social conflicts the intolerable evil of "thinking fanatically," and therefore of acting fanatically.

A third reason for the rise of collectivist thinking, according to Dicey, is "the general acquiescence in proposals tending toward collectivism." This acquiescence he attributes to "the combination of an intellectual weakness with a moral virtue. . . . For sixty years"— remember that Dicey wrote this in 1914, so he means since the middle of the nineteenth century—"For sixty years novelists, newspaper writers, and philanthropists have alike brought the condition of the poor constantly before the eyes of their readers or disciples. The desire to ease the sufferings, to increase the pleasures, and to satisfy the best aspirations of the mass of wage-earners has become a marked characteristic of the wealthy."

Dicey's fourth reason for the rise of collectivism is "the advent . . . of parliamentary democracy." This has "increased the power of a well-organized faction or group, which is wholly devoted to the attainment of some definite political or social object. . . . This possible tyranny of minorities . . . is a fact to which in the twentieth century no reasonable man can shut his eyes." The electorate has learned "that political authority can easily be used for the immediate advantage, not of the country but of a class."

Dicey's fifth reason is "the spread of collectivism or socialism in foreign countries."

His sixth and final reason is "the existence of industrial discontent. . . . We must bear in mind . . . that discontent or even violent indignation . . . is often due far less to . . . suffering . . . than to . . . the contrast between given institutions and . . . desires."

A possible lesson from Dicey's essay of more than half a century ago, which found that the tides of public opinion had even then been running strongly for more than half a century in the direction of collectivism, is that the man interested in meeting challenges to the Open Society may well be a King Canute who is a century too late in giving his command to the tides of opinion.

On the other hand, "every tide will have an ebb," according to an old saying, and according to another, "the highest flood has the lowest ebb." Dicey enumerates some counter-currents which should be useful to the Canutes among you.

"Distrust of State interference is still entertained by the mass of . . . citizens. . . . The dogma of *laissez-faire* has . . . stimulated energy of action. It has left room for freedom of thought and individuality. It has fostered the trust in self-help. It has kept alive emphatically the virtues of the . . . people."

Another counter-current is "the inconsistency between democracy and collectivism":

> The ideal of democracy . . . is government of the people by the people, and in accordance with the wish of the people; the ideal of collectivism is government for the good of the people by experts, or officials who know, or think they know, what is good for the people better than either any non-official person or than the mass of the people themselves. Each of these two ideals contains something of truth, but each of these ideals may sooner or later clash with each other. . . . Beliefs marked by essential inconsistency are certain to give rise to most serious and, it may be, very practical and embittered dissension.

Another cross-current, it seemed to Dicey, is "opposition to the . . . financial burdens of collectivism. . . . For the true collectivist . . . does not leave a penny which he can help to 'fructify in the pockets of the people.' "

With those meager clues to ways of meeting the challenge to the Open Society, I conclude Mr. Dicey's keynote address, and add a few words of summary and interpretation.

A variety of real forces has produced the strong movement away from the Open Society and toward collectivism that has been going on for fully a century. Some of these forces are related to obvious social changes—for example, increasing population, increasing urbanization, the growth of large corporations and labor unions, the changed nature of war, the revolution in transportation and communication, and the growth of science. Not all of these changes do in fact require increased collectivism. Indeed, it was the emergence of these trends in the eighteenth century that motivated the replacement of restrictive or mercantilist policies by the Open Society. Nevertheless, a common cliché is that institutions that served when the world was smaller and simpler are necessarily unsuitable now that it is larger and more complex—a non sequitur that ignores the fact that most of those institutions were adopted only after the increasing complexity was well under way and were adopted as a rational means of dealing with it.

Some of the forces making for collectivism arise not from broad social trends but from specific political arrangements, in particular from the tyranny of minorities that is made possible by majoritarian democracy.

In any event these are real forces that must be understood and reckoned with, that cannot be much affected by superficial efforts, and that certainly cannot be appreciably diverted in less than a generation.

Nevertheless, there are significant forces against collectivism that may perhaps, in a generation or two, grow into a real turn in the tide. One of the few interesting things about what has been called the "New Left" is that it seems to be reacting unwittingly against the collectivism of the old left—against the contradiction between democracy and collectivism. Unfortunately, the New Left has been characterized so far by muddle-headedness, irrationality, ignorance, and childishness. It is like a baby screaming in its crib, as yet incapable of analyzing whether its discomfort arises from hunger, an open safety pin, a wet diaper, or its own thumb in its eye. But from this screaming baby there may mature (Who knows? Greater miracles have happened!) a rational, competent adult, capable of analyzing the constructive possibilities of the Open Society and capable of applying its analyses to reforming society.

6

Abolish the Draft

TODAY MARKS THE FIFTIETH ANNIVERSARY of the end of the First World War and the founding of your organization. From the looks of this audience, only a minority of you can remember that historic eleventh day of November in the year nineteen hundred and eighteen.

I am among that minority. The Armistice came less than a week after my sixth birthday. It was significant to me in two ways, both purely personal. First, I was assured that the Armistice meant that my father would soon be home from the Army, in which he was a lieutenant. Second, I could sense a real change in the attitude of grownups—the lifting of doubts, worries, and uncertainties. This dramatic change of spirit was in contrast with my only other vivid recollection of the First World War, the sense of dread and gloom that infected all the grownups during Germany's Argonne offensive.

Of course I do remember some other things about the War: being admonished to eat everything on my plate because "the Belgian children were starving"—an admonition whose illogicality was transparent even to a five-year-old; saving tinfoil and peach seeds; and, of course, the false Armistice a few days early, which is actually more clear in my recollections than the true Armistice, for the false news reached us in daylight while my mother was in the process of buying me a new pair of shoes in a store downtown in Fresno, California.

Delivered to the American Legion of Monroe County at Rochester, New York, on the occasion of the fiftieth anniversary of the founding of the Legion, on 11 November 1968.

The 1918 Armistice came more than a century after the end of the last previous war that had involved most of Europe and the United States. From the final defeat of Napoleon by the British and Prussians at Waterloo on June 18, 1815, until the declaration of war by Austria against Serbia on July 28, 1914, there was a period of 99 years and 40 days of unparalleled peace and freedom, accompanied by social progress such as had never been dreamed of earlier.

So when the Armistice came it was natural that we expected the peace after the First World War to be at least as permanent as had been the peace before the First World War. But we did not just take it for granted that peace would be permanent. We worked to make it permanent. We established the League of Nations. Many treaties were negotiated to insure peace. War was renounced as an instrument of national policy. The major naval powers, including the United States, signed and carried out disarmament agreements, scrapping enough war ships to reduce their navies substantially.

On the first day of September, 1939, all the hopes, efforts, and accomplishments of twenty-one years were wiped out with the invasion of Poland by Germany.

Ironically, one of the major causes of the destruction of the peace for which so many had worked so hard and so well was an excess of passion for peace. It became apparent that for many citizens of England, France, the United States, and their friends, peace outweighed all other goals, values, and purposes together. No evil could be so great, we declared, as deliberately killing one's fellow man in war.

Even when Hitler had already imprisoned hundreds of thousands or perhaps millions of people, and even after he had begun their systematic torture and annihilation, young men in England, France, America, and other countries took the "Oxford pledge" not under any circumstances to fight for flag or country. As a result of the pledge, and of the basic spirit of which it was only one manifestation, the leaders of these countries were deprived of credibility in international negotiations when they tried to suggest that their countries would not countenance unbridled aggression and tyranny, but would draw a line where they would stand and fight.

We know now that when Hitler's Army occupied the Rhineland they carried orders to retreat if any resistance were encountered. Hitler had issued these orders to back up the guarantees he gave his poorly armed generals that they would meet no resistance from the overwhelmingly better-armed French and the other signers of the Treaty of Versailles.

It is now more than twenty-three years since the end of the Second World War. This peace has already proved to be at least two years more enduring than that after the First World War. But of the Vietnam conflict's many disastrous consequences for the United States, none seems to me so fraught with lasting peril as the fact that it has demonstrated clearly to the world that it is still true, as it has been true throughout our history, that we will not follow our leaders when they judge that the national interest requires resort to arms.

The Revolutionary War was marked by dissent no less violent than that of today. So was the War of 1812, and the Mexican War, and above all the Civil War. Only in the two World Wars, when we considered ourselves the victims of attacks initiated by aggressors, has this country shown the unity, determination, and perseverance required for the successful prosecution of a war.

Do not misunderstand me. Though I recognize that the basic pacifism of Americans is fraught with peril in the modern world, and I regret that Vietnam has etched it in the minds of our enemies, it is one of the things that I cherish most about my country. I am one of those who would dearly love to see "America the Beautiful" replace our present national anthem—not only because it can be sung even if you are not an opera star, but because of the sentiments its words express so poetically:

> Crown thy good with brotherhood,
> From sea to shining sea.

How can we preserve our national security in a world in which, unfortunately, "only the strong can be free" (as Wendell Willkie put it twenty-eight years ago) and at the same time preserve one of the most admirable traits of our American character, our deep-seated love of peace and hatred of war and militarism?

We must not again underestimate the strength and the depth of American devotion to peace. Of all the considerations that led our forebears to come to this far-off land with its unknown risks, strange institutions, a language foreign to many, and little chance of ever again seeing home or loved ones, probably none was more powerful than the desire for peace and freedom. These values continue to be instilled in us generation after generation by our parents, our schools, our churches, our literature, and our political leaders.

Just as we must not underestimate the strength of American devotion to peace and repugnance for war, so also must we not undervalue it. To weaken it would be to jeopardize one of the traits of character that makes America great, that makes it loved and admired throughout the world—much to the despair of the rulers of some countries who try strenuously to inculcate hate for America.

Yet we must also reckon with the danger that this peaceful spirit creates for our country in a world in which the preservation of freedom depends ultimately upon a clear and credible commitment and capacity to fight and die if necessary. It will no longer suffice to wait until after a Pearl Harbor before we firm up our resolution convincingly. It may be necessary, as the Israelis have found, to take military initiative. But such initiative clearly imposes almost impossible requirements on national leaders. How can they, much less everyone else, ever be certain that military initiative *really* was essential, or even justified? Unless such certainty is held almost unanimously, and sustained however long the conflict may require, the country is paralyzed and loses its will.

There is one measure we can take and should take immediately that would do much to resolve the dilemma that arises because, on the one horn, one of America's most fundamental—and also most admirable—characteristics is repugnance for war and, on the other horn, the ability to wage war is essential to the preservation of freedom.

The measure I propose will, I fear, shock some of you. I respectfully request that you nevertheless hear me out and think over my proposal carefully, rather than reject it out of hand. It is not a view I have come to lightly or recently, but one I have held for over twenty years. It is not original with me, nor is it without strong support from many respectable citizens of unquestionable patriotism.

A step that would do much toward resolving our dilemma is to abolish the draft—abolish it completely, lock, stock, and barrel; abolish it immediately, with no ifs, ands, or buts.

This ought to be first on the agenda when the new Congress convenes next January 20. The President-elect already is on record unambiguously as favoring abolition of the draft, though he has not, so far as I know, said unequivocally *when* it should be abolished, beyond "as soon as possible." I suggest that April 20 would be an appropriate date—ninety days after the Inauguration.

At the time the draft is abolished it will be necessary to raise the pay of the military forces to obtain enough volunteers. Should a total, or near-total, mobilization become necessary, as in the two World Wars, a draft would again be appropriate.

My objections to the draft are of two kinds. First, it is immutably immoral in principle and inevitably inequitable in practice. Second, it is ineffective, inefficient, and detrimental to national security.

As to the point of principle, conscription involves taking bodily control of a person and subjecting him completely to the will of others. Nothing is more diametrically opposed to all our ethical, religious, and political principles. If this were necessary for the preservation of the nation, if it were necessary in order to assure that each person does his duty for the survival or safety of his neighbors, then the objections in principle would be outweighed by equally cogent conflicting principles, and the draft would be justifiable. This is obviously true in total mobilization. Equally obviously, it has been nowhere near true at any time since 1945.

I will turn in a moment to some of the inevitable inequities in the operation of the draft, but while we have in mind the basic immorality of the draft, we should note that proposals to require some form of universal national service, so that everyone will be equally mistreated, seem to me to magnify the immorality. Under that plan, even more people would be subjected to improper treatment. It implies that all human beings are chattels of the government.

Inequities in the operation of the draft have been well documented in several responsible studies of Selective Service data. Thus, one study showed that 77 per cent of qualified high school graduates serve two or more years in the military, but only 32 per cent of college graduates.

Now it is not clear how inequitable that is. It may be in some ways a greater sacrifice for a college graduate to be drafted than for a high school graduate. The college graduate, for example, loses more money in civilian pay than does the high school graduate. It may not be inequitable that an obligation be imposed mostly on those on whom it rests most lightly.

One of the most extreme inequities is to draft a star professional athlete, for example a heavyweight boxing champion. Such a person usually has only a brief period, often only two or three years, of peak earning power; he will probably not be able in all the rest of his life to earn a million dollars, much less a million dollars in one or two years. The burden on him is incomparably greater than on others. On the other hand, actual cases taper off gradually and continuously from this extreme to the man who simply has a good chance to become champion or otherwise to earn a million dollars, or the man who is in the midst of a period of rare artistic inspiration and achievement, or the man for whom internal psychological factors make this the most critical year of his life.

Local boards, of course, make some effort to allow for these special circumstances. But every human being is special, and evaluations of circumstances are subjective. If a boy's mother is dying, his board would probably defer him. What if it is his aunt? Or simply a dear friend of the family?

A lottery, which some have suggested, would not be more fair or equitable than the present arrangement. It is simply not fair to subject someone who is heavyweight boxing champion, or whose mother is dying, to exactly the same risk of being drafted as everyone else, because the consequences for them are so much more serious than for others. If we had one dish of diabetic ice cream, and one of regular ice cream, and you want the diabetic serving because you have diabetes but I want it because I have a slight preference for its flavor, would it be fair simply to toss a coin?

One of the most serious inequities of the draft is that the draftee bears not only the personal hardship of the armed forces, but also a large part of the financial hardship. With voluntary armed forces, other taxpayers would transfer to the men in the forces enough money to make up for what they lost in civilian pay, adjusted upward or downward for the special disadvantages or advantages of the armed forces. This would come about simply by setting the pay at levels where sufficient men would volunteer.

Draftees make for ineffective armed forces. A large proportion of their whole time in the armed forces is required for processing, training, and travel. Furthermore, they may be forced into combats of which they or their relatives disapprove, thus helping to demoralize the country in pursuit of any necessary military activities.

Although there are many other arguments in favor of volunteers instead of draftees, it would not be fair to use my short remaining time on those arguments and not have time to acknowledge that there are objections to an all-volunteer force. Some of the objections seem at first glance to have merit; but on examination none that I have heard really do have merit. The case against the draft is about as lopsided a case as one ever encounters in questions of public policy.

The most common objection is that all-volunteer forces would cost too much. Actually, the true cost would probably be less than with the draft, but more of the cost would be out in the open and paid by the taxpayers. Draftees bear large hidden costs, namely the loss of civilian earnings they could have made. In addition to the obvious unfairness of adding the monetary to the personal costs of serving in the armed forces, a less obvious unfairness arises because draftees are usually young and impecunious in comparison with the taxpayers who avoid these hidden costs.

General Hershey and others have referred to volunteers as "mercenaries," "hired killers," and "in there just for the money." Actually, at present 90 per cent of the commissioned officers and all of the highest-ranking noncommissioned officers are volunteers. As Professor Harry Gilman of the University of Rochester Graduate School of Management has asked, "Why . . . are officers who are encouraged to enter and to remain in the service by reasonably high levels of pay called 'dedicated career men' but privates who would volunteer when they too received higher levels of pay called 'mercenaries'?"

In conclusion, let me reiterate that abolishing the draft promptly is important to the welfare and security of our country. That is precisely why I bring the matter before this audience. You are a group whose dedication to the welfare of our country cannot be disputed, for it is amply witnessed by your services to America and the world. My hope is that if you appreciate fully how much the draft undermines the very things for which you have risked your lives, you can do our country another great service by helping to get it abolished.

It has been an interesting fifty years since 1918, in many ways a great fifty years, in some ways a terrifying fifty years. I hope you will invite me back to celebrate the completion of your next fifty years, and that all of you will be here.

Postscript

Most of the arguments made in favor of the draft say that the alternative of volunteer military forces is objectionable for one or more of the following reasons: (1) Not enough volunteers could be obtained for a major war. (2) Volunteers are ineffective. (3) Volunteers constitute a threat to freedom and democracy. (4) If the mili-

A Letter to the Editor of Science, *28 March 1969, responding to letters commenting on an editorial of 17 January 1969 that summarized the preceding speech.*

tary were volunteers, the general population would be less concerned with foreign policy than when the military are conscripts. (5) Volunteers would be predominantly the poor and Negroes.

1. No one has seriously proposed relying on volunteers during a major war, but the draft can be abolished even if as many men are kept under arms as now and even while the Vietnam War continues. This does not imply, however that the armed forces should be as large as they are now. Indeed, one important effect of the draft is that the armed forces are larger than they need to be for their present effectiveness, because (i) the military, like anybody privileged to purchase a service or commodity at bargain prices, is wasteful in its use of manpower, and (ii) the two-year tours of draftees are much less efficient than the longer tours of volunteers. Proposals to abolish the draft contemplate retaining for emergencies the present Selective Service registration system and the present system of reserves.

2. As to the charge that volunteers are ineffective militarily— tell it to the Marines, who are almost all volunteers. Or listen to Housman's 1915 "Epitaph on an Army of Mercenaries," brought to my attention by Professor George H. Ford of the University of Rochester Department of English:

> They, in the day when heaven was falling,
>   The hour when earth's foundations bled,
> Followed their mercenary calling
>   And took their wages and are dead.
>
> Their shoulders held the sky suspended;
>   They stood, and earth's foundations stay;
> What God abandoned, these defended,
>   And saved the sum of things for pay.

3. To the extent that a military force endangers freedom and democracy, the danger comes from the higher ranks of commissioned officers, all of whom are volunteers, as are most of the lower ranks of officers and all of the higher ranks of non-commissioned officers. Using conscripts instead of volunteers in the lowest enlisted grades—and those are the only ranks in which we use appreciable proportions of conscripts—is no protection, as was illustrated by recent coups in Greece and South America.

4. As a device for interesting the population in foreign affairs, the draft has the weakness that it affects so few people—and most of those who are directly affected, the draftees themselves, are not voters. A volunteer force affects every taxpayer, though each is affected less intensely than is a draftee or his parents. While the risk of being drafted may tend to sharpen interest in foreign policy, there is no basis for hoping that it also imparts the infor-

mation, perspective, and objectivity necessary for wise judgments about the national interest. In any case, there are distressing ethical implications in using the draft as an instrument in the battle for public opinion. If this use is accepted, would it not be proper to double or quadruple the number drafted in order to have a greater impact on public opinion?

5. Men are more attracted to hazardous work—whether in the military, police and fire forces, professional boxing, construction, coal mining, university administration, testing aircraft, auto racing, or treating contagious disease—if they are not qualified for equally rewarding but less dangerous work. We all regret that inequalities of opportunity exist; but it is hardly fair to deprive a man of the opportunity he considers best among those available to him, simply because we regret that he does not have better opportunities or does not rank differently the opportunities he has. That is what we are doing if we refuse to pay enough (in money and in nonpecuniary advantages) to attract enough volunteers, but rely on conscription instead.

To pursue these subjects, I recommend the documents relating to S.503 inserted by Senator Hatfield in the *Congressional Record —Senate* for January 22, 1969, and especially the article by Walter Oi of the University of Rochester Department of Economics inserted on January 23 and taken from *Current History*, July, 1968.

7

The Rise and Fall of
the Price of Steel

THE UNHAPPY EPISODE of the rise and fall of the price of steel in early
April did not go entirely unnoticed, even outside Pittsburgh. Nor
has it been entirely forgotten two and a half months later.

But what was noticed at the time was trivial compared with what
was not noticed. And what the incident is remembered for today is
minor compared with its major permanent effects.

To be specific: At the time, in early April, what was noticed was
that the price of steel stayed down. What was far more important
was that our whole economic system, sometimes described as a price
system, sometimes as a system of free markets, was shaken.

Now, eleven weeks later, what the episode is remembered for is
the stock market crash. But a far more serious effect was that our
whole governmental system, sometimes described as a system of individual civil liberties, sometimes as a rule of law, was shaken.

The rest of what I say will be an attempt to explain and expand
what I have said already.

First, consider the short-lived increase in steel prices. Frankly, to
an economist like myself, outside the steel industry, this increase did
not make sense. I am not questioning whether the steel industry
"needed" a price increase. What I question is whether market conditions at the time would have supported a price increase. In point of
fact, steel was not bringing even the full prices already in the official

*Presented before the Tax Foundation in Pittsburgh, Pennsylvania, on 26
June 1962.*

lists at that time, and the industry was operating well below capacity. Under such circumstances, it just does not seem reasonable to think you can get a higher price than the one you are already failing to get. The electric refrigerator industry learned that lesson this spring. Like steel, they announced higher prices, only to have to cut them back. Furthermore, when costs and market conditions do support price rises, they are not likely to support uniform percentage increases for all products.

Finally, an industry that has been described as "a lightning rod for the wrath of all recent Presidents" would seem well advised to achieve a higher average price by lowering some prices while raising others, in such a way as to provide the White House both with bewilderment and with possibilities for face-saving. Such an industry would also seem well advised to announce price changes the evening *after* a Presidential press conference rather than the evening before.

My own opinion is that the Administration's actions had nothing to do with the failure of the price rise to stick. That resulted from weak market conditions, just as in the case of refrigerators. If the President had said to the steel industry, "Congratulations, gentlemen, you need the increase if you are going to play your part in the growth of our economy," or if he had said, "This price increase is due to the wage increase negotiated by Richard Nixon, but no price increase will be necessary when the Goldberg wage increase goes into effect next July," I think that steel prices would still be no higher today than they actually are. I am talking, of course, not about published lists of prices, but about actual transactions, taking account of extras, quality, delivery, the cash actually paid, and the speed of payment.

So I think the price increase was a mistake. But—and this is the important point—it really does not matter whether I (or anybody else) is right that the increase was a mistake. If it was a mistake, it was a harmless mistake. It was harmless because it would not have caused inflation. Remember that inflation is a term that refers to a rise in the average level of *all* prices, not just to a rise in some one price. And the notion that when steel prices change all other prices change proportionately is just poppycock.

It was harmless also in a more important way, namely, that if it was a mistake it was a self-correcting mistake. Another piece of poppycock is the notion that the steel industry is characterized by enough collusion and market power to enforce a price rise that market forces will not sustain.

That is my first point then: that the real reason the price of steel returned to its previous level, and in some instances even fell below it, is to be found in market conditions, not in the words and acts of the Administration.

If that is so, why do I say that the Administration's actions were a blow at the foundations of our economic system? Because those actions were an overt, explicit move toward the further regulation of individual prices by the federal government.

Now let me be clear about the fact that the federal government has a right and a duty to control the general level of prices—in other words, to prevent inflation and deflation. That is the duty of the Federal Reserve Board through its control of the quantity of money, and of the Congress through its control of government deficits. But the government has an equal duty to see that individual prices remain free and flexible. Our system of market prices is the very heart and secret of our economic strength.

It is probably true that the Russian economy can do anything we can do, and even do it better. I mean that they can do any specific thing better, not everything simultaneously. For example, they could unquestionably build a bigger, better supermarket than any now in the United States, or a bigger and more automated bank. All they have to do is take a few dozen top scientists and engineers off their space programs and put them to work on a supermarket or on a bank.

But a far more important capacity, and one in which we excel them by far, is the ability to decide properly whether to build a supermarket and how super to make it, or whether to automate a bank and how automatic to make it. Even more fundamental is the ability to devise things like supermarkets and automation in the first place.

Consider the problem of distributing food to the residents of a certain area. Is it more efficient to have one supermarket or a dozen "Pa-and-Ma" type stores? The supermarket will involve a good structure, lots of capital equipment, and fairly high quality labor. It will need land for parking. People will come to it from considerable distances in their cars.

The "Pa-and-Ma" type stores can be in half-basements using little capital and the labor of retired people. Customers will come only from short distances and on foot.

Which is the more efficient way of distributing food? Obviously, that depends on literally thousands of details. For example, it may be that some elderly couples who could do nothing else productive could run small grocery stores. If so, the supermarket has to be enough more efficient to offset total loss of the labor of the elderly couples. On the other hand, the type of employee who works in a supermarket may have many other oportunities that are just as productive. In that case, the "Pa-and-Ma" type store needs only a small margin of efficiency to dominate.

Again, the small stores can perhaps be tucked into space that has little if any alternative use, whereas the supermarket requires land and good buildings that might be more valuable if used for other purposes. The comparison requires knowing what else could be done with the land and buildings and being able to evaluate the other uses accurately.

Another range of complications arises because not only do the two kinds of stores use up different kinds of resources, whose values must be compared, but they render different kinds of service. Some customers may strongly prefer one kind of service, others may prefer it only slightly or even prefer the other kind of service.

For each kind of store the total value to all the customers must be compared with the total cost. Only then can the two kinds of stores be compared and the decision made that is best for the country.

Decisions like that must be made millions of times every year. The over-all efficiency of the economy and our rate of economic growth are greatly affected by the accuracy and promptness of these millions of individual decisions.

The Russian economy, like all collectivist economies, makes these decisions poorly. But everyone understands the machinery by which the decisions are made. It is an administrative machinery, based on handing down orders from above.

Last fall *The New York Times* had a fascinating article on how badly the Russian economy performs. The article said:

> Soviet leaders speaking at the Communist party congress in Moscow have explained the apparent contradiction between their claims of rapid production growth and Premier Khrushchev's concession that a shortage of capital will bar the initiation of new investment projects for a year or so.
>
> The explanation is that ... failure to coordinate properly all parts of the complex Soviet economy causes vast amounts of capital to be frozen uselessly for many years in plants and installations under construction.
>
> Premier Khrushchev indicated the magnitude of the problem by presenting the following data: As of January 1, there were many millions of square feet of completed factory space that could

not be used because the machinery required for those factories was not available. At the same time in other parts of the country there were hundreds of millions of dollars worth of machinery of various kinds standing idle because the factories, mines, and other installations for which this machinery was designed were not yet ready. . . .

Gennadi I. Voronov, Communist party Presidium member, said: "Who does not know that the national economy suffers great difficulties with the supply of metals, that the supply of pipes is inadequate, that insufficient supplies of new machinery and mineral fertilizers for the countryside are produced, that hundreds of thousands of motor vehicles stand idle without tires, and that the production of paper lags? . . ."

The American economy makes these decisions well, but the method of making them is seldom understood and is widely misunderstood. We make them through the price system. The price system, in fact, may be called our economic secret weapon.

In our economy, prices are the messages that tell people what ought to be done. If the price of something is high, that is a message to producers to try to produce more and to consumers to try to use less. How high the price is tells how hard to try. The prices of raw materials, labor, land, and equipment are the messages that tell how things should be produced, for these prices reflect the amounts of the inputs available and the importance of the alternative uses for them.

Not only are prices the instructions that tell people what to do, they are self-enforcing messages. A producer who does not produce what is wanted, or produces it inefficiently, or does not adjust to change, soon finds that he is not taking in enough money to continue to buy his inputs. He is forced to stop wasting our resources. He is stopped just as forcefully as if he had received a cease-and-desist order from a Federal Bureau of Efficiency—indeed, more forcefully, for his Congressman or his trade association might have more influence with the bureau than with his bank—and anyway it would take the bureau five years to process the order.

The price system functions efficiently only insofar as the prices are free and voluntary. If the prices are set other than through free markets, either because of private monopoly or government intervention, the over-all efficiency of the economy is reduced.

Now the threat of direct price control made explicit by the President's handling of the steel situation, and more recently by the Solicitor General's speech at Harvard, and earlier by bills introduced in Congress as early as 1959, is a very direct threat to hobble and eventually cripple our economy. Not only the Administration but the public also are alarmingly willing to move toward direct price controls, at least if the Gallup poll is any criterion. The Gallup poll of June 8 reported that, of the 86% of voters who have an opinion about whether prices and wages ought to be frozen, 47% are in favor and only 53% opposed.

So my second point is that the major economic consequence of the steel episode was not the effect on the steel industry; it was to jeopardize the central source of our economic strength.

Now I come to my third point, about the relation of the steel episode to the stock market. Let me say first that the only thing I really know for sure about the cause of the crash is that nobody knows the cause, including me. (If anyone tells you he knows, ask him whether he sold short last winter.) But since no one knows, we can all speak freely.

We have to take into account the fact that the relation of stock prices to earnings was out of line with previous experience and with rates of return on less risky investments. We can discard the idea that the collapse resulted from diminishing fears of inflation. For one thing, there has been very little, if any, inflation in the U.S. in the past ten years. For another thing, the prospects of inflation within a couple of years are greater now than at any time in a long while.

We have to admit, also, that the market may simply be foreshadowing a recession; it has foreshadowed all postwar recessions, though recessions have not followed all of the market's drops. But we have to consider—and I myself think this is an important factor—that the basic threat to our economic progress that results from the likelihood of direct price and wage controls may have been a major cause. Furthermore, my fourth point, the threat to our system of government, may be the most important cause of all.

To bring out my fourth point, let me contrast the actions of Presidents Truman and Kennedy when they got mad at steel. President Truman took certain actions to control the steel industry in ways to which it objected. The industry thereupon resorted to the courts, for ours has been a government of laws, in which the citizen's rights are protected against the government by the courts. The Supreme Court ruled that the President did not lawfully have the power he had tried to exercise, but that is irrelevant; the important point is that the courts could be appealed to by those who felt that their rights were violated.

President Kennedy, on the other hand, used powers that are perfectly legal, but he used them to achieve purposes that are entirely outside the law. Since the powers he used, such as investigating individual income tax returns, are perfectly legal, redress through the courts is probably impossible and certainly improbable.

Rather than press this point myself, let me quote several passages from an article by Professor Charles Reich of the Yale Law School in *The New Republic* of April 30 on the chance that a few of you may have missed that particular issue:

> Each of the powers the President used was a legitimate one, and nothing he did was beyond his lawful authority. That is not the issue. The issue is whether the President made proper and responsible use of his powers. The evidence is overwhelming that the actions taken or inspired by the President were primarily for the purpose of intimidating and coercing the steel industry. The previous indulgence of steel industry practices, the use of so many drastic powers in concert, and the willingness to relent after the surrender all confirm this.
>
> Such use of power, whether its objectives are good or bad, is dangerous. Income tax investigations are legitimate, but should they be undertaken specially, with dramatic fanfare, to frighten someone who opposes Administration policies? Should a man's passport application be delayed if he does not fall into line on some economic issue? Should the goodwill of a business be destroyed by official denunciation if it proves stubborn in collective bargaining? The very immensity of government power demands, on the contrary, that it be used in a disinterested manner, and only for the exact purposes intended. Any other use gives a President the ability to force people to do things which under the law he has no right to require. It means that people offend the President at their peril.
>
> The spirit of our Constitution is the spirit of limitation on all powers, of disinterested enforcement of the laws, of equal protection, of due process. It was dangerously wrong for an angry president to loose his terrible arsenal of power for the purposes of intimidating and coercing private companies and citizens.
>
> ... [T]he President has no right to *force* his economic policies on an unwilling industry *without legislation*. Unless Congress acts, the fact is that in a free society there can be no unitary public interest, no single, authoritatively fixed idea of "the public good." Freedom has little meaning if it only allows action that "responsibly" conforms to the President's idea of the national interest. ...
>
> Even if everything that has just been said about President Kennedy's methods and objectives is wrong, his victory is still disquieting. It demonstrates how much power government has today. Such power, no matter how wisely exercised, is hardly less

frightening because the victim forced to surrender was a group of corporate giants and not a small business or a private citizen.

Who, no matter what his legal rights, will challenge the President hereafter? ...

Much of what Mr. Kennedy accomplished by pressure of government power he will hereafter be able to command by the subtlest suggestion. . . . President Kennedy's victory may have advanced peace and plenty, but it did no service to freedom.

So my fourth and final point is this: Far and away the most important and most distressing aspect of the steel episode was not the effect on the steel industry, nor the effect on the stock market, nor even the threat to our economic system, but the fact that it represented a long step toward authoritarianism. The very root and essence of authoritarianism is the idea that a central government has the authority to determine what is in the national interest, and to pursue that interest as defined by itself through any and all means.

But there is a silver lining. A long step was taken toward authoritarianism, yes; but it leaves a considerable distance yet to be traversed. Second, it was not a step from which there is no turning back. I am inclined to believe that it was an inadvertent step, an amateurish step, into which the Administration felt almost pushed as an unforeseen consequence of earlier steps taken, when they rather naively assumed responsibility for labor negotiations, for guidelines on wage settlements, and for avoiding strikes.

The job before us, then, is to make sure that the turning back occurs. That requires a fuller understanding, by the Administration and by the public, of the processes of a free economy and of the long-run evils of many short-run benefits. Economic education is a difficult challenge but not an insuperable one. I, for one, retain some hope.

8

Ends and Means at Watergate

WATERGATE IS DEPLORABLE, disgraceful, immoral, shocking, inexcusable, alarming, reprehensible, and quite a few other things besides, none of them nice.

But the saddest thing about Watergate is that in important respects it is far from unique, or even unusual. It is another of those many instances in which the end is regarded as justifying the means. One thing different about Watergate, however, is that the end is not acceptable to the academic-journalistic complex, as were the ends pursued by Daniel Ellsberg, the Berrigan brothers, the antiwar rioters, the Black Panthers, and innumerable others stretching back to the sit-in strikers of the 1930's.

The proper relation between ends and means is a profound question in moral and social philosophy. The assertion we frequently hear that the end justifies the means is clearly not tenable; but neither is the opposite assertion, that some means are absolutely wrong in all circumstances, no matter what end they may serve.

If we say that the end never justifies the means, we are immediately refuted by the little white lie which protects the dying mother from knowing of a disaster that has befallen her most beloved child; or by the medical researcher who, by sacrificing the lives of a hundred animals, saves the lives of a thousand humans; or by the would-be assassin of a Hitler.

Presented before the Roberts Wesleyan College Commencement in Chili, New York, on 10 June 1973, midway between the burglary at the Democratic National Committee and the resignation of President Nixon.

On the other hand, if we say that the end justifies the means, we face the problem of how ends are to be justified—the problem, in other words, of knowing the proper means for determining what ends are right, and what priorities should govern ends that conflict.

Frequently, especially in social and political life, means that would lead to an end that seems desirable can be seen to lead, if they are generalized, to bad ends more often than to good ones. Similarly, methods that would lead to results which initially are good, may lead in the long run to results that are bad. Thus, even if we were to start with a simple notion of the proper relation between means and ends we would face complex problems in applying that simple notion. No wonder, then, that views on the ethics of ends and means differ widely.

During the nearly two centuries since the Declaration of Independence and the Constitution were written, there has been a great shift of American political thought away from primary emphasis on means and toward primary emphasis on ends. Emphasis has shifted away from adjusting the rules of the game, to use an analogy, and toward adjusting the score.

When the Constitution was written, political thought was strongly influenced by the mercantilist policies which had prevailed for two centuries. Under mercantilism, governments prescribed in elaborate detail what would be done, how it would be done, by whom it would be done, what raw materials and machinery would be used and where they would come from, who could consume what, and in general what the outcome of social, political, and economic processes should be. Results did not always come out as prescribed, of course, and this led to stronger and even more pervasive controls, to fiercer punishments, and to controls on who could say what, to whom, and how, who could travel and where, and who could associate with whom and for what purposes.

By the end of the eighteenth century, enlightened political thought turned to specifying the rules rather than the results of social life. The American Constitution lists a small number of specific things to be done by the federal government, explicitly withholds from it powers to do *any* other things, and mostly concerns itself with the rules of the game. That is, it concerns itself largely with means rather than ends, the Bill of Rights being the most important and obvious of these means.

By the end of the nineteenth century a great transformation had occurred among the leaders of American political and social opinion, and during the second quarter of the twentieth century this became a transformation not just in opinion but in law and practice. It was a transformation in opinions about how social progress and social justice can best be assured. The earlier view had a profound distrust of coercion of some men by others, so it regarded progress and liberalism as almost synonymous with limiting the power of government. The modern view has a profound faith in the omniscience, omnipotence, and beneficence of government, so it regards progress and liberalism as almost synonymous with expanding the power of government. That transformation, I suggest, made Watergate inevitable.

By "Watergate," I refer not just to the intrusions on the Democratic National Committee in 1972 and activities related to that. I refer also to the reaction by journalists and politicians to the Watergate break-in, which—as I shall explain later—has been morally even more corrupt than the Watergate activities themselves. I refer still more broadly to a pattern in American public affairs which has been growing since the Second World War—the McCarthy craze; income-tax corruption in the Bureau of Internal Revenue, the Department of Justice, and the White House staff during the Truman administration; eavesdropping by government prosecutors on conferences between defendants and their lawyers; military conscription in peacetime; the biased perspective of the press and television; the politics of expectation and the exploitation of subsequent disappointment; the litigation explosion; restrictions on freedom that are regarded erroneously as necessary or even desirable in a modern, complex, urban, technological society; the rise of self-selected, self-righteous groups (contemporary counterparts of the Ku Klux Klan) responsible to no one and successfully influencing public policy, sometimes through intimidation, obstruction, suppression, assault, arson, bombing, maiming, and killing.

When the role of the government was restricted mostly to setting the rules of the game—that is, to setting conditions of social, political, and economic life—individual citizens gave their attention to improving their lives within those rules, and legislators gave their attention to improving and enforcing the rules governing the relations among individuals.

But as government began increasingly to control activities with a view to determining outcomes, groups with common interests began to turn their attention to influencing government to use its unlimited powers of coercion for their special advantage. For, as

Walter Lippmann pointed out a third of a century ago, and others long before him, "The attempt to regulate deliberately the transactions of a people multiplies the number of separate, self-conscious appetites and resistances." It leads people to channel their energies into seeking political power by any means. This is, again in Lippmann's words, "the sickness of an over-governed society." That sickness is the underlying cause of the Watergate symptom.

Journalists have commented with astonishment on the absence of pecuniary motives in the Watergate incidents. Their astonishment reflects the extreme lopsidedness of those who report and comment on public affairs. The same lack of pecuniary motives in Ralph Nader has been noted without surprise (though General Motors' skepticism on this point resulted in one of Nader's greatest pecuniary triumphs). The same journalists are not surprised by an apparent absence of strong pecuniary motives in the Berrigans. What motivates all of these people is power. And "the object of power," as Orwell has said, "is power." "Power is not a means, it is an end." It becomes an overriding end when government embraces the whole life of society, for the power attainable through government dwarfs and overwhelms all other sources of power combined, being the only power not subject to a greater power.

To cure the sickness of our over-governed society will require a renewed recognition that ends do not justify means, and that it may be worse to obtain a desirable end promptly by means of coercive government power than to attain the end more slowly through noncoercive, nongovernmental means. Unlimited government is unlimited evil.

Unfortunately, the prognosis is that the sickness will get worse before it gets better. Few people any longer understand the enormous powers for progress that lie in the actions of free individuals operating under minimal coercion or constraint. The progress of the nineteenth century, which is unparalleled in human history, bears striking witness to these powers. Not only do people not understand these powers for progress, they misinterpret progress which has occurred *despite* government intervention as occurring *because* of government intervention. Thus many people, especially young people, are literally unable to think of any other means of improving society than government action.

Some of the younger generation are beginning to chafe under the inefficiency, incompetence, and oppressiveness of pervasive government. So far, however, young people show no signs of learning how to cure the sickness, nor in fact any signs even of diagnosing correctly the source of their frustrations, much less of prescribing a cure. On the contrary, for every evil (and evil has come to mean merely lack of perfection, real or imagined, with no perspective on conditions at other places or other times) they suggest only new laws and new bureaucracies—more of the over-governing that has sickened society. For the obvious failures of existing bureaucracies the only remedy commonly suggested is a super-bureaucracy.

Recovery must commence, as did the sickness, among our leaders of thought and opinion. That requires a solid foundation of constructive, scholarly criticism and a body of imaginative, analytical knowledge of society: not knowledge of specific social problems— that must come later—but knowledge of basic facts and principles of economics, political science, sociology, history, and ethics. If the research universities and institutes develop the basic knowledge, if the undergraduate colleges and high schools disseminate it, then eventually the columnists, editorial writers, commentators, authors, and ministers who serve as intellectual middlemen will purvey it to the public, and finally politicians will respond to the opinions of the electorate. It will be at best a long, slow road, not an uninterrupted one, not a clearly marked one. Recovery will not come in my lifetime, but I hope that it will come in yours.

Until the Watergate affair shackled him at least temporarily, President Nixon appeared well launched on a movement of heroic proportions to reverse the trend toward over-government. Special privileges for small groups at the expense of the public have become nearly universal. To attack these one or a few at a time has become hopeless. Each small group has so much at stake that it protects its privileges with its maximum political strength. To each individual in the public at large, the cost of any one special privilege is so trivial that no appreciable counter-force is generated. The President therefore attacked special privilege on a breathtakingly broad front. If many special privileges can be reduced simultaneously, the total effect of all of them becomes significant to the individuals in the public at large. Furthermore, even members of small special-interest groups find their losses from the abolition of their special privileges largely offset by reducing the costs of the privileges of many other groups. Paradoxically, it may be easier to clean the whole Augean Stable at once than to clean it one stall at a time.

The President's own unparalleled abilities, augmented by the superb and dedicated service of Messrs. Haldeman and Ehrlichman, were achieving amazing progress. Total spending, which is a good index of the degree to which a government is encompassing the totality of society, was coming under control. Obsolete programs, ranging from forty years old down to five or six years, which—whatever may once have been the case—are at best sheer waste and often worse were being stopped. Programs were being decentralized from Washington to the states, to the counties, and to the cities.

There is, in fact, no doubt in my mind that the persistence and ferocity with which the Watergate affair has been pursued is related to the President's domestic reforms. Despite the self-congratulation of the newspapers that the exposure of Watergate is a triumph of a free and unbiased press, it is at most a triumph of a free and biased press. The *Washington Post,* the prime mover in exposing Watergate, has been unsurpassed in its vitriolic hatred of Richard Nixon ever since he attained prominence twenty-five years ago. Furthermore, quite apart from personal animus, the *Post* is one of the most ardent advocates of bigger, more pervasive, and more centralized government (the views which sell best in its market), and no paper in the country is more opposed to the President's efforts to reduce government.

Had the *Post* made comparable efforts in the Chappaquiddick affair, perhaps we would know as much about that as we know about Watergate. The Chappaquiddick affair, after all, was simpler and less effectively hidden. I do not doubt that if the *Post* had had the same animus toward Senator Kennedy that it has toward President Nixon, or even if it had been neutral instead of friendly toward the Senator, and that if it had had the same opposition to the Senator's policies that it has to the President's, or even if it had been neutral instead of friendly toward those policies, we would have known long ago more about Chappaquiddick than we now know about Watergate. The difference mocks the self-serving claims being made by and for the press. It has to be conceded for the *Post,* however, that exposing Chappaquiddick probably would not have been looked on by the Pulitzer Prize judges with the same admiration as exposing Watergate.

Was the press, in fact, primarily responsible for the exposure, as the press claims? I think not. That credit must go to Judge Sirica. But what of the means that he used to attain this worthwhile end? After the defendants had been convicted or pleaded guilty, he threatened them with inordinately long prison sentences if they did not provide evidence extending beyond the indictments which had been disposed of in his court. This differs only in degree from the medieval practice of exacting information by threatening torture. By this means a useful end was served. But does the end justify the means?

Even beyond this, the perpetrators of Watergate appear to be men of good character by their own lights, who put conscience and patriotism above civil law. In that regard they are exactly like Daniel Ellsberg. Yet the press, the ministers, and the politicians who condemn the Watergate convicts praise Ellsberg, the Berrigans, and others who have used comparable means for different ends.

Even spying and eavesdropping, which are viewed with such horror in relation to Watergate, seem to be acceptable when used for other ends. When Jack Anderson, who first attained notoriety about fifteen years ago by being caught red-handed "bugging" a room in the Carleton Hotel in Washington, recently published transcripts of grand jury sessions, the government did not indict him but instead negotiated a treaty with him by which he would, at his discretion, use paraphrases instead of direct quotations. In the Coplon espionage case, more than twenty years ago, the government listened through hidden microphones to conversations between the defendant and her lawyer; and while this ultimately resulted in the defendant's release, no one even suggested seeking to punish those responsible. Is it less reprehensible to spy on lawyer-client relations than on psychiatrist-patient relations, or merely less reprehensible to spy on those of whom we disapprove than on our darlings? It is clear that spying and eavesdropping simply are not objected to as improper means. They are objected to only if done for ends that are unpopular with the objectors.

This is why I said earlier that the reaction by journalists and politicians to the Watergate break-in has been morally even more corrupt than the Watergate activities themselves.

Forty years ago, willingness to overlook means if the ends were acceptable played a significant role in the rise of Hitler. He claimed that the Treaty of Versailles, which settled the First World War, was unjust and there was widespread acquiescence in this view in France, England, and the United States. When Hitler took the law into his own hands and invaded the Rhineland, the western countries were paralyzed by the idea that since there might be some merit in his claims, his means should not be resisted.

Similarly, during the Great Campus Craze of the Sixties many colleges and universities tolerated outrageous behavior, including violence and suppression of speech, on grounds that amounted to little more than that perhaps something on the campus (or even just in the outside world) was less than perfect, therefore any behavior should be tolerated.

While I started by recognizing that it is untenable to maintain that the end never justifies the means, I am concluding by arguing that we have departed far, far too distantly from what is sound in that precept. We have resorted so frequently to coercion—which is another way of saying that we have turned too often to government power—when we thought it could obtain a desirable end quickly that coercion has become a way of life. In that way of life, individuals inevitably diminish their efforts to make or do what others will value and voluntarily reward them for, and increase their efforts to gain power over the machinery of coercion—that is, the government. When attention is focused on gaining power, surreptitious and ruthless activities, of which Watergate is merely one of many, inevitably proliferate.

Another quotation from Walter Lippmann will serve to summarize my remarks: ". . . the collectivists and authoritarians," Lippmann wrote, ". . . may have taught a heresy and doomed this generation to reaction. So men may have to pass through a terrible ordeal before they find again the central truths they have forgotten. But they will find them again, as they have so often found them again in other ages of reaction, if only the ideas that have misled them are challenged and resisted."

Let us hope and pray that the ultimate effect of Watergate will be to lead people to challenge and resist the ideas that have misled them, and thus to commence to cure "the sickness of an over-governed society."

9

Power to the People

DURING THE PAST FOUR YEARS you have participated in a remarkable and heartening transformation of spirit on campuses—not just this campus, but most campuses. There has been a resurgence of good temper, of good humor, of kindness, of honor, of courtesy, of mutual confidence, of considerateness, of tolerance, of objectivity, of generosity, of rationality, of regard for the future, and of personal responsibility. All of this has been accompanied by a restoration of respect: respect of students for faculty, of faculty for administrators, of trustees for faculty, and of faculty, administrators, and trustees for students.

This recovery of confidence and mutual respect on campuses has occurred just when confidence and respect have nearly vanished from public affairs. Opinion polls show that at most one fourth of American citizens have confidence in and respect for the President, and that even fewer have respect for Congress. A survey last fall of the public's esteem for various institutions showed that, except for the military (which was at the top of the list, just an eyelash ahead of universities), all government institutions ranked at the bottom—federal, state, and local governments, the courts, Congress, and the Administration. Among private institutions, only labor unions ranked as low as did the various branches of government.

That this loss of confidence in and respect for government is not just a consequence of Watergate or of Vietnam is apparent from

Presented at the 124th Commencement Exercises of the University of Rochester on 12 May 1974.

earlier surveys. That it is not just an American phenomenon is apparent in England, Ireland, Germany, France, Italy, Russia, or almost any country in Africa, South America, or Asia.

Now the fact is that those who distrust governments are right. For governments everywhere undertake to do many things that cannot be done by governments—least of all by democratic governments—and they even undertake to do some things that cannot be done at all, by either governmental or non-governmental means. Governments promise, as a matter of course, good incomes, good health, good morals, good taste, and good relations among individuals. They promise equality, justice, tolerance, and safety, as well as peace, progress, prosperity, and purity, and even truth, goodness, beauty, and salvation. They attempt to protect us from our own follies: from the folly of smoking tobacco or marijuana, from the folly of watching indecent movies, from the folly of selling too cheap or buying too high, from the folly of buying too cheap or selling too high, from the folly of wasting our money, from the folly of failing to fasten seat-belts, from the folly of buying pills in containers that can be opened by children or arthritics, and from the folly of setting the wrong temperature on the laundry machine. The list is endless in number, infinite in detail, and growing exponentially.

It is a striking paradox that the more people distrust the government, the more powers and responsibilities they heap upon it, many of the new powers being designed to counterbalance other powers that the government already has. The more powers the government has, the more ruthless, corrupt, and pervasive become the efforts to control those powers, the more numerous and harmful become the failures of the government, and the smaller become the respect and confidence that the government receives or deserves.

The appropriate remedy for excessive governmental powers, for abuses of governmental powers, for ruthlessness and corruption in gaining control of governmental powers, is not to create new governmental powers but to dismantle those that now exist. *Return the power to the people.* Give each individual the right and the responsibility for making his own free choices and decisions. Inevitably, some individuals will make unwise decisions, even decisions that harm other people; but in the long run the harm done in this way is likely to be neither as great in the aggregate nor as hard to correct as the harm done by overgovernment.

Perhaps your generation will bring about as dramatic and beneficial a reversal in public affairs as has occurred in campus affairs during your four years here. If you do, it will be a reversal of the tides of law and opinion without precedent in the history of Western civilization. If you do not, what remains of the freedom and democracy that my generation once cherished will hardly last until 1984, much less throughout your generation.

IO

Doctors and Lawyers

YOU WHO ARE RECEIVING DEGREES in medicine or in the sciences related to medicine undoubtedly realize that throughout the country at this season thousands of others are receiving similar degrees in token of their preparation, like yours, for devoting the best parts of their lives to improving the health of their fellow men.

Most of you are vaguely aware, also, that all over the country even larger numbers are emerging from professional schools of another sort, namely schools of law. Probably few of you realize, however, that before your careers have run their courses those lawyers may have more influence than you have over what you do, how you do it, and how you are rewarded.

You may find lawyers defining the range of treatments that you are allowed to use in specified circumstances. Lawyers may prescribe the criteria by which you are to choose among the allowable treatments. Lawyers may specify the priorities you must assign to different patients. Lawyers may require you to keep detailed records to establish at all times that you are in full compliance. Lawyers may punish you unless you can refute beyond a reasonable doubt their presumption that your failures result from not following all of their rules, regulations, and requirements. And lawyers may decide what incomes you deserve.

Should you have the temerity to differ with the lawyers, you will be backed by the authority of your knowledge, your science, your

Presented at the Commencement Exercises of the School of Medicine and Dentistry at the University of Rochester on 26 May 1974.

skill, your art, your experience, your judgment, your dedication, and your conscience. Which is to say that in the eyes of the law you will have precious little backing; for knowledge, science, skill, art, experience, judgment, dedication, and conscience—whatever else their merits—do not constitute due process of law.

This control of health care by lawyers will come about through a process in which many of you, and most of your contemporaries, believe unquestioningly. That is the process of turning to the government to solve all problems, real or imagined, large or small, widespread or confined. If research funds or training funds are less than you would like, have the government get them from other people by force. If you think that smoking tobacco or marijuana is bad for health, have the government prevent it. If you think that cars are too big, get the government to limit their sizes. If you think that people should not see obscene movies, get the government to ban them by force. If you think that professional wrestlers are often frauds, have the government license them. If you think that doctors do not always perform perfectly, have the government establish professional standards and enforce them.

Scarcely anyone has confidence in any branch of government (except, ominously, the military), so we create new government agencies to monitor the old ones. Increasingly, confidence in private institutions and professions also is eroding, and the accepted solution is to regulate them through government, even though government is respected and trusted even less than the institutions it is charged with regulating.

It is this process of putting the least trusted of all institutions, government, in charge of less distrusted institutions and professions which may result in lawyers acquiring a far larger measure of control over health care and research than they have today. For what we call "government" is, after all, made up of people, and not necessarily superior people, much less perfect people. While not all people in government are lawyers, lawyers usually participate in writing rules, regulations, orders, guidelines, and directives, and the adjudicators and enforcers almost invariably are lawyers. So we can expect the work of those now receiving degrees in health to be closely regulated by those now receiving degrees in law.

Some of you may think that I am introducing a depressing note into an otherwise joyous occasion. For two reasons, however, I am not worried about dampening your spirits. First, if you do not take me seriously, as many of you will not, then of course your spirits will not be dampened. Second, if enough of you do take me seriously, my forecasts may happily become self-defeating, for to be forewarned is to be fore-armed and thus perhaps to forestall developments. The lawyers have you outnumbered, but on the average they are no match for you in intelligence, industry, or dedication. Just don't let them ambush you while you are absorbed in caring for the sick.

II

Goals

I I

What Do We Really Want
from Our Economy?

Aims of Economic Policy

What we really want is an ever freer, richer, better life for everyone.

Our economy must provide conditions that develop the mind and the spirit, as well as an abundance of material comforts and mechanical marvels. It must provide expanding opportunities for every individual to realize his own potentialities to the utmost and to open wider vistas for his children. It must encourage initiative, independence, and integrity. It must preserve and enlarge the dignity and moral worth of the individual. Our economy must, in short, strengthen the basic ideals and traditions of American life.

Our ways of working and of consuming constitute a large part of our whole way of life, and are closely intertwined with nearly all the rest. The goods and services provided by our economy, and growth in the economy, provide the means for preserving and enlarging the dignity of the individual. They make it possible to approach more closely our ideals of personal freedom, justice and fair play, broad and equal opportunity, the rule of law, and mutual respect and charity. Those very ideals and traditions are themselves responsible above all else for the unparalleled economic progress which our country has experienced under our Constitution.

A statement by President Eisenhower's Cabinet Committee on Price Stability for Economic Growth issued by The White House on 17 August 1959. I was the principal draftsman of its statements.[1]

These truths, old and familiar and almost commonplace, need to be restated here because policies for our material well-being must always be dominated by the fact that ours is a nation in which idealism, not materialism, is fundamental, a nation in which the government is the servant, not the master, of the people. If we think at all deeply about problems of economic policy we must recognize that economic growth is not an end in itself but a means of advancing toward more fundamental ends. In considering our economic goals, and in evaluating policies for achieving them, we must always keep in mind their contribution to the things we really want.

What then should be the economic aims of the American people? Their aims should be:

- economic growth—that is, a large and expanding output of goods and services
- maximum employment opportunities
- reasonable stability of the price level

While maximum employment opportunities and reasonable price stability both contribute to economic growth, they are worthwhile aims in their own right because they contribute directly to our ideals of self-reliance, integrity, and opportunity.

Economic Growth

A large and expanding output of goods and services makes possible:

- a high and rising standard of living: rapid improvement is as characteristic of the American standard of living as is its high level
- national security and adequate roads, schools, and other public facilities
- expanding job opportunities for ourselves and our children
- an increasing range of choices of cultural, educational, recreational, religious, and social activities

A large and expanding output requires:

- improving health, education, skills, and job opportunities
- discovering, developing, and conserving natural resources
- expanding science and technology

- increasing and improving our stock of tools, machines, buildings, and other equipment
- improving organization and management, so that men, machines, and resources produce the things that are most useful, and produce them ever more efficiently

Economic growth is complicated, and defies valid measurement. Numbers purporting to indicate what the rate of growth is, has been, will be, or should be require intricate interpretation. Economic growth is measured sometimes by increases in the nation's total output of goods and services. These increases are partly due simply to population growth, so for some purposes a better criterion of economic growth is average output per person. Even this is unsuitable for some purposes, for it fails to reflect increases in leisure due to shorter working hours, later ages of starting work, earlier ages of retirement, longer vacations, and other results of economic growth that are valuable but are not measured in terms of money. This difficulty is partly overcome by using still another measure, average output per hour of work. That average, too, may understate our real growth because as our incomes grow we spend more on services (education and medicine are examples) and other things for which measured productivity grows comparatively slowly. Thus the average may appear to grow more slowly or more rapidly merely because of shifts in consumption, not because of any real retardation or acceleration anywhere in the economy.

Maximum Employment Opportunities

For economic growth it is essential that our people, our machines and equipment, and our natural resources all have the fullest practicable opportunities for employment.

Not only is it important that they have maximum opportunities for employment, but also that they be employed efficiently. They must be used to produce more useful rather than less useful things, and outputs must be as large as possible in relation to inputs.

Finally, they must be employed under conditions of economic freedom. People must be free to choose for themselves among a variety of occupations, industries, areas, and jobs; free to decide whether to venture into a new business or risk their savings on a new idea; and free to choose according to their own tastes the ways in which they will spend their incomes after paying the taxes necessary to support essential public needs.

Even the ideas of maximum employment opportunities and of unemployment are not as simple as they sound. Much unemployment—sometimes nearly all of it, especially during recessions or in depressed areas—involves the hardships and lack of opportunity that we all associate with the word "unemployment." Some unemployment, however, especially in prosperous times, represents people who have just recently made themselves available for work and have not yet found their first jobs, or people who have given up or declined jobs with confidence that they can get other jobs that will suit them better. This latter type of unemployment—which, paradoxical though it sounds, reflects breadth of opportunity, not hardship—accounts in part for the fact that no one who talks about "full employment" ever means "full" in the literal sense of one hundred percent. It also explains why maximum opportunities for employment is a more appropriate goal than simply maximum employment.

An understanding of these matters is particularly important in considering the relation between maximum employment opportunities and price stability, for policies to eliminate unemployment do not need to raise prices unless an attempt is made to eliminate the unemployment that results from free choice rather than from lack of opportunity.

Price Stability

Reasonable stability of the general price level supports prosperity and growth. It also accords with our ideals of fairness and justice and the rule of law. A continuously rising price level, on the other hand, strikes at the roots of our way of life, economically and morally, for it:

- inflicts unjust hardships on the many families whose incomes, pensions, or savings are fixed in dollars, or do not rise in proportion to prices
- violates our standards of fair play by harming families whose incomes are average or below average more than families whose incomes are above average
- contradicts promises implied when people put aside income in insurance, government bonds, retirement funds, and other forms

of saving, for when the money is returned it fails to buy the goods and services that people were led to expect when they put the income aside

- creates expectations of further price rises and thus causes transfers of energy, ingenuity, and resources from productive to speculative activities
- distorts the accounts of business firms, creating at times an illusion of profits when in fact capital is being consumed, thereby threatening jobs
- reduces the nation's ability to sell in foreign markets, further threatening jobs

Resistance to rises in the general price level is bound to cause temporary inconvenience to some and to limit the gains of others, but reasonable price stability will powerfully promote the welfare of all.

Our economy has grown since the founding of the republic because we have had faith in ourselves, because we have developed institutions that reward enterprise and efficiency, and because we have believed in progress sufficiently to put aside enough from our current income to expand the productive plant and build the technology needed by a venturesome and growing population. Increases in the price level have not contributed to our economic growth. On the contrary, prices have risen most during war periods. In other periods price rises have often led to speculative booms, which have been succeeded by recessions and, sometimes, by prolonged and acute depressions. We surely do not want booms followed by depressions. What we want and need is sound, sustainable economic growth. The lesson of history is that orderly growth is most likely to occur under conditions of price stability.

Price stability is an idea that involves more than meets the eye. It certainly does not mean that every individual price is stable. On the contrary, freedom of individual prices to change is essential to economic efficiency, for prices are the messages that tell producers and sellers what things should be made in greater quantities and what in smaller quantities, and what materials and services are abundant and what are scarce in relation to the uses for them. "Price stability" must refer to the *general level* of prices. Even this is oversimplified, however, for the general level normally ebbs and flows with prosperity. The idea of price stability must refer to the *average* over a period of time of the general level of prices.

Conclusion

Policies for promoting economic growth, maximum employment opportunities, and price stability must be consistent with the fundamental goals and ideals of Americans.

Discussion of economic policies for promoting growth, employment, and price stability can proceed intelligently only on a basis of sound understanding of the many facets of the broad problem.

12

Challenges to
the American Economy

IT IS A CURIOUS AND STRIKING fact that when challenges to the American economy are mentioned the specific examples that come to mind are more properly called threats than challenges. Thus, we hear much about the dangers of labor monopoly. We hear about taxation that stifles incentive and directs energies into nonproductive channels. We hear about special privileges to certain industries, regions, or occupations that burden the rest of the economy. We hear about the menace of inflation.

But these, and many of the other difficulties of which we hear much, seem to me to be threats, not challenges. A threat to my mind, is something negative that may curtail, hamper, or impede the economy. A challenge, on the other hand, is something positive—an invitation or a goad to new undertakings, to expansion, to further accomplishment.

This insignificant and pedantic matter of terminology points up something significant and substantial about the American economy, and especially about American attitudes toward the American economy. The fact that most of the problems we recognize as confronting our economy today are threats and dangers rather than challenges and opportunities reflects, I think, the enormous confidence we have in our economy. Implicitly, we take it for granted that our economy

Presented before the Committee for Economic Development in Washington, D.C., on 19 November 1958.

is capable of infinite prodigies. We take as hardly more than a striking way to put a familiar fact Fabricant's extrapolation that our economy is headed toward an average family income of $25,000 per year within the lives of our own grandchildren (or even within the lives of the children of the youngest and most virile of active businessmen). Some people even take for granted something that in fact is fantastically beyond the capabilities of our economy, namely the provision of enough capital to the rest of the world to raise the material standard of living of all humanity to our own level. No one seriously doubts the ability of our economy to toss multimillion-dollar spitballs at the moon while simultaneously converting most of our air transport fleet to jets—and all of this while raising our standard of consumption rapidly, reducing the number of hours worked, and expanding education and research. Most of us are confident that there will never again be a depression like that of the 1930s, the 1870s, or the 1830s—or even like that of 1921 or 1938. Our confidence in this proposition about depressions is, in fact, now so great as to be almost comparable to the confidence attached to the same proposition thirty years ago.

You understand, I hope, that I am not myself accepting without qualification the foregoing propositions about the miracles our economy can perform. Indeed, I have deliberately exaggerated and caricatured a bit, in order to sharpen my point, which is that even these prodigies are commonly regarded not as challenges to our economy, but as matter-of-fact descriptions of what it can and will do—what it can and will do if no monkey wrenches are thrown in the machinery. To put my point another way, the fact that we seldom worry about challenges, but only about threats, reflects supreme confidence that we have a champ who will do more than we would ever dream of, and who needs only to be protected from poison, booby traps, and lilliputian shackles.

Now it seems to me that the greatest and the most profound challenge faced by the American economy currently is that of rising above these threats of monkey wrenches from within. If we examine the most serious threats to the economy, we find that almost all of them, whether they relate to laboristic policies, to unsound taxation, or to deleterious regulations, are manifestations of a single underlying point of view. Characteristic of this point of view is the idea that activities carried out by business in pursuit of profit are at best narrow, selfish, and only inadvertently socially useful, and more often are dishonest and socially harmful; and that, on the other hand, activities carried out through the authority of the government are wise and socially beneficial. A man who makes his career in business is regarded as somehow less exalted, less admirable, less devoted to his fellowman than one who enters science, the arts, the learned professions, religion, education, skilled crafts, or—above all—government.

Furthermore, participating in business is widely regarded as constraining the human spirit, as deadening the moral, esthetic, and intellectual sensibilities. Business is contrasted unfavorably not only with writing or painting on the left bank of the Seine, but with just about every other activity.

Very few people, at least among those likely to be taken seriously, would acknowledge explicitly such views as I have described. But I submit that deep down, and even near the surface, most people regard business as dehumanizing to those who participate in it and as antisocial in its effects on others. Certainly this view pervades our literature. And this view is widely held despite the extraordinary accomplishments of the economy during the last century and a half and despite the almost universal assumption that the economy will accomplish even more in the next century and a half.

It may seem that I have picked the wrong audience for belaboring this point. Perhaps so. But ask a successful business leader what is his greatest pride in his business career. Is he likely to make some such claim as that the achievements of his firm have added one one-hundredth of one per cent to consumer incomes? That, incidentally, would be a colossal contribution to human welfare, of a magnitude rarely achieved by an individual, equivalent to distributing to the population at large roughly 25 million dollars a year. But in my limited experience the answers not only are not like that explicitly, which I would hardly expect, but they are not like that in the sense of mentioning anything remotely bearing on the important social contributions of the business. Instead, the answers relate to cafeterias or Christmas bonuses for the employees, harmony with unions, or large contributions of time and money to worthy causes, such as universities. The last is something I heartily admire and encourage, of course; what disturbs me is the idea that directors and officers might consider supporting education and other worthy causes their only, or even their major, contribution to social welfare.

It is easy to see why the social contribution of business is so generally underestimated. The reason is that understanding the social consequences of a business economy is an intellectual task comparable with understanding the solar system. Indeed, the real genius of our economic system is that for a business to be socially useful it is not necessary for the management to understand the workings of the economy as a whole, or for them even to understand what is socially useful. Similarly, it is not necessary, or even helpful, to examine the management's social conscience. If Adam Smith were still alive, and had been observing the economy continuously since 1776, he would still have to say, as he said then, that he had never known much good to be done by those who affect to trade in the public interest. To understand how the public interest is served by those who trade in their own private interests, and to judge what institutional arrangements will make this more true, requires a great deal of observation, study, and thought. Businessmen themselves seldom have time for this kind of analysis; they are, quite properly, too busy doing business.

Unless there is far more widespread comprehension of how the economy ticks and what makes it tick, it is inevitable that our economic machinery will have to absorb a steadily increasing stream of bigger and bigger monkey wrenches. These monkey wrenches in the machinery, however well-intentioned, will slowly but surely arrest the prodigious flight of the economy and bring it gradually down to earth. We see this happening before our eyes in England, as it happened in France earlier, and in Spain and Italy before that. The greatest challenge facing our economy today, therefore, is to get itself well understood right here at home.

13

Business and Government

I WAS INSTRUCTED TO HAVE "a short prepared statement of position and ideological persuasion, and a brief statement of the approach to follow (five minutes maximum)."

The most important position I want to take is that I am happy that this place has been greatly changed since I was here first, 41 years ago next June. This spot where Northrup Auditorium stands was a botanical garden in 1923, a luxuriant, fascinating one with winding paths and a few benches. It was hardly a suitable place for a large public meeting, though it was reputed to be a favorite place for small private meetings. Besides, there was a railroad running along this side of the library, which was then nearing completion, and those steam locomotives were noisy.

As to describing my "position" and "ideological persuasion," I am somewhat dismayed. No brief statement could fairly describe the substance of anyone's position on any serious or complicated question, unless it were the simple statement that he is ignorant and admits it. If a person presumes to have more than superficial knowledge, or even if he merely pretends to, his position will be complex and subject to a variety of conditions that will be unintelligible in an exposition limited to a few hours—much less to five minutes.

One way to convey some of the flavor of my "position" or "ideology" is to give you a few quotations that I use frequently be-

Presented before the University of Minnesota Symposium on Great Issues in Government in Minneapolis on 18 February 1964.

cause they seem to me both amusing at a superficial level, and at a deeper level to reflect important truths. I will mention three, and leave you to figure out their relation to government and business.

First, there is the saying attributed to a poular nineteenth century American humorist that "what you don't know won't hurt you, it's knowing so darned much that ain't so."

Second, there is Murphy's Second Law of Social Dynamics. This states that, "if you just let well enough alone, things will go from bad to worse."

Third, a great deal of what is accepted as factual knowledge in present-day orthodox economics has about the same basis in fact as the conclusion of a certain bank teller, who reported that a bundle of dollar bills contained exactly one hundred bills, as labeled. The way the teller reached that conclusion was by counting some of the bundle. He started out "1, 2, 3, 4." After a while he got to "33, 34, 35." Then he came to "65, 66, 67, 68." But there he stopped, saying, "Shucks, if it's right this far, it must be right all the way."

Now I'll admit that it is going to take more time than you have right now to figure out what those stories imply about my position and ideology. Let me suggest that you forget them now and try to figure them out later. In the meantime I'll try another approach— also indirect, but at least different. I'll thrash around for some labels that I think have some meanings, at least to some people, at least sometimes, that might apply to me, at least approximately.

One such label would be "Manchester Liberal." Another would be "Chicago Conservative." In accepting the term "liberal," however, I hasten to refer you to its root meaning of liberty and freedom. I reject the label "liberal" in its common contemporary usage, which is roughly equivalent to "collectivist," "socialist," "statist," or "mercantilist."

Similarly, in accepting the label "conservative," I hasten to emphasize its root meaning of preserving. I reject the meaning now coming to be accepted of "reactionary," "authoritarian," "fascist," or "elite-ist." What I emphasize is not conserving the status quo and protecting existing interests, but conserving the forces of progress, which are liberty and individualism. In other words I am a conservative in the sense that I want to preserve liberalism.

Correspondingly, as between the Manchester school's normative, a priori, and doctrinaire approach and the Chicago school's scientific, factual, and pragmatic approach, I prefer the Chicago approach.

So much for this introduction. If, as I fear, I have exceeded my allotted five minutes, I will try to compensate on my next turn at bat. If, as I also fear, I have been unintelligible, I shall try to be more specific and concrete in my next turn.

Main Talk

I mentioned earlier that things have changed a lot since the 1920's. Some things have. Some things have stayed the same. Nothing in the 1960's is more like the 1920's than the views people have about government and business. The only difference is an overwhelmingly important one practically. Now *most* people say the things, and politicians pursue the policies, that were confined in the 1920's to social scientists, novelists, historians, journalists, ministers, and teachers—to opinion leaders, in short.

The prevailing climate of opinion among these opinion leaders was, to put it rather baldly, that business is evil, inhuman, degrading, and corrupt, and that businessmen are malefactors, robbers, war-makers, and boors. No one, as far as I know, ever stated it that bluntly; but that is the common denominator that ran through the novels, the sermons, the essays of journalists, the plays, the cartoons, and the teachings of sociologists, political scientists, and historians. (Note that I omit economists; their views on economics have always been out of step with the views of other social scientists, as well as out of step with the intellectual fashions of the day.)

Some of the more thoughtful and scholarly members of the intelligentsia of the 1920's and 1930's (they referred to themselves as "intelligentsia" before they thought of the less pretentious designation "eggheads") published research studies in which they purported to show:

- that we had an "economy of abundance" (a phrase that played the role in the early 1930's that "affluent society" played in the late 1950's) in which old-fashioned scarcity economics had no useful role—was, in fact, misleading
- that we were controlled by "America's sixty families"
- that the principal cause of war is munitions makers who idiotically delight in stimulating consumption of their product
- that the American economy was built by "robber barons"

- that our natural resources had been wastefully ravaged and de-
spoiled
- that corporation managers have become, through a "managerial
revolution," a power unto themselves, beyond the reach of
stockholders
- that consumers and labor would be helpless pawns of business
—"100,000,000 guinea pigs"—except for government protection
- that the economy would fluctuate wildly without government
stabilization
- that the Great Depression of the 1930's represented a collapse of
the enterprise system—a "crisis in the old order"
- that government measures in the 1930's ended the Great Depression
- that there has been a "decline of competition" and a rise of
monopoly
- that wealth and income are becoming ever more tightly concentrated
- that (going back into history) the birth of the modern economy
in the Industrial Revolution was a time of worsening conditions
for the poor, for child labor, etc.

This list of a dozen or so propositions that were prevalent in the
interwar period could be extended to great length. I daresay that a
majority of you here tonight would agree with most of them. What
I want to do is not so much dispute them as to point out that each is
an assertion about facts. Each can be checked by careful, painstaking,
and laborious research—research more careful than that of the bank
teller I described earlier, and less quick to jump to conclusions.

Now, as a matter of fact, each of the propositions I listed has been
investigated—though not with the thoroughness and replication that
would be brought to bear on propositions of comparable importance
in the engineering or medical sciences. Not one of the propositions I
quoted is established. I will not say that any of them has been proved
false, because all that I want to argue for my present purposes is that
we rest our views and our policies about government and business on
purported facts that actually are not established facts.

(I may remark parenthetically that, although it is irrelevant for
tonight's discussion whether these propositions are actually false, I
formed my list exclusively of propositions which I think are widely
believed and which, in my judgment, are indicated by the best evidence available to be false. But I repeat: All that I claim for the

purpose of tonight's discussion is that many widely believed propositions important for establishing policy are not in fact well enough established to justify basing conclusions or policies on them.)

But even if we accept the pseudo-facts on which so much of the case for government intervention in business rests, we still have no basis for the conclusions reached. A curious feature of the writing of the interwar period that so strongly dominates our attitudes today is that nearly all of it purports to establish only a single proposition. That proposition almost invariably is one or another of the many facets of the central proposition that our economy and society are not perfect. From that a variety of far-reaching conclusions are drawn.

Now when I was a student at the University of Minnesota I took some courses in mathematics. One useful thing I learned is that to find out which way a function is moving, you need to know more than just one point on it. To establish that things are not perfect is not equivalent to establishing that things are getting worse; yet that is the conclusion usually drawn.

When I was a student here I also took some courses in logic. I learned that in a syllogism it takes more than one premise to support a conclusion. Even if it were established that things are getting worse, it would not follow that the government could or should do anything about it. That conclusion would require an analysis of the likely effects of the proposed remedy, an issue that is seldom raised with any seriousness.

Now why do I go into all this methodology? When am I going to tell you what the government should do about business, if anything?

Well, I am not going to try to tell you *what* to think about that subject. I am going to be satisfied if I can persuade a few of you *to* think about it. What I think myself, and what I would therefore recommend that you think, runs so counter to prevailing preconceptions and patterns of thought that I would be wasting my breath, except for the pleasure it might bring to any of you who tend to agree with me.

What I ask is that you take a reasonably open-minded view—even a positively skeptical view. Examine the basis for your beliefs about the facts of our society and economy. Scrutinize the analysis by which the facts lead to the conclusions. Then check the conclusions in fresh ways, by fresh evidence.

In refraining from telling you *what* to think, and just urging you *to* think, I am influenced strongly by a personal experience. When I first went to the University of Chicago as a graduate student in 1933,

I had been reading *The Nation* and *The New Republic* religiously every week for more than ten years, and believing every word in them. One day at Chicago a professor, Frank H. Knight, brought to class an issue of *The Nation*, and read a brief paragraph which purported to demolish the old saw that "you can't change human nature." The professor analyzed the paragraph into two propositions. First, "Human nature has changed"; second, "Therefore, human nature *can be* changed." He pointed out that the argument was a complete *non sequitur*. It was not his point that the future may not be like the past. To clarify his point let me drop human nature and take up the weather. The logic, applied to weather, becomes "This week's weather is different from last week's; therefore the present weather can be changed by next week." Then "can be changed," already a *non sequitur*, somehow comes to mean "changed in specified desirable ways by the government."

Beyond these weaknesses of fact and logic there is another fatal flaw in most arguments for government intervention in the economy. That is the almost total failure to examine actual experience with government intervention, to see what experience shows about the kinds of problems and the methods in which government intervention is successful or unsuccessful.

Back in the 1930's, when I was studying here, at Chicago, and at Columbia, there was perhaps more excuse than there is now for failing to analyze the record of government control; for at that time recent experience with intervention was limited. There wasn't really *much* excuse, however, because almost all human history has involved extensive government intervention, and the noninterventionist period of the nineteenth century was more or less unique. Furthermore, even in the nineteenth century nonintervention was only comparative; there was a good deal of experience that could have been analyzed.

But in the mid-1930's, intervention again became the prevailing policy, and now in the mid-1960's we have had more than a quarter of a century of experience that ought to be analyzed. Yet there has been no real analysis of this experience. We still operate on the faith of our fathers and grandfathers of the 1920's, a faith rooted in wrong facts and bad logic.

Of course, everyone realizes in a general way that the farm program has been a mess. How many know, however, that only a few commodities are regulated, and that those that are regulated are the ones that make all the trouble? And which way does the causal relation run, if there is one? Is it because commodities are regulated that they are troublesome; or is it because commodities are inherently troublesome that they are regulated?

Since the Federal Reserve Board was established 51 years ago, has our monetary system behaved better or worse, from the point of view of cyclical stability and economic growth? Have investors been taken to the cleaners less often or less severely since the Securities and Exchange Commission was established?

Are consumers served better in states where public utility regulation is strong and effective than in states where it is weak or nonexistent?

We have tried to set minimum prices and maximum prices, minimum wages and maximum wages. What have the effects been?

Some of these questions are only now beginning to be investigated, on a small scale. One of the leaders in this effort is a former member of the Minnesota economics department, George Stigler, now president of the American Economic Association. About a year ago at Swarthmore College, in a spectacle something like this one involving Stigler and Paul Samuelson, Stigler summarized some of his tentative, preliminary judgments by giving five rules to be applied when judging what economic tasks a government can perform and what it can't. Let me summarize Stigler's five rules for you:

1. The government cannot do anything quickly.
2. When the government performs detailed economic tasks, the responsibile authorities cannot possibly control the manner in which they are performed.
3. A democratic government tries to treat all citizens alike, ignoring individual differences.
4. The ideal policy from a government's viewpoint is one with identifiable beneficiaries who each gain a lot at the cost of many unidentifiable persons, none of whom is hurt much.
5. The government never knows when to quit.

This concludes my message. I'm not trying to tell you what to think, I'm just trying to tell you to think. The reason that I have so much to gain by just getting you to think is that widely accepted arguments for government intervention in the economy are largely based on erroneous views of the facts, incorrect drawing of conclusions, and complete failure to examine the record of intervention.

14

Economics of Ignorance,
and Vice Versa

I AM GOING TO START WITH the "vice versa," that is, with ignorance of economics and then turn to the economics of ignorance, but I will change the spelling of the last word so that it ends with "-ts."

There are two charges that I have been hearing for the thirty years that I have been involved in the teaching of economics both as an active participant and as an administrator, and that I hear over and over against the colleges' teaching of economics. One is that our graduates are ignorant of economics and the other is that the faculties in the colleges tend to make the students too "liberal" or "leftish." There have been two factual studies which have not been publicized much but throw some light on these two propositions. One was made by the Opinion Research Corporation of Princeton, New Jersey, about four years ago, and the other by the National Opinion Research Center (NORC) of Chicago about three years ago. The first mainly studied college students and what they know about economics, what their attitudes are about economics, what kind of study they do in economics. The other mainly studied the faculty that teach economics, what their views and attitudes are on the teaching of economics, what their personal backgrounds are, their education, and so forth.

The study of the students came to a very simple and clear conclusion as to why so many of the graduates of the colleges are ignorant of economics. The reason is that when they enter college they are

Presented before the Robert Morris Associates in Montreal on 28 September 1964.

ignorant of economics and when they are in college they do not study economics, so when they graduate, they know about as much as when they came. The ignorance is not instilled in them in college, it is something they arrive with. The facts on the study of economics by college students are somewhat shocking. For example, even of college seniors who have majored in one of the social sciences—sociology, political science, history, anthropology—about two out of every five have not taken one single course in economics. If you turn to the people who graduate in the natural sciences—physics, chemistry, geology, biology—about two out of three have not taken an economics course in college. As for the people in education, the high school and grade school teachers of the future, four out of five have not taken any economics during their college careers, and four out of five is also the figure for those in the humanities—foreign languages, English, art, music. The shocking fact is that the students in the colleges for the most part do not study economics.

That is the explanation of their ignorance. In this study a quiz was given to college students with a hundred questions of a factual nature about economics to see how much they knew. The entering freshmen had an average score of 49. The graduating seniors who had not studied economics had an average score of 52. The seniors who had studied some economics scored an average of 63 and those who had majored in economics averaged 72. It is clear at least that those who do study economics in college do learn something more than they knew when they started.

It may be, as is often charged, that the college graduate of today is somewhat liberal or left-wing. I do not know whether that is true or not, or even exactly what it means, but one thing that is clear is that those who study economics are less liberal afterward than they were before. That is, the effect of studying economics in college is to leave the students somewhat less liberal or more conservative than they were when they started. That was tested by a series of questions to which the answer would reflect the student's attitude. They were asked whether they agreed or disagreed with certain statements; I mention three of them to show the kinds of things that were interpreted as reflecting attitude. One was, "Our economic system shares fairly between workers and owners." Of the seniors who had not studied any economics, 62% agreed, but of those who had majored in economics, 89% agreed. The effect of studying economics is to put them more on the conservative side on that question. Another was, "Our business system cannot function without the profit incentive."

Of the seniors who had not studied economics 57% thought that was correct, whereas of those who had studied economics 81% thought it was correct. Another was, "Competition is a better regulator of prices than government control." Of the seniors with no economics, 54% agreed; of those who had studied economics, 78% agreed.

You may still think the other 22% represent a shocking problem, and I agree, but if you are wondering how people get to be liberal, one thing is clear: It is not through the study of economics in college. That tones down and tends to reverse the general attitude. If our college graduates are generally liberal in their economic attitudes, I think we have to look for the explanation somewhere else: not so much at the professors of economics as at the professors of history, sociology, English, mathematics; not so much at the noneconomics professors as at the high school teachers—it turned out that the future teachers were the weakest of all both on knowledge of facts and principles and on attitudes; not so much at the teachers as at the ministers, the journalists, the novelists, the playwrights, the union leaders, the advertising and public relations profession—in other words, the whole intellectual climate of the times.

I do not deny that the great majority of college teachers of economics would be categorized as liberal. The NORC study shows that they classify themselves as Democrats five to one, that in the 1960 election they voted for Kennedy four to one, and in the 1956 election for Stevenson three to one. I would guess, without having taken or seen any polls or even talked to anybody about this, that in the 1964 election, the ratio for Johnson will be at least six to one and possibly eight or ten. The study showed that about three out of four felt that the government should expand its role in the economy; needless to say, education was the favorite area for expansion. About six out of seven thought, however, that in the teaching of economics in college, certain basic values ought to be emphasized and ought to dominate the teaching; when they were asked what these values are about a fifth said individual freedom, about a fifth said efficiency, and about two-fifths said scientific knowledge of economics, that is, a factual and analytical approach to the subject of economics. Thus, whatever their own views on economic policy, they felt that the emphasis in teaching should be on objectivity and basic social values such as freedom and efficiency.

The evidence is that the great majority of the college teachers of economics do a very creditable job of teaching objectively. It is not as objective as it might be, and all the people with different points of views would not be fully satisfied, but on the whole the performance is creditable. The best evidence of that is the fact that they leave their own students less liberal than before they studied the subject.

I turn now to the economics of the ignorant.

I have a list of ten beliefs. I think that at least half of the people here will agree with at least half of them. They are all false in my opinion. For some of them, the most I can say is that there is no evidence that they are true. In other words, I think they are all false, but for some I admit that I can not honestly claim the evidence is definitive, or that only an ignoramus could believe them. I have picked statements that are widely believed by respectable people like bankers, professors, and economists.

1. It is almost universally believed that the Securities and Exchange Commission (SEC) in the United States has brought somewhat greater protection to investors than they enjoyed before its creation. That is so widely accepted that no one even thought of investigating it until a year or two ago, when a professor at the University of Chicago got interested in it, George Stigler, President of the American Economic Association. It was not an easy thing to investigate, but he is a very ingenious, conscientious person and has some research assistants, and he found ways to get at it. If anybody wants to look it up, there is an article in the *Journal of Business* last April that describes it. He finds that the losses to investors in new issues of industrial securities in a period before the creation of the SEC, the 1920's when business was generally good, were about 20% in the first year. In the 1950's, under the SEC, the losses during the first year were 20%. That is, the losses seem to be just the same since the SEC has been operating as before. Yet virtually everybody will give lip service to this innovation of the New Deal, even if they find others hard to admire. The only objective study that has been made suggests that it has had no beneficial effect in its main intent. I hardly need to say that it has had many detrimental effects and has jeopardized important freedoms, not only the freedom to invest your money where you please, but also freedoms closer to those covered in the first ten amendments to the Constitution.

2. A second and related general belief is that the state utilities commissions cause electric, telephone, and gas rates to be lower than they would be if they were not regulated. This also has been investigated recently by the same people, and there is no evidence that it is true. There seems to be no difference in rates. The researchers have been able to compare circumstances where rates are not regulated

with those where they are, and also they have studied rates before
and after regulation went into effect. Not all the states even now have
utility regulation. I am not saying that there are no consequences,
but whatever the consequences are they are not lower prices to the
consumer, and that is the main objective and one that everybody
takes for granted. Certainly the utility people do, and enormous
amounts of money are spent by lawyers on both sides fighting these
things, and maybe that is why they have no effect. It seems to stand
to reason that there must be some effect—surely this many regulatory
commissions would not be just playing a game—but if you just look
at the record, there is no evidence that there has been any effect, and
some that there has not.

3. A third popular belief is that automation is a technological
force that causes unemployment among the unskilled. It is much
more nearly true to put it the other way around and say that government policies force the unskilled out of the labor market, and that induces automation. Because the unskilled have been forced out of the
labor market it is necessary to automate to find some way to produce
things without them. How are the unskilled forced out of the labor
market? Let me call your attention to the fact that in the last decade
in the United States the average hourly wage for all workers in
manufacturing went up 42%, but the minimum rate went up 67%.
The price of the cheapest workers has been boosted 67% by law,
from 75 cents an hour to a dollar and a quarter an hour, whereas the
highest priced labor has not gone up nearly so much.

There has been a similar effect with higher priced labor also,
particularly due to some unions forcing wages up and inducing
automation and reducing employment in their industries. Automation is not an autonomous technological force like contagious diseases, the weather, or some vast social force that cannot be stopped
and that moves independently. It is an economically induced phenomenon. How far automation is carried or where it is introduced
is a matter of price incentives and costs, and of artificial pricing that
forces the cheapest labor out of market.

4. The next is an old one that those of you who studied
economics must have come across in class. There is a widespread
belief that if one country could produce everything more efficiently
than a second country, then the second country couldn't hope to
sell anything to the first country. That is obviously nonsense, as
you can see on a small scale by looking within a bank. If the president of the bank is a healthy, husky fellow he can probably do

everything more efficiently than the janitor can, or than the tellers. Everything that they do in the bank, like sweeping the money up off the floor and counting it, he could probably do better, by applying a little brains to it. Yet the janitor and the tellers have no trouble selling their services to the president.

A similar situation holds with international trade. The absolute cost within one country in comparison with the absolute cost in a second country has nothing to do with whether there will be any trade. That is the old law of comparative advantage. More specifically, suppose the Canadians are supermen. In one man-hour of work, they can produce a thermometer or in five man-hours a camera, to take a couple of our Rochester products as examples. And suppose that in the United States, even with the same capital, it takes ten man-hours to make a thermometer as compared to one in Canada, and twenty man-hours to make a camera as compared to five in Canada, so that the U.S., on these assumptions, which I hope are unrealistic, is less efficient in both. Still the fact is that, with free trade, the U.S. would sell cameras to Canada and buy thermometers from Canada. The fact that Canada could make cameras cheaper than we could would not prevent us from selling cameras to Canada, because their advantage is even greater on thermometers and they will prefer to get their cameras by making thermometers and trading them to us for cameras. On the other side of the coin, we will prefer to get our thermometers by making cameras and trading them to the Canadians for thermometers.

The question of whether trade will occur depends on a comparison of *relative* costs. If the relative costs in one country are different from the relative costs in the other country, trade will be advantageous to both countries. This is known as the "law of comparative advantage." Most of the talk I hear about international trade is mistaken because it ignores this basic fact, which has been known for two or three hundred years. I observe that even the very professors who teach the law of comparative advantage sometimes do not understand it in practical situations when they step out of the classroom; so I do not criticize the students too much.

5. A fifth proposition that is widely believed, maybe not so widely in this audience, is that there is an increasing concentration of control in the American economy, a rise of monopoly, as people say, speaking loosely. Literally speaking, there is hardly any such thing as monopoly, and it is more accurate to talk about concentration of control.

There have been three studies in the last fifteen or twenty years by different people using different criteria of what constitutes concentration. Some writers say that if the four largest firms produce half the output, that is a concentrated industry. Others say that if the two largest produce 25%, that is concentration. Some writers measure the importance of an industry by the number employed in it, others by the value added by it, others by the share of the national income originating in it. All the approaches that have been tried come to the same conclusion, namely, that there has been no growth in concentration in the private sector of the American economy as far back as we have data that can be used for this kind of study, which is to 1899.

There has been some increase in concentration, but only within the public sector. Government monopoly has grown greatly during this period, but in the private sector there has been no appreciable increase in concentration of control.

One thing that misleads casual observers is that there certainly has been a strong tendency towards larger firms; but the economy has been getting larger, and the existence of large firms is not the same thing as concentration of control. Estimates made by different investigators are that something like 15% to 25% of the private economy might be called concentrated or quasi-monopolistic, meaning that the bulk of the output is controlled by few enough firms so that no one of them will take an action without regard to what the others might do in response. I mention that figure, which is not relevant to the question of the trend, because it is much smaller than many people think. If it surprises you, you might recall that wholesale trade, which is competitive, is twice as important as auto production, which is concentrated.

6. A sixth proposition that is widely believed is that unions cause inflation. I think they do not. One thing that amuses me is that apparently most union leaders privately believe that they are guilty, so a lot of circuitous talk results. First, unions do not raise wages as much as is commonly believed. There have been some careful studies of how much higher wages are than they would be if there were no unions; these studies show that few if any unions raise wage rates as much as 25%. The best estimates, or maybe I should call them "guesstimates," made by competent experts who are familiar with the facts, are that unions on the whole probably raise wages about 10% to 15% above what they would be if the unions were

not there. Unions cover only 20% to 25% of workers, so that cuts
down their effect on the average of all wages to 2% to 4%.

Whatever this figure may be, however, it shows nothing about
inflation. Inflation refers to a rising trend in the level of prices; it
does not mean that prices are high, but that they are going up.

Union control may cause wages to be a little higher than they
otherwise would be, but there is no reason to think that there has
been an increasing degree of union control—if anything, slightly the
opposite. The unions would have to be gaining strength to account
for rising prices.

What really causes inflation is an increase in the quantity of
money, including in money bank deposits as well as currency. If
unions raise wages "excessively" when there is not an inflationary
increase in the quantity of money, there will be a rise in unemployment, as I indicated earlier in talking about automation. This has
certainly happened to the lowest wage groups, more through legislation than through union action, and there is evidence that it has
happened in the higher wage groups in industries like the auto industry. Employment has not expanded as much as it would have,
workers have not been able to enter that industry in the same numbers that they otherwise would have, and they have been pushed into
other occupations where their productivity is lower, so that the
over-all productivity of the economy is lower and the economy's
growth has been retarded. Many workers are earning less than they
would if there were no unions, because they are not able to get into
unionized industries. Many things can be said about the effects of
unions, but inflation is one thing that cannot be blamed on them.

7. The seventh point is that it is very widely believed that the
Federal Reserve System since its establishment half a century ago
has brought about an increase in economic stability. When you examine the facts you find that the fluctuations in prices and in the
level of output have been decidedly less stable in the fifty years since
the Federal Reserve System was created than they were in the fifty
years before that. Furthermore, if you leave out the periods of the
First World War and the Second World War, it is still true that
there has been greater instability in the behavior of the stock of
money, in price levels, and in total output in the fifty years since the
Federal Reserve was established to stabilize those things, than there
was in the fifty years before that when we did not have much
machinery to stabilize them. In fact, there has been no twenty-year

period in our whole history like that from 1920 to 1940, when we had three depressions as acute as those of 1920–1921, 1929–1933, and 1937–1938. You will find a great deal of material on this question in a book published by the National Bureau of Economic Research about a year ago called *A Monetary History of the United States,* by Milton Friedman and Anna Schwartz. I am afraid that Mr. Friedman is *persona non grata* in the Federal Reserve Board these days, although one of the things he tries to emphasize is that, if you say that the people involved were stupid or wicked, you have missed the whole point.

8. Another widely held belief is that the Great Depression of the 1930's represented a collapse of the private enterprise system. A book was a best seller a few years ago under the title *The Crisis in the Old Order,* and its general thesis is that the business system, the banks, and the businessmen utterly failed, and that they were so demoralized by having caused the greatest economic disaster in modern history, with all its political ramifications, that they gave up the ghost, so to speak, and turned to the government for help. Ask somebody what he thinks caused the Great Depression, and you will get lots of explanations; but one thing that nobody will tell you is that the Federal Reserve System allowed one-third of the stock of money to be wiped out during that period. There has never been a time in any country when a third of the stock of money has been wiped out or even a far smaller fraction, without causing a major depression; and, incidentally, there has never been a major depression that was not accompanied by a reduction in the stock of money. Any explanation of the depression in simple terms like consumer installment credit, or a real estate boom, or the break in the stock market (which did not come until after the downturn in general business) is beside the point if it ignores this one overshadowing factor. It is widely believed that the enterprise system showed at that time that it could not work. What actually happened was a failure of government.

9. My ninth point is a debatable one, and I want to emphasize my earlier remark that while I am asserting these beliefs are false, I have to admit that some of them have not been disproved definitively. It is widely believed that the tax cut last winter caused the lively spurt in business that we have had this summer. It may have contributed; nobody knows. The record shows that when tax cuts have been made in the past, approximately half of them have been followed by spurts and approximately half of them have been fol-

lowed by rather lackadaisical business activity. The simple historical record suggests it is like tossing a coin; if you have a tax cut and you want to know whether business will then spurt, you toss a coin, and if you get heads you predict it will, and you will do just as well as predicting from the tax cut. If you try to analyze the effects of the recent tax cut, the first complication that you have to take into account is that the stock of money grew over this summer at an extraordinarily rapid rate. It was growing at a rate of more than 7% per year, in contrast with an annual rate of growth of about 1.3% over the winter. It is well established that changes in the rate of growth in the stock of money are followed by changes in the rate of business activity. An increase in the rate of growth of the stock of money is followed by an increase in the level of business activity. A decrease in the rate of growth in the stock of money is followed in due course (there is a good deal of variability in the lag) by a decrease in the rate of business activity. If you are interested in this subject, the current monthly letter of the St. Louis Federal Reserve Bank has a brief summary article on it. It does not refer to the tax cut, but the facts it presents have to be taken into account in trying to analyze the effect of that tax cut.

10. The final proposition is that in the modern corporation the stockholders have lost control, and the managers are in complete charge. Of course in any organization, if you are only one of a thousand people, or one of a hundred thousand people, your voice will be small; but there is no important organization I can think of in the modern world where you can get out as fast and as simply and as cheaply as you can get out of a corporation if you do not like the behavior of the management. If I were fortunate enough to own some stock in U.S. Steel, which I do not, and if I were to take a dislike to Roger Blough, which I have not, it would be very simple to call my broker and say, "Fire him and his whole crew and hire me Joe Block's team." This is not just an academic possibility, either. Stockholders know it—not every single one of them every day, but every day some of them do ask whether a business is being managed effectively, and even if it is, whether others have even better prospects.

Contrast that with political organizations. If I do not like the way the city of Rochester is run, I can move to the suburbs, and a lot of people do. If I do not like the way Monroe County is run, I can still manage, but not so easily, to get out of the county and commute. If I do not like the way the state is run, things become com-

plicated, for I will have to find another job to get out. And if I do
not like the way the United States is run that is a very complicated
matter. Mismanagement of the United States would have to be very
bad indeed for me to consider moving out, even to a lovely country
like Canada. My freedom in the political sphere to dissociate myself
from managers I do not like and make arrangements with others is
far more restricted than in the corporation.

I conclude from all of this, from what I have found out about
students not studying economics, and from the fact that they learn
a lot when they do, and that it does not seem to affect their basic
attitudes adversely, that it is extremely important for more students
to study more economics. In spite of the emphasis on the importance
of science, it is nowhere near as important for the citizen to understand science as it is for him to understand economics. The government is increasingly involved in scientific matters, but neither the
public nor its elected representatives make scientific decisions. They
do not really decide in Congress, much less in a referendum, whether
our missiles ought to have solid fuel or liquid. They do not decide
whether our space capsules should carry one man or two. They do
not decide in Congress or in the electorate what would be a good
approach to cancer or leukemia. We have come a little bit close on
the smoking and cancer issue, but even there so far Congress has
not made any decisions. But in the field of economics, we do have
the citizens themselves often making or determining the basic decisions, and certainly that is what our elected representatives do. We
expect them to make the technical decisions about taxation, minimum wages, monetary policy, the regulation of business, depressed
areas, and international trade. These are not turned over, and in the
nature of the case could not properly be turned over, to technical
bodies, as are scientific decisions. Indeed, the government just makes
a contract with Cal Tech or somebody to hit the moon, if that is
what they want done, and the basic technical decisions will be made
there. We cannot do that in the economic field and therefore economic education is far more important than scientific education.
The progress of our economy depends on the skill and competence
and understanding of the managers of individual firms, and it also
depends on the skill and competence of professional economists in
analyzing economic programs and advising the electorate and our
elected representatives. The thing that ties my original subject and
the vice versa together is the great importance of economic education.

III

Prices

15

The Price System

HERE IN THE U.S. is an area of about 3 million square miles contain-
ing 150 million people. Suppose you were asked how to organize
these people to utilize the resources available to them for their material satisfactions. You can imagine you have a fairly detailed inventory of the natural resources of the country, of the people and their
knowledge, energies, and abilities, and of their wants. Imagine that
all these resources are as unorganized as a set of chessmen just poured
out of their box and awaiting organization on the chess board. Your
problem is to organize the resources so that wants will be filled as
well as possible.

If you can get your head working at all in the face of so staggering a prospect, it will occur to you that one of the first things you
are going to need is some way of establishing goals and measuring
achievement. Which of the many things wanted are going to be
produced, in what quantities, and with what priorities?

And after you establish these goals and priorities, you will need
a method of assigning the various pieces of capital, the various natural resources, and the various people to particular activities. Each
will have several alternative uses; you will need a method of deciding
which use to assign it or him to, and of coordinating the resources
assigned to cooperate in each task.

Then, third, you will have to have some system for dividing the
product among the people; who gets how much of what, and when?

*Presented before the Citizens Board of the University of Chicago on 29
March 1950.*

Fourth, you will probably realize that for one reason or another your system will not work absolutely perfectly but will sometimes turn out to have overproduced some things and to have underproduced others. You will need some system of adjustment to these temporary shortages and abundances, until your method of measuring achievement and your method of allocating resources can get the basic situation corrected.

A fifth kind of problem you may worry about is that of providing for the expansion and improvement of your capital equipment, and technological knowledge.

These five functions have to be provided for when you establish any organization, even a small and relatively simple one. When we consider the large and complex organization of an entire economy, what are some of the alternative ways of arranging for them?

The most obvious way to arrange things is the way an army does. You set up a commander and a general staff. They decide on goals, they decide who shall do what to attain them, they decide how to apportion the product, and they issue orders accordingly.

Another method is that used in beehives and ant colonies, in which caste and custom determine who does what. Things go on in the same way, generation after generation.

A third way is to introduce money and let each person decide what activities that others will pay for he will engage in, and what things that others offer for money he will buy. This is a method that no one really invented. It requires careful and sometimes complicated analysis to discover how it will really work. Indeed, it was only with the recognition that this is in fact a method of organizing society that the scientific study of economics began, back in 1776.

Under this system, goals are set by the money offers of individuals for goods and services. Resources are allocated to one activity or another by the desires of their owners for money income. Goods are distributed to individuals according to their willingness and ability to pay the prices. Thus prices become the crucial organizing element in such an economy. Indeed, this system is often called the "price system."

The price system has two outstanding features. First, it is by all odds the most efficient system of social organization ever conceived. It makes it possible for huge multitudes to cooperate effectively, multitudes who may hardly know of each other's existence, or whose personal attitudes toward one another may be indifference or hostility. Second, it affords a maximum of individual freedom and a minimum of coercion. And since people can cooperate effectively in production even when their attitudes on other issues are hostile, there is no need for unity and conformity in religion, politics, recreation, and language—or even in patriotism and goodwill except in the very broadest senses.

Although one of the big features of the price system that commends it is the voluntary nature of individual actions, the system nevertheless exerts powerful inducements and even compulsions.

A consumer who has it in mind to use up a lot of a scarce commodity highly prized by others is forced to forgo consuming other commodities to an extent judged by others to be equivalent. A producer who tries to get more income than his services are judged by others to be worth is prevented from doing so by the freedom of buyers to buy elsewhere and of other sellers to underprice him. A business manager who tries to waste labor, capital, and raw materials, either by producing something less desired than other things that could be made with the labor, capital, and raw materials, or by using the labor, capital, and raw materials inefficiently, is prevented from doing so because he will find himself taking in less money than he pays out. As long as he can make good the deficit, by giving up his own right to consume, this can continue; but when he can no longer make good—that is, when he can no longer pay for the labor, capital, and raw materials—he is forced to stop wasting them just as firmly as if a cease and desist order were issued by a Federal Bureau of Efficiency. Maybe more firmly, for his Congressman may be more influential with the federal bureau than with his creditors.

The freedom of the system produces inducements or compulsions for individuals to act efficiently in the general interest. It is not by any means true that each enterprise is free to do what it pleases. It is restricted by the freedom of consumers to buy elsewhere; of the owners of labor, capital, and raw materials to sell elsewhere; and of business managers to enter the same business in competition with it.

This freedom of others to compete for advantages is effective in checking individual self-aggrandizement because economic information is effectively disseminated by prices. Prices represent one of the most efficient communication devices ever invented.

Indeed, we might look on the problem of organization as hinging on communication. The problem is to bring to bear on each decision two very different kinds of information. On one hand, any decision depends on general, over-all economic data; for example, how much a certain product is wanted, and how abundant the resources are from which it could be made. On the other hand, it depends on minute special knowledge; for example, knowledge of peculiar abilities, of unused resources, of possible changes in ways of doing things.

Now the problem is whether to transmit the detailed knowledge of special circumstances to a central agency, or to transmit the general information to the individuals who have the detailed knowledge. The detailed knowledge is too voluminous and nebulous for transmittal or for assimilation, and no one could know what parts should be selected. The general information, however, is summarized in prices.

Just that part of the general data that is relevant to an individual's decision is summarized in prices. If a price goes up, that tells him everything he needs to know to guide his action; he does not need to know why the price went up; the fact that it did go up tells him to try to use a little less or it tells him to produce more of the commodity, and how far to go in his efforts.

Not only do prices convey information on how an individual *should* act, but they provide at the same time a powerful inducement for him to do so.

In conclusion, let me acknowledge that I have given only a sketch, and only of an ideal free enterprise or price system at that. I do not apologize for that, however, for an understanding of the theory of a price system is essential to any efforts to improve our economic organization or to any comparison of alternative modes of economic organization. To me the most depressing thing about the prospects for a free society is not the hydrogen bomb, or international politics, or communist agitation; it is the fact that so very few have any understanding of economics.[1]

16

Wages, Productivity, and Prices

BEFORE DISCUSSING THE IMPORTANCE of productivity, I want to dispel a common illusion by explaining one way in which it is *not* important. Improving productivity will not help fight inflation.

There are two reasons why improving productivity will not reduce inflation appreciably. First, look at the simple arithmetic of the situation. Productivity grows on the average by something like 3 percent per year. Even a miracle could not raise the average rate of growth within a few years by 10 percent. A 10 percent increase in the average rate of growth would amount to about three-tenths of 1 percent per year. Inflation has been running well over 4 percent per year. So, such a miracle would reduce the rate of inflation by less than a tenth—by well under one-half of 1 percent per year.

But, second, inflation reflects the relation between the rate of growth in the supply of money and the rate of growth in the supply of goods and services. If the supply of money grows faster than the supply of goods and services, then the amount of money per unit of goods and services will increase. But the amount of money per unit of goods and services is what we call the price level, and a rise in the price level is what we call inflation. Variations in the rate of growth of the money supply are enormous compared to variations in the rate of growth of productivity. During the first half of this year, for example, the money supply grew at a rate exceeding 10 percent per year. For the past month or two the rate has been essentially

Presented before the National Industrial Conference Board in Chicago on 1 November 1960.[1]

zero. Thus, fluctuations in the rate of growth of the money supply completely dwarf fluctuations in the rate of growth of productivity. Furthermore, fluctuations in the rate of growth of productivity account for only a tiny part of fluctuations in the rate of growth of the output of goods and services, which mostly result from fluctuations in the rate of employment of labor, raw materials, and capital.

While improving productivity will not help with the inflation problem, it is nevertheless of the greatest importance to the welfare of the American people. Gains in productivity are the principal source of gains in our standard of living. Increases in earnings, including the "fringe" benefits that go with them, help provide wage and salary earners with a higher standard of living.

Clearly the only way that general purchasing power can go up is through greater production. The purchasing power of wage and salary earners can also go up if their share of the total national output increases; their share has, in fact, been increasing gradually for several generations, and is now nearly 80 percent of the total. This increase has resulted primarily from advances in productivity. From any viewpoint, the role of productivity in providing gains in the standard of living is crucial.

The average level of prices can be stable only if the average level of earnings is reasonably in line with productivity. It does not follow, however, that for any specific job, occupation, firm, industry, or region, productivity and earnings must be related in the same way that average productivity and average earnings are related. On the contrary, the relation of productivity to specific earnings is complex. To examine the relation between earnings and productivity, we must consider:

- measures and meanings of productivity
- sources of gains in productivity
- productivity and earnings in one industry, job, or occupation
- productivity, wages, and prices in the economy as a whole

Measures and Meanings of Productivity

As our population grows and more hands and heads go to work, production is almost sure to rise, but productivity need not necessarily rise. *Production* refers to output, without regard to the amounts of labor, capital, and natural resources used to get that output.

Productivity, however, refers to output per unit of input; it is a measure of efficiency. The importance of maintaining maximum employment opportunities for our labor, capital, and natural resources is generally recognized. It is equally important to use them efficiently, for this means that more goods and services are produced from the same labor, capital, and natural resources.

Several different measures of productivity are in use. No one measure is the right or the best measure. The choice among measures depends on the purpose involved and the data available (which are nearly always inadequate).

The most familiar measure of productivity is output per man-hour. Even this measure has several forms. It can be based on man-hours paid or on man-hours worked. The results differ because of paid vacations, holidays, and sick leave. Output per man-hour paid is useful in cost calculations, while output per man-hour worked is useful in evaluating the efficiency of machinery or working arrangements.

Output per man-hour is based sometimes on production workers only, and sometimes on salaried workers and self-employed workers as well. Since the number of salaried workers has been growing faster than the number of production workers, productivity rises more slowly when salaried workers are counted in the labor inputs. Salaried workers are as essential as other workers, but often it is hard to assign specific output to their work; hence it is difficult properly to account for them in measuring productivity.

Measures of productivity for the whole economy usually reflect both changes in productivity within industries and changes arising from shifts in the importance of different industries. Special measures of productivity have been devised that to some extent exclude the changes resulting from the changing importance of different industries. Such measures show how much better we can do the same things, but do not reflect the extent to which we have shifted to doing different things.

Another measure of productivity is sometimes used: output per unit of labor and capital combined. This measure attempts to show how efficiently the economy is using both labor and capital. Historically, measures of output per man-hour have risen faster than measures of output per unit of labor and capital combined, because the amount of capital per worker has been increasing.

Any answer to the question, "How fast is productivity rising in the United States?" depends on the definition of productivity that is used and the time period selected; it depends also on the quality of the data available, which varies with the definition and with the time period. In selecting a time period, the opening and closing dates must be at comparable stages of the business cycle; otherwise, we make an error which is like measuring the rate of tidal rise on the ocean by comparing the peak of a wave at one time with the trough of a wave at a later time. Successive peaks represent the course of economic growth better than successive troughs.

It is estimated that output per man-hour paid for in the private economy rises about 3.1 percent per year (a rate that would double output per man-hour paid every twenty-three years), while output per man-hour worked rises 3.7 percent per year (equivalent to doubling every nineteen years). Output per unit of labor and capital combined rises about 2.1 percent per year (equivalent to doubling every thirty-three years).

Despite the inexactness of data about productivity changes, there are a number of important statements about our experience in the United States to which most experts would agree:

1. Productivity in the American economy has been increasing for as long as there have been data, and probably longer.
2. There seem to be long-run fluctuations in the rate of productivity increase which are not yet well understood.
3. The rate of growth in output per man-hour has been in an upswing in recent decades, rising more rapidly since the First World War than before, and still more rapidly since the Second World War.
4. Improvement in productivity is slower in many service industries than in manufacturing or agriculture.

Sources of Gains in Productivity

The long and rapid rise in productivity in the United States has occurred not because people work harder (in fact, our grandfathers almost all worked longer hours at heavier tasks than we do), but because people work more effectively. The increase in the effectiveness with which people work results in considerable part from increases in education, in skills, in health, and in general well-being. The rising quality of the labor force, in short, is an important source of productivity increases.

A related source of productivity increases is new knowledge, some produced by research in industrial, university, and government laboratories, but much developed in an informal way on all kinds of jobs where ingenious people make innumerable small or large improvements in their methods of doing things.

Productivity increases also as more and better capital equipment is used. One man with a steam shovel can move more earth than many men using only hand tools. Even without improvement in the quality of equipment, an increase in the amount used can bring a rise in output per man-hour. In general, however, as we accumulate capital, we incorporate in it the findings of research, so that we have not only more but better capital equipment. But capital includes more than just tools and machinery. For example, the improvement of roads, harbors, communication networks, water supplies, and sanitary facilities can all contribute to rising productivity.

Just as the tools with which people work are important to their productivity, so too are the natural resources at their disposal. Ask a farmer about the importance of good land or a miner about the importance of the richness of the seam he works. The discovery and development of more and richer natural resources result in increased productivity.

Increased productivity also results from more effective organization of the nation's human and material resources, so that each input is used where it can produce the most value. The organizing job is performed mostly by management, and improved methods of management increase the rate of growth in productivity. An important contribution of managers is in seeking and developing new products and new methods, and especially in risking the funds necessary to try innovations that often prove costly failures.

The responses people make on their own initiative to differences in wages and prices also result in labor, capital, and natural resources moving toward their most effective uses.

As manpower shifts from, or avoids, low-productivity jobs where pay must be low, and moves to higher-productivity jobs where pay is better, productivity increases for the economy as a whole, even though productivity in each industry separately may remain unchanged. Similarly, the efforts of owners of capital and natural resources to get a high return lead them to employ their property where the demand for it is greatest. Competition for the buyer's dollar and the incentives offered in a free economy by wages, prices, and profits play a vital role in directing our efforts and stimulating efficiency, as well as in rewarding them.

Increases in productivity arise, then, from the efforts of people in all walks of life. They are not attributable to any single group. Even a group whose measured productivity happens to be rising cannot necessarily claim special credit, for its rises may be due primarily to increases in the quantity and quality of the people, capital, natural resources, management, and technology with which it works. Labor, capital, natural resources, management, and technology jointly produce our output, and an increase in the quantity or quality of any one of them will increase the output per unit of input of the others.

Productivity and Earnings in One Industry

The various measures of productivity all give us some insight into the process by which our standard of living rises, and they therefore have some bearing on the average gains that workers can expect to obtain through increases in average earnings or decreases in average consumer prices. In evaluating specific wages and salaries, however, there is no similar rule or formula of broad applicability.

One important barrier to any general rule is that productivity and its growth, however measured, vary tremendously from industry to industry. There are many reasons why productivity increases more rapidly in some industries than in others. New industries typically present many opportunities for improvement, since, as they grow, economies are realized from mass production or simply from new ideas. New technology and new resources affect some industries more than others. Arrangements by governments, labor, or management stimulate productivity gains in some industries but retard them in other industries. Many direct-service industries are by nature difficult to change; for example, productivity cannot be expected to rise as rapidly in barber shops as in automobile factories.

If wages were tied to output per man-hour, industry by industry, the result would be both unfair and impractical. Wages would go up rapidly in some industries, stay about the same in others, and even decline in a few.

Since many occupations and types of jobs are found in virtually all industries, people doing the same work would receive different pay. In fact, many plants produce in several industries, so wages might differ for the same work in the same plant. Industries with constant or only slowly rising wages would have increasing trouble persuading people to work for them, while people would be on waiting lists to work in the high-wage industries.

Also, tying wages to output per man-hour in each industry would reduce the incentive to industry to introduce the innovations which raise productivity in the first place, and would discourage expansion in the successful industries by preventing exceptional productivity from being fully reflected in reduced costs and prices.

Thus, if wages are not tied to the productivity of individual industries, the outcome is likely to be more equitable and more practical. The ordinary processes of wage determination, and of choosing among jobs once rates of pay are established, tend to bring about roughly equal pay for equal work.

Not only would it be impractical to tie wages in each industry to productivity in that particular industry, but it would also be impractical to tie wages in each industry to average productivity in the whole economy. This would ignore differences in the need for labor and in its availability. In an expanding area, industry, or occupation, employers frequently raise wages more than the national average increase in output per man-hour. These large wage increases serve the useful purpose of inducing labor to enter the area, industry, or occupation in question, and they help pay moving or retraining costs. In a declining area, industry, or occupation, a chronic labor surplus may develop, and attempts to increase wages in line with the national average increase in output per man-hour would reduce employment opportunities and make it less likely that new industries would move into the areas of labor surplus.

These considerations and many others like them make it clear that it is difficult or impossible to prescribe general criteria for proper rates of wages and salaries. Those on the spot with knowledge of all the special circumstances must find the best solution for each case.

Productivity, Wages, and Prices in the Economy as a Whole

Even though the special circumstances surrounding each particular wage or salary may make it impossible to judge any one rate, certain judgments can be made about the general or average result of all the separate rates. There is an analogy here to the judging of baseball players: The shortstop, for example, does not necessarily cause a game to be lost if he scores fewer runs than the opposing shortstop; but the team as a whole certainly loses if it scores fewer runs than the opposing team as a whole. In wage negotiations, as in baseball, even though we have no clear-cut criterion for evaluating any one contributor, we can apply certain clear-cut criteria to the total result.

For the economy as a whole, productivity is related to wages in the following broad terms: If the average level of prices is reasonably stable, wages can rise only as much as productivity, appropriately measured, rises. (Increases in the total share of national output going to wage and salary earners do modify this assertion; but such changes are so slow and the possibilities for further increases from the present 80 percent so limited, that they can be overlooked in discussing short-run practical questions.)

Productivity and changes in productivity throw little light on what wages should be, or what changes in wages should occur, in any particular job, firm, industry, occupation, or region. For example, above-average increases in productivity in any one industry may to some extent:

- raise wages in the industry
- increase employment in the industry
- decrease employment in the industry
- increase output in the industry
- lower prices in the industry
- raise wages in other industries which compete for similar workers
- lower wages in other industries
- raise prices in other industries
- lower prices in other industries

The extent to which each of these adjustments is appropriate in any instance depends on literally thousands of details and special circumstances, and can best be worked out by individuals who have freedom and opportunities to choose among jobs and among the goods and services they buy. Since the public interest may be little concerned with each separate adjustment in each instance, and since the maintenance of free institutions and free collective bargaining are paramount goals of public policy, attainment of the appropriate over-all result for the whole economy must be sought by controlling the environment in which wage and salary negotiations occur.

The key to a proper environment is to maintain a legal and institutional framework such that the self-interest of each party is either consistent with the public interest or balanced and checked by opposing interests of other parties. If excessive wage and price increases would cause severe losses of employment, sales, and public goodwill, for example, one side or the other will resist them. Where excessive concentrations of power in the hands of labor or business produce too many results or a net result contrary to the public interest, remedies should be sought through eliminating the power to injure the public interest, rather than through direct control of unions, businesses, or collective bargaining.

Another important key to an environment that will hold wages and salary settlements in line with the public interest is sound management of money, budgets, and debt by governments. When mismanagement creates pervasive inflationary pressures, little success can be achieved by those who attempt to hold down particular wages or prices, for neither party to transactions gains any advantage from preventing increases—and to the extent that they do succeed they may do as much harm as good, since "gray markets" appear under these conditions.

Conclusion

Productivty is the basis of prosperity. Increases in productivity, on which depend the rapid improvements that characterize the American standard of living, spring from many different sources: more effective workers, more and better capital equipment, better natural resources, better management, new knowledge and technology, and a social organization that affords broad opportunities, encourages competition, and provides incentives and rewards to individuals for efficiency, thrift, and industry.

For the economy as a whole, increases in wages and salaries, including fringe benefits, must be matched by increases in productivity; for if they are not, prices or unemployment must rise. But this general principle for the economy as a whole throws little light on what earnings should be in any specific job, firm, industry, occupation, or region. If the millions of indivdual wage and salary determinations made each year in millions of special circumstances are to turn out in the aggregate to conform with average productivity increases, they must be made in an environment in which neither party has the power to force unsound settlements on the other, and in which governments are managing money, budgets, and debts properly.

17

Price Stability

EVERYBODY SEEMS TO BE AGAINST inflation as they are against sin, but seldom do people try to analyze why they ought to be. I should like to review briefly several important reasons for opposing inflation.

Why Inflation Is Harmful

1. Inflation harms those whose incomes do not rise proportionately with the general price level. During a general price rise, all prices and incomes do not move in unison; those whose incomes lag behind suffer most.

2. Inflation tends to injure low-income groups somewhat more than the upper-income or even the middle-income groups. Theoretically this should not necessarily be so, but it works that way because lower-income groups cannot, or do not know how to, protect themselves as do people at higher income levels. For example, in several public opinion polls, people have been asked how they think they can best protect themselves against inflation. A surprisingly large number reply that the best way is to invest in government bonds. This view may make the Secretary of the Treasury happy, but it does not make good sense as a hedge against inflation. Answers of this sort come much more frequently from low-income respondents than from those at higher income levels, who are generally more

Presented at the Farm Foundation National Agricultural Policy Conference in Lake Hope, Ohio, 12–15 September 1960.

sophisticated financially. Another common answer from those with low incomes is that protection can be provided by saving more and by getting out of debt, whereas higher income groups are much more likely to say the opposite—"buy now, pay later; go into debt if you can."

3. Inflation results in unfulfilled implied promises. I am not moralizing; I refer simply to the economic inefficiency caused by inflation. When people lose confidence in the value of money, they change their savings habits and refrain from making the kinds of commitments—insurance policies, purchase of fixed money claims, and the like—upon which our organized economic life depends.

4. Inflation has harmful effects on business decision making. A rubber measure of value destroys the integrity of the monetary unit for accounting purposes and creates maladjustments in the use of our resources. Under inflation some businesses think they are making money when they are losing money and dissipating their capital. Inflation also diverts an excessive amount of resources to speculation. Speculation is not bad in itself, but inflation causes excesses and overcommitments, which in turn create economic disturbances and lower efficiency.

5. Inflation creates a balance of payments problem by reducing our exports and stimulating our imports. Needless to say, the resulting serious financial difficulties and adjustment problems impair our economic efficiency and growth.

The Meaning of Price Stability

So we are all against inflation. We want and need a stable dollar. But what is a stable dollar? What exactly do we mean by reasonable price stability? Clearly we do not want each individual price to stay fixed, for prices perform an important function. High prices indicate that more of certain things are wanted or are hard to get. Low prices indicate that the things to which they are attached are in surplus or have a low priority. Individual prices not only convey information about relative needs and scarcities, they also serve as a strong force in compelling people to do what they should do in the social interest. The efficient operation of the economy depends on the flexibility of individual prices.

Price control has an intuitive appeal for many people—they like the idea that if you do not want prices to rise you can pass a law to prevent it. Of course, such a procedure is self-defeating. When we have price controls, prices no longer mean what they meant when we wanted to stabilize them. Under price control, amounts of goods and services wanted are no longer available at the stated prices; and furtive auxiliary considerations enter many transactions. The fact that a number stays constant does not achieve stability of individual prices, nor of the average level of prices. The average will be based on fictitious prices.

The notion of price stability is further complicated by the fact that, not only does it refer to an average of all prices, but it refers to this average only "on the average." That is to say, we do not want the average to remain the same day in and day out, month after month. Mild ups and downs are normal and to be expected. What we want is the average to average out at a fairly constant level over a period of time. With this double form of averaging necessary even to define the concept of price stability, no wonder it remains so elusive for the public to grasp.

Historical Price Patterns

People often talk as though a mild or extreme inflation has been going on ever since the Pilgrims landed and that more is inevitable. What has been the history of prices in the United States? We have data on wholesale prices as far back as 1720 and on retail prices as far back as 1800. To be sure, some of the data are not very accurate or reliable, but over the sweep of history they give us a pretty good picture of the price record.

If we plot these average prices on a chart, we find the predominant impression is one of stability. Over the whole period from 1720 to 1960 wholesale prices have gone up, on the average, about one-half of 1 percent each year. The second striking aspect about such a chart is the tremendous peaks scattered along the long-term trend. People not accustomed to reading charts will often be impressed by these great peaks without noticing the basic trends.

Every such peak in American history, every large rise in the average level of prices, has been associated with war and the immediate aftermath of war. After each war, however, within ten to twenty years, prices have dropped again, at least briefly, to their prewar level. The only exception has been the period since World War II. A comparison of the peacetime years with wartime years shows that in peacetime years prices have declined about one-half percent per year—speaking very roughly, of course.

Another characteristic of the long-term record is that during periods of as much as thirty years prices have moved gradually and cumulatively up or down. From 1865 to 1897, for example, the index of consumer prices declined by nearly one-half and the index of wholesale prices by nearly two-thirds—a generation of creeping (and sometimes galloping) deflation.

Finally, if we look at the record still more carefully, we find smaller movements associated with business cycles. Typically, in a period of economic expansion, the price level is stable after the trough and during roughly the first half of the upswing; but toward the peak, prices begin to go up, and they continue to rise after the peak level of economic activity has been reached and even after a downturn is in progress. Later, as a recession develops, prices stabilize; and if the recession is long enough or deep enough, prices may fall. Typically, only a severe recession can break down the price level; in a mild recession the level only stabilizes for a time.

Recent Price Patterns

I stress these characteristics of our long-term price history patterns (which are similar to those recorded by other countries) for two reasons: (1) Our recent experience, at a first superficial glance, seems somewhat different from the normal pattern; and (2) we are badgered today with many special explanations for our recent price history which seem to me to be either specious or amateurish or both.

Consider first our postwar experience. As recorded by our price indexes, prices have doubled in the past twenty years. After World War II and after the Korean War, they showed no sign of coming down as they did previously. They evidently are not going to come down. If they did, the result would be disastrous. Historically, some sharp deflations and some severe depressions were required to bring prices down. The recessions we have had since World War II have all been very mild—extremely mild by historical standards. In these postwar recessions, price behavior has been entirely typical. Our success in coping with recessions has given us an inflation problem which we did not have before. By controlling recessions, we have strengthened the normal tendency for price increases to become cumulative. This simply means that our improved ability to control recessions has made it much more important for us to control general upward price movements during periods of business expansion. As we become more proficient in dealing with the major problems of recession, we become much more alert to the serious, though smaller and related problem: price level stability. This is as it should be, but we should not be misled about the magnitude of the problem.

Though I believe we face the danger of persistent upward price pressures in the future, this does not mean that I place much stock in the new and special explanations of the recent past. What has happened since World War II can be explained in the same terms that explain the price history of the past two hundred years. One distinction between an amateur and a professional in the field of economics, or in any scientific endeavor, is that the amateur always thinks up *ad hoc* explanations for everything that has happened, while the professional looks for the pervasiveness of basic forces and first tests the validity of proven generalizations.

In public discussion *ad hoc* explanations naturally have popular appeal. Two of them receive sufficient attention to merit examination here. According to one widespread belief, a basic change in the structure of the economy is creating new rigidities in wages or in prices which exert persistent upward pressures. According to other views, inflation results from a change in national economic policy occasioned by the Employment Act of 1946. Let us take a moment to look at each of these explanations.

On the question of new rigidities, some people argue that inflation is largely caused by unions which have prevented lowering of wages and have pushed wages (and costs) up excessively by monopolistic power. The other variant is that businesses with monopolistic power have "administered" prices generally upward.

Whatever may be wrong with unions, and that may be a great deal, I think it is a bad mistake to blame everything that goes wrong with the economy on unions. One quarter of the labor force is unionized. Wages have gone up more in many nonunion occupations than in strongly unionized occupations. Of course, unions have brought blame upon themselves by their sales campaigns and internal politics. But the impact of the unions on general wage levels has been greatly exaggerated. One labor expert has summed up the results of the recent studies something like this: About a quarter of union members have had their particular wages raised substantially, perhaps 15 percent above what they would have gotten without their unions; half of the union workers may enjoy wages 5 to 10 percent above what they otherwise would have gotten; and about a quarter of union workers belong to organizations that have not had any appreciable effect on their wages.

The fact that unions have had some, albeit overrated, impact on the structures of wages among different groups of workers does not mean that they have pushed up the average level of wages and costs for the economy as a whole. Indeed, what has happened to wages on the average would have happened in any inflationary situation and can be explained without recourse to witch-hunting.

With respect to business monopoly—or business concentration to use a more neutral term—three separate studies in recent years, using different concepts and criteria, all come to the conclusion that concentration of business power has not been increasing during the twentieth century and may be decreasing. Therefore, administered pricing does not seem to be a likely "new" inflationary force in the economy. Besides, despite popular misunderstanding that it could be, no systematic analysis has been adduced to show how or why.

Let us turn now to the other alleged explanation: the Employment Act of 1946 and the policies used to implement it. Here there is a grain of truth—not as to cause but as to effect. As I indicated before, to the extent we are successful in eliminating major depressions, we are confronted with a problem of cumulative price rises during expansions. Surely, no one would say, "Let's go back to some serious depressions in order to deflate the price level!" The moral of this story is that, with or without the Employment Act, we simply have to make comparable progress on the inflation control front. The situation is similar to that in other fields. In medicine as we reduce infant mortality almost to zero, we turn our main attention to cancer or heart disease. As we eliminate smallpox, the common cold becomes a subject of greater attention. As we solve the inflation problem, we can be sure that other problems that now have lower priority will become increasingly urgent.

Compatibility of Price Stability and Other Goals

Some people feel strongly that the Employment Act raises a serious issue of conflicting goals—that price stability, high employment, and economic growth cannot be achieved simultaneously. I do not believe that a major conflict exists. The compatibility of these goals depends largely upon how we set them and the means by which we pursue them. Historically the record shows no conflict between price stability and economic growth. As I have pointed out, a reasonably stable dollar is necessary for rational decision making and orderly economic progress. Price level stability, properly conceived, implements rather than hinders growth.

As with price stability, "full employment" is not a simple concept, and it means different things to different people. But no one seriously holds that it means 100 percent of the work force at work. Some people put an acceptable level of unemployment at 3, 6, or 2.94 percent. My feeling is that no percentage which includes me and my friends is acceptable. But whatever level we settle for, it will vary from time to time, and it will not mean what the public at large seems to think when they hear the word "unemployment." This term conjures up visions of the 1930's with its massive unemployment—visions of children at home with no food, no shoes, no fuel for the furnace, and what not. While we still have some unemployment that causes severe economic hardship, this type of unemployment has been vastly reduced since the war.

A detailed study by the Bureau of Labor Statistics for 1956–57 (prosperous years) showed that about 20 percent of our unemployment was of a seasonal character, in construction particularly. About 20 percent consisted of new entrants into the labor force, young people and others who had not previously been employed (these people would not even be counted among the unemployed in most other countries). About 10 to 15 percent consisted of people who were voluntarily changing jobs. In other words, about half of the unemployed were not really hardship cases. During a recession a much larger proportion of those unemployed would be layoffs and heads of families who cannot remain long out of work without their families suffering privation. The duration of unemployment would also increase. But with improved unemployment compensation systems, much of the sting can be and is removed from this form of unemployment. If we can keep our recessions mild and short, we shall certainly have achieved a reasonable full employment goal. Such hardship as may remain, and some is unavoidable, can be alleviated by welfare measures.

18

Price Control

To AVOID MISUNDERSTANDING, let me make it clear at the outset that many of the people on the Office of Price Administration are able and admirable; in fact, some of my best friends work for the OPA.

There has been remarkably little coherent criticism of the OPA, but there is a vast amount of just plain bellyaching or griping. In fact, I doubt whether many of you here in Washington realize how bitterly and widely the OPA is despised. This hatred, incidentally, is a factor to be reckoned with, not only in relation to wartime morale, but much more seriously in relation to postwar problems. People now hate the Nazis and the Japanese so much more than they hate the OPA that there is no real problem. But after the war, I venture to predict, the whole structure of the OPA and every vestige of economic control will be swept away, lock, stock, and personnel, in a blind flood of resentment. Since OPA activities so far have for the most part only postponed (and enlarged) the problem of inflation, such a sudden and total abolition of economic regulation may well have tragic consequences.

Now what causes this hatred of the OPA? The OPA in defending itself always assumes—though perhaps disingenuously—that the resentment is really resentment of wartime scarcities, or that it is resentment of government regulation as such. Actually, not 10 per cent of the criticism is of this character; nearly all of it is resentment of

Presented before the American Economic Association in Washington, D.C., on 12 January 1943.

the particular way OPA and its officials have gone about their business.

The OPA has adopted a procedure that involves its participation, overtly or covertly, in all the technical and organizational details of millions of enterprises. To bring about necessary wartime readjustments efficiently under its scheme of operation requires knowing more about each firm—more about its plant, its machines, its sources of materials, its labor, its markets, and so on—than is known by those who have made livings for years by knowing such matters in minute and thorough detail. Those in the business, instead of straining their accumulated knowledge, skill, ingenuity, and resourcefulness toward facilitating efficient readjustment, devote all their energies to persuading or "educating" OPA officials that it is impossible. This tendency was illustrated by an advertisement in the New York *Times* last spring offering for $7.00 a month to keep businessmen abreast of the OPA; one prominent feature was the latest information on "how to appeal effectively to OPA officials."

The businessman's antagonism is personalized. He does not run into the kind of business problem he has met before; he runs into an economist, a lawyer, or an administrator who does not talk his language. The unhappy official, however competent, is sure to reveal himself ignorant of some minute and petty detail of business practice, from which the businessman jumps to the conclusion that his orders are incompetent, irrelevant, and immaterial.

A workable approach to OPA problems would be to regulate the economic environment in such a way that businessmen will exert all of their technical and managerial skill toward devising ways to further the war effort. The objective should be to channel rigidly the resourcefulness of American business, not to dam it up for the duration. To put the point in more general terms, the necessary wartime control should be achieved, not by putting an enormous staff to work participating directly in the millions of economic decisions and actions that occur daily, but by setting up a general economic environment in which each individual in every transaction has a clear indication of where the national interest lies and at the same time has an almost compulsory incentive to act accordingly.

Now a mechanism for this kind of control is already established and functioning; namely, the price mechanism. By intelligent manipulation of this mechanism businessmen could be led to select that line of activity at which they could produce the most—this being measured by the urgency of the need and by the availability of other suppliers—and to produce it with the least use of critical materials.

Incidentally, I am told that the Germans have recently abandoned the price control program inaugurated in 1936—of which our OPA is a very close copy—and are now switching to a price and profit technique. Since the survival of the United Nations in 1940 and 1941 is attributable largely to German bungling, stupidity, and inefficiency, we may well be grateful that they did not revise their economic program earlier. There is reason to hope that it may now be too late.

Regulating the economy through the price mechanism is a process in which economists could be useful, as contrasted with the present OPA procedures, which requires administrators, lawyers, and technicians, none of whom has much appreciation of the general over-all economic implications of his work. As an illustration of the kind of thing that could be done, consider the problem of rationing consumers goods and controlling their prices.

The present crazyquilt method involves a very personalized form of control; it is a form of regulation based on direct meddling. One has to explain to local commissioners just why he needs ten pounds of sugar extra, and he may have to explain to numerous snoopers on the roads why he is driving his car. At the same time, large quantities of sugar are being virtually wasted by those whose needs fall short of the ration, and sizable amounts of gasoline and rubber are going to waste. The supply of meat available for consumption has often fluctuated as much as it has during the past six months; yet never within the memory of the oldest person present have there been such gross inequalities in its distribution geographically.

Any number of sensible ways can be devised for accomplishing the objectives the OPA seeks—that is, economizing of scarce goods and stabilizing the price level—without the inefficiencies and bureaucracy of the OPA. An excellent review of some of these schemes was given by de Scitovsky in the August *Review of Economic Statistics*. I regret that there is not time now to discuss any of these in specific terms, but I have recently given in the *American Economic Review* a rather condensed statement of the way a progressive spending tax could handle the problem.

In conclusion I should like to make one further remark. Defenders of the OPA are inclined to fall back on political arguments. Now it is true, I believe, that the kind of thing the OPA is doing to meet its problems is exactly the kind of thing the man in the street would think of—if he did not put much thought on the problem and if he knew no economics. "If prices are going up, prohibit it," he would say. "If goods are scarce, everybody line up and we'll ladle them out." But when the price-control bill was before Congress, no such simple view was taken. Indeed, it was only with the greatest reluctance that the bill was passed after months of discussion, and it was clear that almost any workable alternative would have been preferred. As it was, the bill got through only after OPA officials had argued that no great exercise of its powers would be necessary, as the country could easily have all the butter *and* guns it wanted, price control being needed only at a few bottlenecks. During the period the bill was pending, some individuals in the OPA opposed measures to control the inflationary gap, denying that there really was one; though the bill was hardly passed before they proclaimed the impotence of price control unsupplemented by control of general purchasing power. There is no reason from this record to suppose that the economists of the OPA are any better judges of political feasibility than of economic feasibility; and there is reason to hope that their economic recommendations would be sounder if based only on economic considerations, leaving general policy considerations to the responsible political officials.

19

How To Ration Consumers' Goods and Control Their Prices

THE GROWING SCARCITY of consumers' goods makes the problem of rationing them increasingly urgent. Sugar, typewriters, bicycles, automobiles, tires, and gasoline are already subject to direct administrative rationing. Although no widespread infringement of the sugar regulations is apparent, the experience with tires and gasoline, if it should become more general, would be tragic. Even with sugar the cost of administration is not to be blinked at in a country straining every nerve toward war production.

A fundamental difficulty with administrative rationing is that equal allotments do not result in equal treatment or equal sacrifice. This has been recognized for tires and gasoline, and varying quantities have been allowed different classes of consumers. But no administrative board can appraise the merits of claims for allotments above the minimum, nor can it control the disposition of the commodity once allotted. Perhaps it can determine that a gasoline user's work is important for defense and that no public conveyance is available; it cannot judge whether he could shift his residence, change jobs, ride with a neighbor. And most of its problems are far more complicated than this one. For success a rationing board requires a nearly unanimous feeling by the general public that rationing is necessary, that the board's methods are proper, and that its administration is competent, uniform, and impartial.

Published in the American Economic Review, *Volume 32, No. 3, September 1942, pp. 501–512.*

In our economy goods have normally been apportioned through
the price mechanism. The commodity goes to those who want it
badly enough to pay the price, this being dependent upon need or
taste for the commodity, upon the acceptability of substitutes, and
especially upon incomes. The income element in determining the
distribution of goods and services is always a source of social concern.
This concern occasionally results in direct allocation of goods and
services outside the price system, notably free education and medical facilities, and more often it leads to efforts to redistribute income,
notably through progressive income, gift, and inheritance taxes.

In wartime the rôle of income in rationing through the price
mechanism becomes crucial, whether the peacetime distribution of
income be regarded as admirable or abominable, for the wartime
lowering of total consumption would push considerable fractions of
the population below the subsistence level if peacetime differentials
in living standards were maintained. In wartime, furthermore, the
amount of money which consumers have and try to spend exceeds the
amount of goods and services for sale. The excess, or "inflationary
gap," causes a general rise in the level of prices, which may become a
serious impediment to economic mobilization, by retarding the shift
of resources, discouraging saving, encouraging hoarding of goods, and
erratically shifting the burden of the war. To rely on the normal operation of the price system during the war thus would cause great
inequities in consumption and serious obstruction of the war effort,
and this in ways that would cumulate, weakening morale, encouraging further injustices in the distribution of goods, aggravating the inflationary movement.

Measures to restrict these disruptive tendencies so far adopted
fall into two general categories: (1) over-all measures to reduce the
inflationary gap, such as increased taxation, restriction of consumer
credit, and government borrowing from consumers; and (2) specific
controls, such as price ceilings and rationing coupons. The second
kind of measure cannot control inflation; indeed, it was clearly recognized in the statement accompanying the Price Ceiling Order of
April 28, 1942, that measures of the first category are essential for
that. But the over-all measures are unwieldy, slow in their effects, and
not sufficiently flexible to keep up with rapid and unforeseeable
alterations in the magnitude of the inflationary gap—though they
can doubtless be improved in detail, as for example by withholding
income at its sources instead of waiting, as now, from two-and-a-half
to twenty-three months to complete collection of income taxes. The

specific controls embodied in the Price Ceiling Order and accompanying rationing devices, while they might alleviate gross inequalities if they functioned smoothly, actually cause great waste of whatever consumers' goods are available; in addition, the huge cost of administering them reduces the amount of consumers' and of war goods available. The waste of goods which they cause can be discussed best in relation to a constructive proposal.

The proposal set forth here is an amalgam of over-all measures and specific controls. It would effect the optimum allocation of scarce goods among consumers with infinitely less cost, friction and waste, and with far greater simplicity and flexibility than other methods. At the same time it would prevent inflation and facilitate economic mobilization.

Let us approach the general plan by steps. First, consider the problem of rationing meat. Beef yields various cuts in proportions which are not easily altered. With consumer income rising and its usual outlets in durable goods closed, nearly everyone will try to buy the best cuts. Because of the price ceiling, the price cannot rise above its highest point in March, and at that price the demand will exceed the supply. Perhaps butchers will favor special customers, or perhaps a first-come, first-served policy will prevail. Either will cause considerable injustices and grumbling, all the more because those engaged in war work are likely to be too busy to shop early and wait in line, or are apt to have moved recently and so not to have established claims to a butcher's favor. As in the case of sugar, administrative rationing will become necessary. But it would be preposterous to assign to each person so many ounces per week of sirloin steak, so many of porterhouse, so many of top round, so many of bottom round, so many of rib roast, etc.

A far more intelligent policy is that of the English, who limit each person to a certain value of meat per week. Those who prefer quality to quantity can exercise their preference, as can those who prefer quantity to quality. Suppose the prices of different cuts are left to demand and supply, subject to the important restriction that each person's total demand is limited to, say, 75 cents per week. Then, if there is a general preference for quality, the prices of better cuts will rise enormously *and* the prices of poorer cuts will fall correspondingly. For, if everyone tried to spend most of his 75 cents on good cuts, their price would have to rise since their quantity is fixed; but no one would have much money left to offer for poor cuts and their prices would have to fall to dispose of them. As the differential increased a growing number of persons would be repelled by the rising price of good cuts and attracted by the falling price of inferior cuts. Finally, those who cared so much for quality that they were willing to restrict themselves to minute quantities of meat would get the good cuts; but as a penalty they would have released the great bulk of the meat to others. Those who decided to forgo the quality cuts would be rewarded by more than proportionate shares of the quantity.

Suppose, on the other hand, a general preference for quantity and indifference to quality. Then everyone would try to buy the cheap cuts, consequently having little money left to spend on good cuts. The result would be to push the price of inferior cuts up and of superior cuts down, until the differential became very narrow; and meat would be divided almost equally on a poundage basis.

In either case, there would be real equality in the degree to which each person's needs and tastes were satisfied by the quantity and quality of his meat. Equality of sacrifice must take account of quantity and quality, and of the fact that the amount of sacrifice entailed by curtailing either is a subjective matter varying from individual to individual. This is taken into account by restricting each person's total expenditure on meat, which in turn makes it possible to leave the prices of different cuts free to indicate the relative scarcity and desirability of the various cuts. The relative prices of different cuts might change freely, but no increase in the level of meat prices in general could occur, because the total amount of money spendable on meat would be fixed. If the amount of meat available were to increase or decrease, the allowable expenditure on meat would be increased or decreased by the same amount.

Now, there is no point in confining the merits of this system to meat. Much better results will be secured by extending it to all food, by limiting total weekly expenditures on food to, say, $3.00 per person. Those who greatly prefer meat to any other food then can expand their expenditures on meat beyond 75 cents. If they do, they will have less to spend on other foods, and those who give up meat in the face of the price rise caused by the meat-eaters will be rewarded by being able to buy more than their proportionate share of, perhaps, vegetables. The prospect of this greater amount of vegetables induces those who have no great craving for meat to leave the meat for the meat-lovers, and the rising price of meat reinforces this inducement.

Still more generally, the scheme should be extended to all consumption goods and services. Then those who are easily satisfied with little food—that is, with either small quantity or low quality—have an inducement to forgo food and take their consumption in forms less desired by their more ravenous countrymen. There could be no inequality in total consumption: Inequalities in consumption of different commodities would balance out for each individual, just as inequalities in quantity would be balanced by inequalities in the reverse direction in quality. The measurement of consumption would be in value terms, and value would reflect the relative scarcity of each good in combination with its relative desiredness by all consumers as a group. There could be no rise in the price *level*, of course, for the aggregate of the consumption allotments would equal the aggregate of the consumption goods and services available. Shifts in *relative* prices are highly desirable, for they give each consumer the data for balancing his wants against the wants of others, taking into account the relative scarcities of various goods; and they provide a powerful incentive for him to do the balancing in such a way that he consumes as little as possible of things that are scarcest or most desired by others.

Another important feature is that this system would not tie up any considerable amount of resources in its administration, and that it relies on control mechanisms which are already established and functioning in our economy, merely governing their action instead of replacing them entirely. To put the point in more general terms, the necessary wartime control is achieved, not by putting an enormous staff to work participating directly in the millions of economic decisions and actions that occur daily, but by setting up a general economic environment in which each individual in every transaction has a simple measure (price) of how important each commodity is to the nation and at the same time has an almost compulsory incentive (the necessity of getting the most for his limited funds) to discover how he can best adjust to the national emergency—in whatever the degree of his patriotism.

Finally, it should be observed that shifts in relative prices can serve to shift the amounts of different commodities available. Sugar and coffee, for example, compete for whatever shipping space is allotted to such things. Should consumers, under their curtailed level of living, desire to increase the ratio of sugar to coffee this would be reflected by a much greater rise in the price of sugar than in the price of coffee (or perhaps a greater decrease in the price of coffee than in the price of sugar, if consumers were cutting down on both more than on other things). This change in relative prices would indicate that consumers would be better satisfied if some of the shipping space being used for coffee were transferred to sugar. Whether the transfer could actually be effected would depend upon a host of matters with importing, but at least the possibility of decreasing consumer sacrifice with no increase in shipping would be definitely known.

A uniform total-expenditure ration is, however, more drastic than is required in this country, at least in the immediate future. The degree to which it would equalize consumption exceeds by far what is necessitated by war conditions, and a sudden equalization of consumption would produce serious secondary shocks, both economic and psychological. Those who exert the greatest efforts during the war have, furthermore, a prior claim on current consumption (as well as on future consumption). Some flexibility in the maximum total consumption is desirable also to provide for extreme cases, whether arising from emergencies or peculiar needs and tastes. But administrative boards for these purposes would be dangerous: With the best of intentions and abilities equity would be impossible, and the mere suspicion of favoritism or of unevenness from time to time or place to place would be fatal. The amount of the total-expenditure ration should be fixed differently, however, for different ages, family compositions, etc., on a uniform basis, just as are personal exemptions for the income tax.

Flexibility in the total-expenditure ration can be introduced if, instead of prohibiting expenditures in excess of the total ration, a tax is levied on excess expenditures at a steeply progressive rate. A family of four, for eample, might be allowed a basic total expenditure ration of $2,000 per year. (The figures used here, as in the foregoing examples of meat and food, are purely illustrative and do not reflect even guesses as to practical figures.) Any expenditures beyond $2,000 would be subject to a 10 per cent tax, expenditures beyond $2,500 to a tax of 15 per cent in addition to the 10 per cent, expenditures beyond $3,000 to an additional 20 per cent tax, etc. Thus, it would be possible to consume more than the basic ration if current income were high, which by-and-large would be when individuals or their properties were engaged in war activities. As a matter of fact, as we shall see later, the present proposal itself would make it more true than it now is that high incomes correspond with intensive war work. But because of the tax, expansion of current consumption would entail a disproportionate and rapidly mounting contraction of post-war consumption; that is, the tax would cut heavily into savings which could be spent, free of the tax, after the war.

The problem of administering this plan for rationing consumer goods and controlling their prices reduces to the problem of administering the progressive consumption tax. To require individual accounting for consumption expenditures would not be feasible. It could be presumed that all income not saved is subject to the consumption tax.

The present income tax laws already provide for reports on income. No evidence of saving should be recognized, except government bonds. Thus, the government would minimize the problem of regulating all the diverse forms in which savings occur, and would be better able to control investment during the war. Altogether, the consumption tax might not increase appreciably the administrative burden of the Treasury—and certainly would not add to its burden in anything like the amount by which present and prospective Office of Price Administration operations would be eliminated.

Each individual, then, would file a federal income tax return in the usual way. To it would be appended a calculation of his consumption tax, consisting of four steps: (1) any adjustments necessary to bring his total net income figure into line with an income definition more appropriate to the consumption tax than are the income tax definitions; (2) deduction of the part of this income used for purchasing United States government bonds; (3) deduction of the basic expenditure ration, and of amounts used for any purposes specially exempted from the consumption tax; (4) computation of the tax on the balance obtained in the third step. Measures to speed collection, incidentally, would be as desirable in the case of the consumption tax as in the case of the income tax, and at least as feasible.

Perhaps the most difficult question in administration would concern liquidation of assets. In so far as assets, whether securities or such consumers' goods as tires and toasters, were paid for by other consumers out of their current income, no harm would result, for no upward pressure on the price level would be exerted. It would be necessary to guard against liquidation by sale or mortgage to businesses, banks, or in general out of any funds not subject to the consumption tax. Without working out here all the details which would be necessary to implement the plan, it may be asserted confidently that a little legal, accounting, and administrative ingenuity can minimize the difficulties and the possibilities of evasion. In one respect at least, evasion of the consumption tax would be more difficult than evasion of the income tax: One's neighbors do not know either one's actual or reported income, but the only object of evading the consumption tax, increasing current consumption, would tend to make one conspicuous in a war community.

It is much easier to estimate the volume of production of consumers' goods and services, all that would be required for determining the basic or tax-free expenditure ration, than it is to estimate the inflationary gap. The only adjustment would be to allow for spending above the basic ration in the face of the tax. This could not be of great importance, because the number of people having sufficient incomes to spend much above the basic ration would be very small if the tax were sufficiently progressive, and most of them would be deterred by the tax.

The consumption levy is not a tax in the usual sense. It is a transitionary device for reducing and equalizing consumption to the degree that may become necessary during the war. The income tax, because it affects consumption only indirectly, is not sufficiently flexible to do this efficiently, especially without impairing the power of differential earnings to transfer resources into war activities. The consumption tax, however, cannot be relied upon for revenue—indeed, the better it fulfills its function, the less tax revenue it yields —so it would not diminish the necessity of income taxation. Sales of government bonds induced by the consumption tax, together with the income tax, would guarantee adequate government finances during the war. But if the bond sales were to carry the principal burden, the structure of the government debt might create post-war problems of income distribution. The inequalities of consumption that were suppressed during the war would cumulate, to be released with exaggerated force after the war. If excessive concentration of government bond holdings is limited by proper use of the income tax, the funds saved to avoid the consumption tax could constitute a powerful aid to post-war economic adjustment.

Having arrived at a basic total-expenditure ration and steeply progressive consumption taxes, let us for a moment forget the route by which we traveled and survey an alternative path which sets out to levy a progressive sales tax—that is, to charge higher prices to high-level consumers. The scheme set forth above accomplishes this neatly.

Consider, for example, three purchasers of the three tires remaining on a car that has worn through its other two. Let us suppose that A, B, and C are each entitled to a basic total-expenditure ration of $2,000 per year, and that supply and demand, as controlled by total-expenditure rationing, have set a valuation of $25 on each tire. A, B, and C each purchases one to round out his own set of three remaining tires.

Before considering the situation described, let us digress to note that this situation implies that the seller has decided the things he can buy with $75, plus what he can get for his car, are more desirable to him than the services of the car, especially in view of the high costs of operating it. The reason he can get so much money for his tires and car and so many other things with the money is that people like A, B, and C, who need cars—or think they need cars, and what man can distinguish between "real" and "illusory" needs?—are spending so much on car operation that they have been forced by the ceiling on total expenditures to withdraw from the markets for other things, thus letting down the prices of other things and attracting our tire-seller into the vacuum they have left.

Returning to the purchasers: The apparent price of a tire to each buyer is the $25 the seller receives from each. If A's total expenditures are under $2,000, $25 is the real price to him. But to B, who is spending between $2,000 and $2,500, the real price is raised by the tax he must pay, say 10 per cent, to $27.50. And to C, spending $3,100, the price is raised by the tax, say (using the arbitrary figures set down earlier) 10 per cent + 15 per cent + 20 per cent = 45 per cent, to $36.25. The reason D, whose total expenditures are a trifle over $10,000, is not in the market for a tire is that it would cost him, with tax, $237.50 (projecting the figures used earlier, which rise by 5 per cent for each $500 of expenditure).

The reason for charging higher prices to higher income groups is, of course, that they require a greater stimulus to curtail consumption, since they have the possibility of simply reducing saving. It is to be recalled that if they refrain from consuming now, they can get full value in goods after the war when consumption rationing is halted, and this possibility reinforces the stimulus to minimize current consumption.

There would be little danger from purchases by those for whom the tax is low in behalf of those for whom it is high. Such a transaction would be an effective evasion only if it were based on a promise by the high-level consumer to repay after removal of the consumption tax. The actual purchaser would have to forgo current consumption equal to the price of the commodity to him, and in return he would receive an illegal credit instrument of indefinite maturity. People who can rely on one another to fulfill obligations of that nature are likely to be of more or less similar social and economic status, hence affected approximately alike by the tax; and the integrity required will not often accompany sly circumvention of emergency war measures that are obviously uniform and objective in their incidence. But the most effective obstacle to arbitrage is that the person who extended credit would have to do so out of his own total-expenditure ration and income; and, if his expenditures were low enough to make his tax low, he could not extend much credit—because he would have to cut into his own consumption, or else he would incur taxes curtailing his income and hence his power to extend credit.

In evaluating a proposal of this kind it is essential to consider not only its primary effects but its secondary repercussions. In considering these, however, it is important to distinguish between consequences that are fundamental characteristics of the war situation and its attendant hardships and consequences not inherent in the war situation but only in the particular plan of meeting it. The object of any plan is, of course, to smooth the course and spread the impact of consequences of the first kind, with a minimum of undesirable consequences of the second kind.

As an extreme example of the secondary repercussions of the plan, imagine its effects on a luxurious summer hotel so located as to be of little potential use to the military forces even as a convalescent home. Perhaps it had been patronized exclusively by persons with incomes in excess of $10,000 per year. If its nominal rates were $20 per day, extrapolation of the illustrative progressive consumption tax figures used before would raise the minimum effective price to the patrons to $190 per day. The management would be faced with the necessity of lowering its rates to serve lower income groups. To curtail costs it would have to reduce the size and quality of its staff and of the articles furnished. The staff, in order to continue receiving incomes, would be forced to look for other jobs, and the place to look would be in war work. Indeed, the management might well decide to liquidate its mobile assets, selling plumbing, hardware, rugs, vacuum cleaners, dishes, tableware, linen, furniture, and its whole inventory of things no longer being produced but badly needed because of population shifts under the war program.

In effect the hotel staff would have received notice that its former services were not contributing as much to a nation at war as they had to a nation at peace. It would have a full range of accurate information as to how it best could contribute to the war: If its assets were mobile (the cost of removal and shipment would indicate how mobile they were from a national point of view) and were scarce and urgently needed elsewhere (the prices being offered by consumers out of their total-expenditure rations would show how badly they were wanted in relation to their scarcity), it would have a strong incentive to dismantle; but if the losses entailed in this were greater than those of continuing to operate at lower rates it would have evidence that its services are more useful (less useless!) as it is. The owners and employees would find themselves in unfortunate circumstances, like those already confronting automobile dealers and operators of tourist cabins; but their burden would be an unavoidable result of the fact that their services did not contribute materially to the war effort, and it would be alleviated by the opportunity, through the freedom of the prices of their assets, to recover some of their losses.

This example is perhaps an extreme one. It has been chosen deliberately to show the worst possible secondary repercussions and indicate that even in such circumstances the proposed plan may alleviate an unavoidable hardship and expedite adjustment to the requirements of the war economy: the hotel management being under compulsion (financial) to apply all its ingenuity to discovering uses for its assets.

The program should be put into operation without delay. If it is put into effect now, it will not have to set the initial total-expenditure ration extremely low and the progressive features need not be severe, because the volume of available consumers' goods and services has not yet declined markedly. As the decline proceeds, people will be able to organize orderly retreats from their peacetime standards of living, and shifts in relative prices will be sufficiently gradual to facilitate readjustment of the economy to the new structure of demands. The longer the economic changes due to the war are forced to operate under a system of fixed individual prices, the greater will be the maladjustments; and the larger will be the amount of direct governmental participation in the detailed decisions of individuals that will be necessary for the functioning of the economy under any scheme.

It may seem that, even with the plan in effect, one or two items might become so extremely scarce that even if divided equally there would be barely enough to go around, and that administrative rationing would therefore become necessary for such items. Despite the plausibility of this reasoning, it is fundamentally fallacious. Such extreme scarcity cannot exist apart from a general scarcity, because goods are substitutable both in consumption and production. On the consumption side, there is no single good nor any small group of goods that cannot be replaced more or less satisfactorily by other goods. On the production side, a desired result can be achieved in a variety of ways, and any particular resource has innumerable potential uses.

All these possibilities of substitution quickly convert what would otherwise be an acute specific shortage into a mild general shortage. A shortage of tires, for example, becomes a lack of truck-hauled vegetables, and this leads to greater demands for rail-hauled vegetables, thereby slightly increasing the scarcity of refrigerator cars; it becomes a lack of access to factories, which leads to housing construction near the factories, hence increases the scarcity of building materials; it becomes a lack of urban transportation, which leads to increased use of trolleys and subways, hence to increased demands on electric generators, and so to scarcity of illumination. Every specific scarcity becomes an indistinguishable part of the general scarcity. As the general scarcity accumulates, total-expenditure rationing must become increasingly strict. Lower basic rations and more steeply progressive consumption taxes must come into force, for this is the best means of minimizing the hardships from the general scarcity and of distributing them equally.

Undoubtedly a large number of exemptions from the total-expenditure ration will be proposed. Very few if any of these will bear analysis, though many seem acceptable at first. To establish any exception would be a dangerous precedent. To exempt medical expenses, for example, would benefit only the upper-income groups, since in general the lower-income brackets do not have the money to try to spend even in emergency, but must rely on social facilities. Those whose expenditures are high enough to subject them to a high consumption tax would be those whose standard of living was enough above the general average for them to make the unpleasant adjustments that the vast majority of the population must make even in peace when medical expenses are incurred; otherwise, they could resort to facilities available to families unable to assume the full cost of medical care. Exempting one item would greatly encourage its utilization by the upper-income groups. Medical facilities in wartime are extremely overburdened and their use has to be curtailed below an "adequate" level simply because there is not an adequate amount in existence.

A general class of exceptions probably will be put forward with the object of "directing consumption to those items which do not use up war materials." The fact that this can be accomplished most effectively by fixing the general price level in such a way as to leave *relative* prices free to reflect scarcities and wants is, however, one of the most cogent arguments for the proposed plan. Furthermore, there is nothing to be gained by encouraging the consumption of such goods except in so far as they can replace goods using war resources; so the better able such goods are to satisfy consumer needs the smaller should be the consumer's remaining claim on other goods.

There is perhaps a case for exempting payments on debts contracted prior to adoption of the plan. Insurance payments pose a problem, but not an insuperable one. In so far as they represent pure insurance they are transfers from one consumer to another, hence the premiums should be exempt but the benefits taxed if the beneficiary spends them; in so far as they represent service fees they are consumption, so should be subject to the tax; and in so far as they represent savings they should come under government control. A possible device, which could be extended also to other savings institutions, would be for the insurance companies to buy government bonds to which were attached coupons that could be distributed to policy holders for use as evidence of savings when computing the consumption tax.

On the income side of the picture, it would be desirable but impractical to include the income-value of durable goods. Perhaps in the case of houses, the rental value of owned homes might feasibly be added to income and expenditure. In so far as the amount of other durable goods owned tends to be correlated with income, the progressive features of the tax schedule would compensate for them.

A system of total-expenditure rationing, coupled with a steeply progressive tax on all expenditures in excess of the basic ration, would be enormously superior to the devices now being inaugurated, because it would (1) effectively prevent inflation; (2) achieve the fairest and least wasteful distribution of consumers' goods; (3) be administratively simple and flexible; (4) avoid the disruptive consequences of (a) suspicion of favoritism or incompetence, actual or illusory, by administrative boards, (b) widespread disregard of law, (c) extensive policing investigations and control of private affairs, (d) elaborate red-tape, delay, and frustration in economic matters, (e) concentration of individual efforts on persuading or educating administrators instead of on solving difficulties, and (f) extensive diversion of resources to nonproductive, regulatory functions.

The proposed tax is essentially a progressive sales tax. As such, it bridges the gulf between the advocates of a sales tax, who rightly emphasize the desirability of discouraging consumption by direct taxation and the difficulties of relying exclusively on income taxation; and the advocates of exclusive reliance on income taxes, who rightly emphasize the desirability of progression and the regressive incidence of uniform sales taxation.

20

Guidelines

For the most part, I shall discuss the guidelines for domestic wages and prices separately from those for foreign trade. The two are related, however, and I shall take some note of this near the end of the paper. For each of the two types of guidelines, foreign and domestic, I shall consider what their objectives are, whether they are likely to achieve these objectives, what unintended effects they are likely to have, and what alternatives there are for achieving the objectives.

1. Wages and Prices

The basic scripture on domestic guidelines is in the *Annual Reports* of the Council of Economic Advisers. The wage-price guidelines were first handed down in the 1962 *Report*. For the latest exegesis, I turned to the 1966 *Report*, which contains a 31-page chapter entitled "Prospects for Cost-Price Stability."

This chapter I found distressing. It was not its substance that distressed me—I knew about that in a general way from newspapers and magazines. What distressed me was the unprofessional quality of the economic analysis. I am going to digress on that for a moment.

I want to emphasize that I am referring now to the professional quality of the economic analysis, not to the judgments based on the

Presented before the American Bankers Association in Washington, D.C., on 1 April 1966.[1]

analysis or to the recommendations based on the judgments. It is the
shoddy, slipshod, contrived character of the economics in the 1966
Report that surprised me and distressed me. In contrast, the 1962
Report was a respectable piece of work, certainly worthy of serious
study by the economics profession and worthy of respect even from
those who disagreed with it.

While a layman or a journalist reading in the 1962 *Report* about
the guidelines for wages and prices might come away with about the
same impressions that he would get from the 1966 *Report*, an economist notes important differences. The authors of the 1962 *Report*,
like their predecessors, were under pressure to say something consistent with the popular folklore that what causes inflation is wage
increases, and to construct a weightier club for clouting the unions
than the jawbone relied on by their predecessors. But the economic
and statistical competence and conscience of the authors of the 1962
Report showed through clearly in what Albert Rees has described
as "the fine print in the back." This "fine print" had the effect of
negating the generalities; it was nearly equivalent to a statement
that each particular wage rate or price should be set in accordance
with demand and supply. Similarly, the 1962 *Report* avoided sancti-
fying any specific number. Arthur Burns has traced the deterioration
of this early formulation through successive *Reports*. The glittering
generalities came more and more to the foreground, sloughing off
the "fine print" altogether, and by 1964 the figure 3.2 per cent—the
same magic number that had proved so useful with beer three
decades earlier—had come to be regarded as having some useful
part to play in practical wage determinations.

This is not the place for a full-scale critique of the 1966 *Report*,
or even the chapter of it under consideration here, but I must extend
this digression enough to indicate the reasons why I consider the
economic analyses so sadly shoddy. The reasons are in two categories:
first, fundamental deficiencies and, second, poor economic craftsmanship.

Of the fundamental deficiencies, I will mention two. First, only
once in the 27 pages of text devoted to wages and prices is there any
reference to money. Then it is referred to only in a brief allusion to
monetary policies outlined in the preceding chapter as "intended to
assure that total . . . purchases of goods and services do not exceed
the economy's ability to produce." Actually, the discussion in that
chapter suggests that monetary and fiscal policies are intended the
other way around, to assure that purchases do not fall short of
capacity to produce; it makes no reference to the control of inflation.

Now, there is a good deal of disagreement among economists about the relative importance of various factors that affect the price level; but no one seriously denies that money and credit play an important role. A chapter on prospects for stability in wages and prices that does not mention money and credit can only be likened to the monster without Frankenstein.

A second major deficiency is that nowhere in this chapter is any heed paid to the most important function of prices in our economy, namely their role in allocating finished products, labor, and raw materials among alternative uses; in regulating the rate of expansion or contraction of industries and firms; and in guiding efforts to economize on some things by replacing them with substitutes, either in production or consumption. There are references in the *Report* to the fact that prices are related to "the public interest," yet no awareness that the most decisive impact of prices on the public interest is through their role in directing our economic organization. Prices communicate information on needs and priorities and they provide incentives, verging on compulsions, to act efficiently in response to the information.

As for poor economic craftsmanship, consider only this one example, from the summary: "The guideposts must continue to aim at complete stability of average domestic prices." Does "complete stability" mean *complete* stability—day by day, minute by minute? Was this written with an awareness of the typical seasonal and cyclical behavior of prices, and if so does it imply something far more drastic than is discussed in the *Report*? Again, what is the significance of the adjective "domestic"? Presumably the implication is that products that are imported are not included in the average. But these products may enter, in large or small measure, into the costs of some domestic goods. Is it implied that some other domestic goods must then have lower prices, to keep the average from rising? One can think of various possible interpretations, but none of them make much sense. To spell out an acceptable definition of price stability would, of course, require a little essay, which would have to confront the difficulties of measuring price levels. Similar ambiguity and fuzziness pervade the *Report*—the kinds of things that make life miserable for a mediocre student trying to get a senior paper or a master's thesis approved in a self-respecting economics department.

The objectives of the guidelines are not really stated explicitly in the 1966 *Report*, except for the statement previously quoted that they "aim at complete stability of average domestic prices." Implicitly it is clear that their general objective is to avoid inflation. To most people this means, at least to a first approximation, that the amount of goods and services commanded by a dollar should remain constant. That is, any reduction in a dollar's power to purchase some goods and services should be offset, at least approximately and in proper time, by increases in its power to command other goods and services.

It can be said with assurance that the guidelines cannot accomplish this. More generally, it can be said with assurance—an assurance growing not only from economic analysis but from thousands of years of experience—that if effective demand exceeds supply at the prevailing price level, the purchasing power of the dollar cannot be maintained by any means.

To say that effective demand exceeds supply at prevailing prices is just another way of saying that there are not enough goods and services to be matched up with all the dollars, if goods and dollars are matched at the ratios specified by prevailing prices. Some dollars are left over; there are no goods to match with them. If prices do not rise, which would require fewer goods and services for matching each dollar, the only alternative is some kind of rationing scheme, formal or informal, to decide which dollars will be the ones that get the goods and services. Thus, some of the dollars lose their purchasing power altogether for lack of ration points, certificates of priority, influence, friends, gray-market power, getting in line soon enough and waiting long enough, or whatever consideration it is that determines which dollars are allowed to remain potent. The dollars that are reinforced by the required supplementary consideration buy the same amount as before. Notice, however, that dollars themselves did not command the goods, but dollars plus something else; so as a practical matter the purchasing power of the dollar is no longer as great as when it alone could command the goods. Notice also that when the sterile dollars that can command nothing are averaged with the potent dollars, the average amount of goods commanded by all the dollars has declined. The only possible way to maintain the purchasing power of the dollar is to maintain a balance between total monetary demand and total supply of goods and services.

Inflation can be generated only by the Government. Business firms, labor unions, or consumers with excessive market power can do many objectionable things that are contrary to the public interest; but one objectionable thing that they cannot do is to cause inflation —or, for that matter, prevent it. Within the Government the only important power to cause or prevent inflation lies with the Federal

Reserve Board. If the Government has a large deficit, this will not cause inflation unless funds are supplied for financing the deficit; correspondingly, a surplus will not cause deflation unless the money supply is allowed to lag. There is one, and only one, way to achieve the price stability at which the guidelines purport to aim, and that is to control the rate of growth in the stock of money and credit.

Some subsidiary devices are available, to be sure, for influencing the size of the effective demand that results from a given stock of money, taxes being the most important, but these are distinctly subsidiary to monetary policy—indeed they are simply one of the things monetary policy has to reckon with in judging the proper rate of growth in the stock of money. The guidelines, whether they are met or not, will not make a bit of difference in regard to inflation.

The guidelines allow no room for the notion that a price may injure the public interest by being too low, even if the seller is making a handsome profit. If there is a large increase in the demand for a commodity, to give one illustration, a rise in its price serves the public interest in several ways. First, the price rise induces users to consume the commodity sparingly, especially if it is of little significance to them or easily replaced, so that the supply is left for those to whom it is significant and who cannot easily find substitutes. Second, the price rise induces producers to expand output, by offering higher rewards to the suppliers of its inputs—including labor. Third, the higher price makes production of the commodity still more profitable, and this induces more firms to seek to enter the field. These and similar effects are all in the public interest, for they lead to the public's being supplied with what it most wants, and they open up new opportunities for labor and for producers of raw materials to earn more. Correspondingly, a wage rate can be too low for the public interest, whether or not the worker "needs" more income.

If effective demand exceeds the supply of goods and services, the Government can best serve the public interest by not attempting to interfere with the rise in the level of wages and prices that is then inevitable. The Government's intervention through wage and price control—or "guidance"—will not be without consequences; those consequences will be to lower the efficiency of the economy and to cause inequities and injustice, but not to maintain the purchasing power of the dollar.

Please note that the preceding paragraph does *not* say that the Government can best serve the public interest by allowing inflation. In my judgment, inflation is probably contrary to the public interest. What the paragraph does say is that *if* there is inflation, it is contrary to the public interest to attempt to suppress the symptoms. Analogously, it is contrary to an individual's welfare to have a pronounced tremor in his hands; but if he does have such a tremor, it is against his welfare to eliminate it by fastening his hands firmly into rigid stocks.

"The general guidepost for wages," the Council says in its 1966 *Report*, "is that the *annual rate of increase of total employee compensation (wages and fringe benefits) per man-hour worked should equal the national trend rate of increase in out-put per man-hour*" (emphasis in original). In 1960 I commented on this argument in the following two paragraphs, which I stand by:

> Not only would it be impractical to tie wages in each industry to productivity in that particular industry, but it would also be impractical to tie wages in each industry to average productivity in the whole economy. This would ignore differences in the need for labor and in its availability. In an expanding area, industry, or occupation, employers frequently raise wages more than the national average increase in output per man-hour. These large wage increases serve the useful purpose of inducing labor to enter the area, industry, or occupation in question, and they help pay moving or retraining costs. In a declining area, industry, or occupation, a chronic labor surplus may develop, and attempts to increase wages in line with the national average increase in output per man-hour would reduce employment opportunities and make it less likely that new industries would move into the areas of labor surplus.
>
> These considerations and many others like them make it clear that it is difficult or impossible to prescribe general criteria for proper rates of wages and salaries. Those on the spot with knowledge of all the special circumstances must find the best solution for each case.[2]

The Council made the same point in its 1962 *Report*: "How is the public to judge whether a particular wage-price decision is in the national interest? No simple test exists, and it is not possible to set out systematically all of the many considerations which bear on such a judgment."

Another objection, to which I alluded briefly in the same 1960 speech and which the Council comments on in its 1966 *Report,* is that such a guideline rigidifies the shares of labor and capital in the national income. The Council recognizes this, but it makes a series of contradictory assertions:

1. that under the guideposts the division of income between labor and capital would remain unchanged
2. that the division "has remained virtually unchanged since World War II"
3. that "there have been repeated short-run swings" in the division
4. that public policy is neutral with respect to changes in the division

Perhaps the contradiction between propositions (2) and (3) is a matter of careless and imprecise exposition; perhaps the Council means to say that the trend has been constant and to imply that cyclical fluctuations about the trend are irrelevant—though that implication would be incorrect, in my judgment. But the contradiction between propositions (1) and (4) seems irreconcilable, if the guideposts represent "public policy."

"The general guideline for prices," the 1966 *Report* asserts, "is that *prices should remain stable in those industries where the increase of productivity equals the national trend; that prices can appropriately rise in those industries where the increase of productivity is smaller than the national trend; and that prices should fall in those industries where the increase of productivity exceeds the national trend*" (emphasis in original).

This is followed by: "Within a given industry, the guideposts allow for individual wage and price adjustments that do not affect the over-all wage or price level of the industry. Increases for some groups of workers or products can be balanced by reductions for others."

The Council leaves it to the reader (or perhaps to the Antitrust Division) to imagine the mechanism which will insure that a rise in wages or prices in one firm of an industry will be offset by declines in another firm of the same industry. They leave it to the reader, too, to ask: Why only "within an industry"? Why cannot rises in the average wages or prices of one industry be offset by declines in other industries? And won't wages tend to move by occupations, and thereby to affect different industries differently, and different firms within an industry, in accordance with the extent of their dependence on particular occupations?

There is, of course, no reason why prices should necessarily fall in a firm, much less an industry, where output per man-hour worked has risen more than the national average. The Council scarcely indicates why they think so, but the indication is that they think cost per unit of output falls whenever output per man-hour worked rises. Actually, in the short run the principal causes of increases in output per man-hour are increases in the utilization of capacity, and it is perfectly possible (in fact, in the early stages of a recovery it is usual) that the effect is smaller losses, not "excessive" profits. In the somewhat longer run, the principal causes of increases in output per man-hour are increases in the amount or quality of capital or of management. In a static economy these increases in capital or management would not ordinarily be made unless they lowered cost per unit, but in the actual economy they are often associated with rising costs per unit, and efforts to offset rising costs of labor or raw materials. In any event, prices have an important allocative or rationing effect, and without taking account of shifts in demand as well as in cost it is not possible to say in which direction a price should change in the public interest.

Embedded in the foregoing discussion are the following answers to the four questions posed at the outset:

1. The objective of the wage and price guidelines is to maintain the purchasing power of the dollar.
2. The guidelines can do nothing to achieve this objective.
3. The most important economic consequence of the guidelines will be a lowering of total output below what it otherwise would be.
4. Only the Government can cause inflation and only the Government can prevent it. The Federal Reserve Board can prevent inflation by properly controlling the rate of growth in the stock of money.

2. Foreign Trade

The President in his Balance-of-Payments Message to Congress last year said, "The dollar is, and will remain, as good as gold, freely convertible at $35 an ounce. That pledge is backed by our firm determination to bring an end to our balance-of-payments deficit." As one means for realizing that objective, he said:

I hereby call upon American businessmen and bankers to enter a constructive partnership with their Government to protect and strengthen the position of the dollar in the world today.... Specifically, I ask the bankers and businessmen of America to exercise voluntary restraint in lending money or making investments abroad in the developed countries.

Subsequently, these general objectives were translated into specific guidelines for banks and non-bank corporations. For banks, the guideline was that 1965 foreign loan balances be kept below 105 per cent of the amount outstanding at the end of 1964. Non-bank corporations were asked to generate intracompany trade balances 15 to 20 per cent more favorable than their 1964 balances. While the voluntary nature of the guidelines was stressed, extensive reporting systems were established, designed to enable the Federal Reserve Board and the Secretary of Commerce to ascertain whether individual corporations were abiding by them. (The guidelines apply only to "developed" countries, but special consideration is given to Canada and Japan.)

For 1966, the guidelines have been changed. Banks may expand foreign lending at the rate of 1 per cent per quarter, thus raising total lending capacity to 109 per cent of the 1964 base. Non-bank corporations are asked to limit their direct foreign investment for the two-year period 1965–66 to 135 per cent of their average investment (including retained earnings) over the three-year period 1962–64.

The questions asked about wage and price guidelines are also pertinent to foreign exchange guidelines: What are the objectives? Will the guidelines achieve those objectives? What unintended effects will the guidelines have? What alternative policies would achieve the objectives?

The objective of these guidelines is to reduce and even to eliminate the deficit in the balance of trade that the United States has experienced in 15 of the last 16 years. Recently the deficit has been accompanied by a substantial outflow of gold. The cause of this deficit has not been an unfavorable balance of private trade. Indeed, the balance of trade has been singularly favorable—in 1964 a surplus of $3.6 billion. Instead, it is the Government deficit on foreign aid and military expenditures abroad that has converted an otherwise highly favorable balance into an unfavorable one.

Some painfully elementary economics lies at the heart of the problem of the balance of payments, yet it is seldom mentioned, much less seriously weighed in official analyses that purport to explain or underlie policies.

The balance of payments problem arises because our Government is engaged in a form of price fixing. In this instance, the price it fixes is the price of the American dollar, not only in terms of gold but also in terms of its rate of exchange for other currencies. Fixing the price of the dollar is essentially like fixing the price of any commodity. If the price is set too low, pressures develop to raise it; some means has to be found to ration the dollars available, and black or gray markets develop. If the price is set too high, pressures develop to lower it, potential buyers will have to be rationed among sellers, and black or gray markets spring up (albeit selling at less than the fixed price).

It is the latter situation that prevails today. The pegged price of the dollar is too high. At that price, the number of dollars being offered for exchange with foreign currencies exceeds the amount of foreign currencies being offered for dollars. Through purchases, foreign aid, investments, travel, and military expenditures we are supplying more dollars than foreign purchasers and investors want *at the existing price of the dollar.* That excess is the balance-of-payments deficit.

The primary objective of the guidelines is thus to maintain a fixed exchange rate between the dollar and other currencies. A secondary objective is to maintain a fixed price for gold in the settlement of international balances, but the gold outflow would be of little concern if we abandoned our efforts to fix exchange rates.

The guidelines aim to control the patient's symptoms, not his health. They are administrative constraints limiting what owners of dollars can do with them. In other words, they are a form of rationing. The parallel with the discussion of wage and price guidelines is complete. Just as the wage and price guidelines cannot maintain the domestic value of the dollar in the face of an excess of effective demand, so also is it impossible for the foreign trade guidelines to maintain the value of the dollar in international trade. A stable *price* for the dollar does not imply a stable *value* for the dollar. The value of a dollar depends on its power to buy, and, for example, a dollar that can be invested in a foreign subsidiary or loaned to a foreign firm at 7 per cent interest is more valuable than one which cannot be so loaned or invested. The nominal price may not reflect that difference in value, but you and I know which dollars we would prefer.

Reducing the number of French francs or British pounds that a dollar will buy is only one way to devalue it; another way is to reduce the rights that go with owning a dollar. The guidelines constitute devaluation in the latter sense.

The devaluation is made explicit in the case of military purchases abroad. When the Defense Department pays one-third more to buy something in the U.S. than it would have to pay abroad (a practice it follows), the value of its dollars has clearly gone down. The nation gets less defense per dollar expended than it otherwise would. When an American firm is forced to borrow money abroad at 7 per cent when it has dollars at home that can earn only 5 per cent, the value of those dollars has similarly been reduced.

In brief, the question is not whether the dollar should be devalued—it already has been—but, what form the devaluation takes. As in the domestic case, if the dollar is devalued, the preferable form of devaluation is in its market price.

It is by no means clear that the guidelines will enable us to balance our international accounts even in a nominal bookkeeping sense. In the short run, some improvement may appear, for reductions in lending and investing abroad will not have much immediate effect on the return flow of earnings and repayments. In the longer run, the return flow is bound to decline and thus to affect adversely our balance of payments.

The answer is even more clouded by the interdependence between current lending and direct investment abroad and other components of international trade, particularly exports. Dollars borrowed from American banks by foreign firms and individuals frequently end up being spent for American products. Similarly, direct overseas investments stimulate not only exports of real capital but also exports of semifinished products and raw materials, especially to foreign subsidiaries. (An interesting facet of the Government position on guidelines is the defense it makes of foreign aid, that 85 per cent of the aid is spent in the U.S. Why should not private loans be allowed a similar defense?)

In recent years, the U.S. has experienced a very favorable balance on private merchandise exports and imports. This has been an important factor in enabling Government to finance foreign aid and overseas military activities. In the first year of the guidelines, the excess of exports over imports declined from $6.7 billion (1964) to $5 billion (1965). Exports had risen by 15 per cent in 1964, but rose by only 4 per cent in 1965, while imports increased by 15 per cent in 1965 as compared to 10 per cent in 1964. Part of the decline in export growth can be explained in terms of the shipping strike and other special circumstances, but probably the guideline constraints on lending and direct foreign investment also had a significant impact. When these interdependencies are taken into account, it is by no means clear that the hoped for reductions in the deficit can be realized, even in the bookkeeping sense.

Nor is that the end of the matter. There is a serious threat of retaliation by other nations once they perceive the effects of our program on their economies. Recently, Eric Kierans, Quebec cabinet minister and former president of the Montreal and Canadian Stock Exchanges, said:

> Considerable savings in imports could be achieved if Canada imitated the United States initiative and demanded detailed analyses of imports and prices from the 900 largest American affiliates operating in Canada.... There is no reason why we cannot produce economically thousands of items imported automatically from parent companies.

In establishing the guidelines, we deliberately avoided restricting imports precisely because we feared retaliation. I see no reason to believe that foreign nations will feel differently about our investment guidelines. Increased borrowing by American firms in foreign capital markets is apparently forcing interest rates up in those markets and making foreign businessmen restless. The probability that their governments will ultimately succumb to their pleas for counteraction seems high.

Even more important is the question of political sovereignty. Mr. Kierans, in addition to the remarks already quoted, said that our guidelines represent "a tightening of the American grip on our economy that threatens the attainment of our own economic objectives and an infringement of our political sovereignty." No nation these days is likely to tolerate for long a situation in which a foreign nation directs a firm in its territory to carry out policies in the interest of the foreign nation at the expense of the best interests of the firm and the nation in which it is located. Thus, the guidelines pose a serious threat not only to international trade but—more important —to international relations generally.

It is important to emphasize that whether or not the guidelines are effective in eliminating our bookkeeping deficit is not important. The deficit that the guidelines attack is a symptom, not a disease. Their failure or success may, however, be important through effects on future Government policy. If the deficit persists despite the guidelines, what further steps can be expected? Much more of the same, I fear—controls on dollar spending abroad extended to geographic areas and kinds of commodities or activities not now covered; more restrictive controls in areas already covered; and so forth. The conclusion drawn by politicians when their economic controls fail invariably is that even stronger applications of the controls are required.

Even if the deficit is erased I suspect that the guidelines will prove durable. There is little evidence that left alone our over-all trade balance would fall into the black, even if the pressure imposed by the Vietnamese conflict were suddenly erased. Our one "hope" is that inflation will be much greater in the markets where we sell than in the United States or in the markets where we buy.

So far, I have said nothing about whether businessmen will "voluntarily" succumb to the entreaties of the President, the Secretary of Commerce, and their cohorts. I have no doubt that they will. Their attempts to meet the guidelines may be frustrated by the interdependencies discussed above, but that is a different matter. They will nonetheless have tried to conform. Indeed, it is perilously close to the Newspeak of *1984* to pretend that they have a choice. The president of a firm who receives a personal letter—six and a half pages, single spaced—from the Secretary of Commerce asking for detailed data on how the firm is abiding by the guidelines, and stating that the Secretary would like said president to submit a personal appraisal each quarter evaluating the extent to which the company is achieving its over-all target, is not likely to regard that request as one he can "voluntarily" refuse—particularly if he has read or heard about the use of all the powers of harassment and injury possessed by the Government against other businessmen who have been accused of not conforming voluntarily to the gospel laid down by an official to whom has been revealed a vision of "the public interest."

The language used in discussing the program is often revealing. The January issue of the *Survey of Current Business* of the Department of Commerce, for example, says, "The features of the original program were retained and new ceilings for U.S. private assets abroad in 1966 were outlined." News articles contain such gems of contradiction as "tighter, though still voluntary, curbs on private investment," and one report quoted a discerning statement by a Midwestern banker: "The bulk of all foreign loans are in the top 25 to 30 U.S. banks. Therefore, the voluntary program can be po-

liced very effectively." It is difficult to regard terms like "ceilings,"
"curbs," and "policed" as anything but Newspeak when applied to
the notion of voluntary compliance.

The value of the dollar in foreign exchange has become the
sacred cow of the American economy. Discussions of it are notable
for the emotional and propagandistic language employed—"the
strength of the American dollar," "as good as gold," "an essential
cornerstone of the free world's international monetary system."
Little has been done either empirically or analytically to support
the view that we really ought to walk over hot coals to effect stabilization of exchange rates.

It would be useful, of course, if we could actually stabilize the
buying power of the dollar abroad, since we could thereby eliminate
one source of uncertainty in international exchange. But stabilizing
exchange rates is not equivalent to stabilizing buying power. When
exchange rates are free to adjust, they provide a sensitive measure
of the value of dollars abroad and a strong incentive to act accordingly to conserve or utilize foreign exchange. Fixing exchange rates
is like fixing a clinical thermometer so that it will always read
98.6° F.: Once the thermometer reading is fixed, the thermometer is
no longer useful in judging the health of the patient. I am convinced
that the U.S. could abandon its policy of fixed exchange rates with
hardly a ripple occurring in international trade and finance. Moreover, in the long run I am convinced that such a course would
enhance international trade and promote economic development
throughout the world.

Perhaps it seems presumptuous of me to say to an audience of
bankers that the U.S. should abandon fixed exchange rates, when
you have not only more knowledge in this field than I have, but
infinitely more experience; and I know that bankers generally feel
that to abandon fixed exchange rates would be little short of cata-
strophic. I am goaded to being so presumptuous, however, by recollections of earlier predictions of catastrophe and chaos if freedom
were introduced into markets. Let me remind you of the feeling in
1946 that removal of OPA price controls (which was itself regarded
as a debatable proposal) should be effected in a gradual and orderly
manner, otherwise there would be economic chaos. In fact, I know
of no one who recommended a sudden, unanticipated total abolition; yet by a political fluke that happened, with results that were
dramatically beneficial. In the early 1950's it was widely held that

the Federal Reserve had to peg the price of Government bonds, otherwise there would be dire consequences. When the pegging stopped the only important consequence was that inflation, to all intents and purposes, stopped (though the index continued to creep up, in substantial part because of upward statistical biases in its construction). Only a few years ago it was widely held by bankers, despite their opposition to price fixing, that to allow more than 1 per cent interest to be paid on savings deposits would be disastrous. I believe that a switch to free exchange rates would bring with it no more harm than did those other switches to free markets, and no less gain.

To summarize, then, short answers to the four questions raised at the start of this section are:

1. The objectives of the foreign trade guidelines are to maintain the value of the dollar in foreign exchange and at the same time create a large enough surplus in the balance of payments on private account to offset the large deficit on Government account.
2. The guidelines cannot maintain the value of the dollar, and it is doubtful that they can even bring about a bookkeeping balance between payments and receipts, except possibly for a short time.
3. The guidelines represent a serious restriction on international trade and an even more serious hazard to international relations.
4. An alternative and much preferable policy would be to let foreign exchange rates be determined by demand and supply in free markets.

3. Relations Between the Guidelines

There are basic similarities between the guidelines for wages and prices and those for international trade. Furthermore, wage and price policies affect international trade, and international trade policies affect domestic wages and prices.

It is generally believed that obedience to wage and price guidelines helps solve balance-of-payments problems. The idea is that keeping our prices down makes it easier for us to sell abroad and more difficult for foreigners to sell here. If keeping prices down were really equivalent to preserving the value of the dollar, this simple analysis would be adequate. Where inflation has in fact occurred, and money prices do not constitute the only consideration necessary to buy goods, the effect on foreign trade depends upon what other considerations have to be added to the money price in order to complete a purchase. In other words, the impact on foreign trade depends on how the available supplies are rationed among competing customers. Exports are in a particularly vulnerable position in regard to extra-monetary considerations. When U.S. buyers are unable to obtain as much of a commodity as they want at guideline prices, public officials are likely to feel that foreign customers can wait. Similarly, domestic shortages stimulate measures to increase imports, for example by lowering tariffs and quotas. Thus, the final effect on the balance of payments may be adverse.

Recent developments in copper illustrate this. The U.S. producer price for refined copper is now less than half the world price. If foreigners were permitted to buy all they wanted at prevailing prices, virtually all copper available in the United States would be exported, and no copper would be imported. The large volume of exports and the elimination of imports would contribute to a more favorable balance of trade. The result would nonetheless be viewed as a catastrophe; and rightly so, for we would have bestowed an extravagant gift on the foreigners who bought our copper below the world market price, while bringing to a halt our production of goods that depend on copper.

Needless to say, we have not allowed that to happen. Instead, we have imposed export controls on copper; Congress is being asked to remove the duty on copper imports; we are quietly tolerating a second U.S. market for copper at premium prices; a rationing scheme has been imposed that requires producers to allocate a certain amount of copper to defense uses; and—to top off this chamber of economic horrors—consideration is being given to raising the margin requirements for trading in copper.

Furthermore, the consequences of these actions with copper quickly spread to industries whose products are related to copper in production or consumption—which, eventually, means virtually all economic activity. Policies like those for copper already loom for steel, aluminum, sulphur, shoes, and no doubt other products.

A basic similarity between the two sets of guidelines is that in both cases the problem at which the guidelines aim is created by the Government. The Government is the source of inflationary forces which the wage-price guidelines attempt to control; the Government is the source of the deficit in the balance of payments. (As an *obiter dictum*, I may remark that most major economic problems have grown out of earlier Government efforts to deal with some comparatively minor problem.)

Another basic similarity is that neither set of guidelines can achieve its objectives, except if conditions come about in which the guidelines are superfluous. To be sure, the balance-of-payments guidelines could, at least theoretically, achieve a bookkeeping balance, at least temporarily; what they cannot do is maintain the purchasing power of the dollar abroad. Neither can the wage-price guidelines maintain the purchasing power of the dollar at home.

Both sets of guidelines deal with symptoms, not with the economic health of the country. While it would be preferable if our economic health were unimpaired—that is, if effective demand for goods and services at home and for foreign exchange abroad were in balance with supply—granted that it is impaired, it would be better not to interfere with the symptoms. Interference with the symptoms creates economic inefficiency and lowers the level of economic welfare, but does no good.

Both kinds of controls—or "guidelines"—will inevitably spread without limit. There will be no limit to the number of prices and practices that must be controlled, or to the extent of the detail into which the controls must penetrate. There will be no limit, either, to the amount of coercion and compulsion that will have to be used to enforce the controls.

This last point, the threat to freedom and civil liberties, seems to me the least immediate but most important feature of the guidelines. Even the ordinary protections of due process of law go by the boards, for the guidelines are not laws, and it has been made clear that their enforcement will be by undue processes.

Violators of the prescriptions for voluntary action are not prosecuted for the violations. Instead, every law, regulation, or requirement to which the offender is subject, however unrelated to the offense, may be searched for some possible violation—a process which, even if it leads to nothing, constitutes in itself a heavy penalty in time, money, fear, and notoriety. Every benefit or privilege which the offender may derive, directly or indirectly, from the Government may be withdrawn—or the fear of withdrawal used to secure compliance.

If you have been reading between the lines you may have guessed that my enthusiasm for guidelines is not great. In fact, I can formulate no better summary of my views than George Stigler's statement: "This development is an unmitigated evil from the longer-term viewpoint appropriate to a nation."

21

The Nixon Economic Decrees

THE NEW ECONOMIC POLICY that took effect on August 15 by presidential edict and went into its second phase on November 15 has two main thrusts, one domestic and one foreign. Each of these two thrusts in turn has two parts, one dealing in the short run with pricing aspects of the economy, the other dealing in the longer run with real economic activities.

On the domestic front, the wage and price controls have an immediate impact on the nominal or measurement aspects of producing and distributing real goods and services. The proposals with regard to taxes and productivity are designed to increase the amount of goods and services produced, by stimulating fuller employment of resources and by stimulating more efficient use of resources, but it will take some time for them to be adopted and then to affect the economy.

Similarly, on the international front, floating exchange rates and the 10 percent surcharge on imports cause an immediate effect on prices. Efforts to bring about revisions in the trade policies of other countries are intended to shift the pattern of real economic activities, but this cannot happen quickly.

Thus, on both the domestic and foreign fronts, there are price measures intended to have an immediate impact, and there are real measures intended to improve underlying economic conditions in the long run.

Presented before the Collective Bargaining Conference of the University of Pennsylvania in Philadelphia on 19 November 1971.

The short-run domestic measures are exactly the opposite of the short-run international measures. Internationally, the prescription is to replace rigidity and bureaucracy by flexibility and freedom, that is, to go from governmental price-fixing to free markets for international currencies. Domestically, the prescription has been to replace flexibility and freedom with rigidity and bureaucracy, that is, to go from free markets to governmental price-fixing for wages and prices. The long-run measures, however, are alike on the domestic and international fronts, in that both depend on the ability of the Administration to obtain cooperation by persuasion or inducement of unsympathetic bodies, namely the United States Congress for the domestic economy and foreign governments for international trade.

I shall discuss only the domestic thrust of the New Economic Policy, and only the wage and price controls. Concerning these, I shall discuss, first, the prospects for success; second, why they came about; and, third, when they will go away.

First, the prospects that wage and price controls will succeed in checking inflation are nil. Wage and price controls will affect many things, but inflation is not among them.

It can be asserted with assurance—an assurance growing not only from economic analysis but from thousands of years of history in many countries and civilizations—that, if effective demand exceeds supply at the prevailing price level, the purchasing power of the dollar cannot be maintained by any means.

This is not to deny that some prices and wages will be lower because of the controls. But to the extent that a price is lower because of controls, some of the money that in the absence of controls would be spent on that product or service becomes available for spending on something else, thus increasing the demand for other goods and causing their prices to rise.

Not only will wage and price controls fail to check inflation, they will in fact be harmful to the economy. There is a strong tendency to regard prices simply as incomes to those who receive them. Indeed, this fallacy is reflected in the use of the term "incomes policy" to refer to wage and price control. The same prices that constitute incomes to those who receive them constitute costs to those who pay them. More generally, prices are the coordinating device of the economy, and economic efficiency is strongly dependent on them.

Not only do wage and price controls reduce economic efficiency, they are a major restriction on personal freedom. We intellectuals, who earn our livings by writing and talking, are inclined to rate economic freedom as distinctly secondary to freedom of expression. Freedom of expression, however, is our economic freedom. For the overwhelming majority of the population, restrictions on what they can buy or sell, and on what terms, have far greater impact on their personal lives than restrictions on expression. It is as easy for us intellectuals to write and speak admonishing the rest of the population to sacrifice economic freedom in the public interest as it is for the nonintellectuals to tell us to shut up or else say and write only those things that are in the public interest. We, of course, would respond eloquently and passionately that it is in the true public interest for us to say whatever we please, even if it contradicts official policy and received doctrine—in fact, *especially* if it contradicts them. The nonintellectuals—those who earn their livings by making and doing rather than by writing and talking—being less facile with words and ideas, may actually be led to believe that sacrificing their freedom is in the public interest.

There is one way in which wage and price controls might happen to prove useful. That would occur if they were invoked simultaneously with an abrupt retardation in the rate of inflation. In our economy innumerable commitments and contracts are made every day that will be fulfilled in the future—leases, labor contracts, sales agreements, and catalogues that must be printed in advance are examples. In making these forward commitments it is necessary to allow for possible changes in the price level. If prices have been rising for some time at 4 to 6 percent per year, as in fact they have for the past six years, it is prudent to project a continuation of that rate of inflation in making commitments for the future. Should there be a sharp reduction in the rate of inflation, such commitments might cause hardship. For example, if a wage commitment were predicated on a 5 percent rate of inflation and inflation were to halt, unemployment would probably result.

Thus, if the government knew that inflation was about to halt and the public did not know it, the government might protect people from their ignorance or folly by prohibiting price and wage increases for a period long enough to let the public see that inflation had stopped. Thereafter, the public could be left to its own discretion. Although further commitments might be realistic, continuing commitments made earlier would still cause problems.

This is an extraordinarily fine-spun theory, and there is no experience that supports it. It amounts to saying that people do not believe that the government is going to arrest inflation, so the government will force them to act the way they would act if they did believe it. The paternalistic coercion needs to last only long enough for the government to stop inflation and for people to revise their expectations and consequently their actions. Actually, the government does not know whether it is going to stop inflation, only whether it hopes and intends to stop inflation. Comparison of the instructions about the money supply given by the Open Market Committee of the Federal Reserve Board with the actual behavior of the money supply makes it at least doubtful that the government knows much more than the public does about how government policies will work.

Furthermore, even if the government had the capacity to produce an abrupt deceleration in the rate of inflation, it seems scarcely likely that it would do so. The unemployment that would result from abruptness would be too objectionable.

It is notable that, while the money supply grew during the first half of this year at an annual rate in excess of 10 percent, it has grown little or not at all since the New Economic Policy was adopted. Obviously the rate will not be held so low much longer, because of the unemployment consequences. But it is not impossible, though it is improbable, that monetary policy will be tight enough so that a year from now the rate of rise in the official price indexes will have fallen to the 2.5 percent rate that officials have recently promised. (That will depend in part upon the diligence with which the Price Commission disciplines the specific prices that enter the index; these prices are always subject to special attention under price control.) The odds are that monetary policy will not be restrictive in 1972 but expansionary, partly to stimulate employment and partly to keep interest rates from rising too much in the face of a large Federal deficit.

In the unlikely event that monetary policy does bring the rate of inflation down to the target rate within a year, the long-run consequences might be unfortunate, for the public would have learned a false lesson. The public would conclude that price control is an effective cure for inflation, and Price Commissions would become a permanent, or at least a recurrent, feature of the economy.

Since monetary policy probably will not, and should not, be so restrictive as to haul the rate of inflation down to the level some

Administration spokesmen are anticipating, the Pay Board and the Price Commission are likely to encounter increasingly rough weather. The 5.5 percent rate of increase in wages that is being allowed may be consistent with price stability and full employment now, since productivity increases rapidly in the early stages of cyclical recovery. But the rate of increase in productivity will decline as the economy expands, so it will presumably be felt necessary in due course to lower the allowable rate of rise in wages. Anticipating this, employers and employees both are likely to press for the maximum allowable wage increases now, for fear that they will not be permissible later. But this would make the recovery less vigorous than it otherwise would be, since it would reduce the rise in profits that results from the lag of wages behind productivity and thereby strengthens the expansion.

Similarly, the Price Commission should be able to adhere for a while to the 2.5 percent annual rate of price increase that it is allowing. At the rate of inflation prevailing when the price freeze took effect on August 15, 2.5 percent would cover the increase for six or seven months, that is until about March, if 2.5 percent per year is interpreted as 2.5 percent now. After that—or a little earlier or later depending on the growth of the money supply—pressures will begin to build, but they might not become unmanageable for another three or four months, just as they did not in the recent ninety-day freeze. Eventually, further increases in the ceilings will be required; but if they come just when the allowable rate of rise in wages is being reduced, the apparent inequity will put a great political strain on the whole system—and at a time when the political atmosphere will already be highly charged.

How did we get into this mess? Or, as a *Wall Street Journal* editorial put it a few days ago, "What's a nice country like this doing here?" All the objections to wage and price control that I have mentioned, and many that I have not mentioned, are known and thoroughly understood by the economic leaders of the Administration, including George Shultz, Paul McCracken, Herbert Stein, and—above all—Richard Nixon.

While I have not discussed with those gentlemen, or with anyone else in the Administration, the reasons for the New Economic Policy, I have a conjecture that seems to me highly plausible. My conjecture is that the political pressures for wage and price control were so universal and so powerful that they became irresistible. The head of a country in which 70 to 80 percent of the population believes in witchcraft, simply has to practice a little sorcery. Or, as a friend of mine put it, "When all the world is mad, 'tis folly to be sane." Public opinion polls show that more than 70 percent of the voters believe in wage and price control as a means of controlling inflation.

Indeed, I believe that the President did a good job in staving off controls as long as he did. In the late spring and early summer of 1970 there was a powerful drive for controls by leading newspapers, television commentators, and members of Congress; and in apparent response to that the President established the National Commission on Productivity in the summer of 1970. In August of 1970 Congress passed the bill giving the President power to invoke wage and price controls, and thereafter kept up a steady barrage of criticism because he did not invoke them.

In the late spring and summer of 1971 a heavier and more sustained attack occurred. The attack by liberal Democrats in Congress was joined by twelve influential Republican Senators. The Committee for Economic Development (CED) came out swinging for controls. The President's own appointee as Chairman of the Federal Reserve Board, long one of the most trenchant and devastating critics of price control, publicly urged an "incomes policy," as he had begun to do soon after taking office. In July 1971, in a nationwide television interview, the President of the AFL–CIO said, ". . . if I was in [the President's] position, I would impose controls at this time. I don't see any other way that this situation is going to get under control."

Thus, leaders of business, labor, Congress, economics, and journalism and most of the public were clamoring for controls. What voice was heard on the other side? Only the President's, amplified occasionally by two or three of his close associates. Some may think that the President should have ignored everyone but himself, and quoted George Washington: "If to please the people, we offer what we ourselves disapprove, how can we afterward defend our work? Let us raise a standard to which the wise and honest can repair." But George Washington was not President of the United States when he said that. I personally would have liked to see the President ignore everyone's opinion but his own, since I share it; but on the other hand I'm not sure I'd like to live in a country where the President had that much power to ignore public opinion.

Finally, when can we expect wage and price controls to end? I fear that there is nearly an even chance that controls will not end in this century.

There can be no doubt that the Administration is totally committed to ending controls as soon as possible, just as they were committed to avoiding controls. It is perfectly clear from many statements by Mr. Nixon, some going back a dozen years or more, that he must find the controls wholly repugnant. Invoking them in August represented surrender to overwhelming political force after a long, determined, and skillful fight. In the fight the President repeatedly voiced clear and sound analyses of the objections to controls. He has made many statements, going back at least to the period of his Vice Presidency, that show that he objects to price control on grounds of both practice and principle, of both economic efficiency and personal freedom. Politically, he must be keenly aware that he was first elected to public office with one of the only two Republican Congresses in forty-two years, and in both the elections that the Republicans won antipathy to controls was a major issue.

The conclusion that must be drawn from the President's capitulation is that the forces favoring controls are overwhelming. While these forces will diminish as the inevitable bureaucratic interferences of controls affect more and more people, or as the controls break down, the conclusion many people will draw then is that more extensive and stronger controls are needed, and that present controls are simply being administered badly. It has to be recognized that many liberals believe in controls as a way of life and welcome any extension of them for whatever reason. I see no counterforce of any consequence. When a business group as influential as the CED, a labor leader as influential as George Meany, leaders of the economics profession as influential as Arthur Burns and Kenneth Galbraith, Congressional leaders as influential as the twelve Senators, newspapers as influential as the *New York Times* and the *Washington Post,* and a proportion of the voters as influential as three quarters of them, all advocate wage and price controls, then, even though from time to time some of these groups may become disillusioned (as Mr. Meany did in little more than a month), we have to recognize a consensus that may make price and wage controls a permanent part of the American way of life.

Furthermore, while life under controls will disillusion many who now favor them, it also will arouse new appetites. When a broad system of controls is in force, it is possible for groups with sufficient political impact to manipulate the controls to their own advantage, for any use of controls inevitably has the effect of taking from some and giving to others. A special control that might be too blatantly piratical to survive politically or legally by itself may survive when it is just one bit of a vast and complex administrative apparatus, and when it can come about by administrative action without legislative enactment or even notice.

Walter Lippmann, in his great book *The Good Society*, written more than a third of a century ago, makes this point:

> The attempt to regulate deliberately the transactions of a people multiplies the number of separate, self-conscious appetites and resistances. To establish order among these highly energized fragments, which are like atoms set in violent motion by being heated, a still more elaborate organization is required—but this more elaborate organization can be operated only if there is more intelligence, more insight, more discipline, more disinterestedness, than exists in any ordinary company of men. This is the sickness of an overgoverned society.

A dismaying possibility, suggested by my colleague at the University of Rochester, Professor Karl Brunner, is that our economy may go the South American route: We may incur large government deficits, finance them by printing money, and respond to the resulting inflation by direct controls. That is, in fact, exactly what has happened in the past six years, which has been a classic example of pure monetary inflation. In the six years 1966 through 1971, the public debt (net of debt held by U.S. government agencies and trust funds) has grown by roughly $35 billion, and the amount held by the Federal Reserve Banks has grown by roughly $25 billion. In essence, two-thirds of the deficit has been covered by printing money —the euphemism is "monetizing the debt." The public has liked this apparently costless method of feeding all sorts of appetites at the public trough, but it has not liked the inflation which has resulted. If now it believes that price and wage controls can dissipate inflation, and if experience in the next year seems to confirm that, then we have to fear that the South American way of life might become our way of life. A look at any South American economy can result only in alarm at such a dismal prospect.

I do not want to leave the impression that I am predicting that price and wage controls are here to stay. I do want to leave the impression that the probability of this is too serious for complacency, at least by one who is concerned for the fate of his country and his grandchildren. I fear that there is almost a fifty-fifty chance that some degree of Federal price and wage control will outlive the twentieth century and even my grandchildren.

A more optimistic possibility, one that seems to me equally probable, is that the whole apparatus—Cost of Living Council, Pay Board, Price Commission, and IRS field staff—may collapse in a shambles before this time next year. That might happen if at some time the Pay Board takes a firm stand on a wage contract that is important to labor unions. (Note that while less than a quarter of the labor force is organized, all five of the labor members of the Board represent organized labor.) The labor members might then walk out, in which case the Pay Board would presumably collapse, and after it the Price Commission.

Another possibility for collapse of the whole control mechanism is through Congressional intervention, to provide relief or special privilege for one group or another, or more generally through *de facto* intervention by individual Congressmen and committees in the day-to-day administration of the controls.

To recapitulate the three sections of my talk: *First,* the controls will not check inflation, though if inflation is in fact being checked abruptly right now by monetary policy it is conceivable (though improbable) that a brief period of controls would partly ameliorate the very adverse employment consequences of such an abrupt check. The controls will, to the extent that they have any effects at all, reduce the efficiency of the economy and impair individual freedom.

Second, the controls came about through an irresistible consensus of an overwhelming majority of the American public.

Third, the controls may collapse within a year or they may outlast this century, both alternatives being about equally likely and all other alternatives together being less likely than either of these.

22

Foul-up by Consensus

PRICE AND WAGE CONTROLS should never have been started. They should be ended now. The best way for them to end is the way they ended in 1946: suddenly, totally, and unexpectedly. Considering how well economic policy was handled in the first three years of the Nixon administration, when the greatest peacetime inflation in our history was cooled with only the mildest slowdown in employment and production, it is hard to believe that it could have gotten so fouled up in the past two years. Inflation is even greater than when the administration took office, and is probably beyond the possibility of being checked without a recession. The foul-up can be dated to August 15, 1971, when wage and price controls were imposed in response to an overwhelming consensus of the American people—labor leaders and business leaders, Democrats and Republicans, liberals and conservatives, economists and journalists, producers and consumers. The best that can be hoped for this sorry episode is that some people may have learned something—but, frankly, I doubt that many have.

Written for the Rochester Times–Union *of 27 October 1973.*

IV

Growth

23

Economic Growth

THE STORY OF AMERICA'S ECONOMIC GROWTH is one of the most remarkable pages of history. A free and enterprising people have
achieved a level of material well-being undreamed of earlier, and
not more than dreamed of even today in most parts of the world.
And this high level is still rising rapidly. Unparalleled improvement
in material levels of living, though dramatic, is far from the most
important part of the story of American economic growth. Two
other features are even more significant: first, the non-material
benefits of economic growth, in the form of improvements in the
quality of our life; and second, the broad diffusion of both material
and non-material benefits to all the people.

Growth is not an end in itself. We do not live to grow; we grow
to live better. And we do live better, not only by consuming better
but also by working under better conditions. Most of the brutal
physical toil formerly necessary for man to make even a meager
living has now disappeared.

Economic growth has provided us with leisure to enjoy the fruits
of our efforts and to engage more fully in a richer variety of cultural and recreational pursuits. It has made possible higher levels
of education and enlarged opportunities for creative activity. It has
greatly widened the choices open to the average citizen, and it has
given him vastly increased opportunities for developing and utilizing
his individual capacities. It has given new dimensions to individual
dignity and endeavor. In short, our economic growth has brought us

*Delivered before the Presentation of Loeb Awards to Business and Financial
Journalists in New York on 8 June 1960.*[1]

more and better means of satisfying our wants, and it has also brought us better wants.

Throughout history it has been taken for granted, as it is taken for granted in many parts of the world today, that the inescapable lot of most of humanity is to live out their lives in toil, filth, misery, ignorance, and disease. Even in the greatest civilizations of the past— those that we admire most, such as Ancient Greece or Renaissance Italy—the flowering of civilization was shared by only a comparative handful of people. A unique feature of our economic growth has been the broad sharing of progress among all groups—urban and rural, workers and managers, white and colored, eastern and western. Viewed either by the perspective of history or by the perspective of other contemporary economic systems, we represent, as Vice-President Nixon told a Moscow television audience in 1959, the nearest approach to a classless society.

It is well to review the story of our economic growth, not in a spirit of smug self-congratulation, but in a spirit of humility. What we tend to take for granted, and to regard as the natural and in-destructible state of affairs toward which all social and economic developments inevitably progress, is in fact unique in history. It may well prove transitory unless we understand the sources of our past economic progress and pursue wise policies for preserving and cultivating the forces of progress. We still have pockets of poverty, instances of opportunities foreclosed unnecessarily, and other eco-nomic problems. All of these problems are real, many of them are important, and a few are urgent. But we can tackle our problems with more zest and confidence if we do not confuse lack of perfec-tion with lack of progress, or with being second rate.

Economic growth is one of the catch-phrases of the day. Behind the phrase there are, to be sure, real and important issues; but they are not simple issues, and confusion results from efforts to oversimplify them. Economic growth is difficult to define and more difficult to measure.

Generally, people think of economic growth as an increasing supply of goods and services. This is all right as far as it goes, but it doesn't go very far. As population increases, a larger suppy of goods and services is needed to maintain a constant level of output. An economy may get bigger—or "grow" in an absolute sense, perhaps even as a world power—without adding to individual welfare. Obvi-ously, growth must involve rising levels of *per capita* output if it is to mean increased welfare.

But this is not all. Growth in any meaningful sense must mean not just more things, but more things that are useful and that people want. Today we produce such things as automobiles, television sets, and missiles, instead of surreys, stereopticons, and cannon balls. Evolution in the composition of output is as much a part of economic growth as is expansion of the volume of output. Similarly, if growth is to be meaningful the output must be well distributed among all the people.

In our economy, changes in the composition of output reflect the free choices of the people, and the valuation of the output reflects the values placed on goods and services through voluntary purchases and sales. Private output conforms to choices made in the market, and public output to choices made through political processes by freely elected representatives. In a centralized economy, both private and public output reflect the choices and values of the authorities, and the values placed on goods and services also represent authoritarian decisions. There is no valid criterion of the extent to which the nominal "growth" achieved by a centralized economy is meaningful growth in terms of the aspirations and desires of the people. Furthermore, with centralized economic authority the benefits of growth need not be distributed widely. Total and per capita output can rise, while the living levels of the masses are rising little or not at all.

Clearly, true growth must refer to economic welfare. This means we must consider not only goods and services but non-material aspects of growth. As our productive capacities have risen, we have chosen to take part of our growth in the form of leisure and improved working conditions. In fact, an economy could be growing even though output per capita were stable, if at the same time the amount of time and effort needed to produce that output were declining.

If the concept of growth is complex and elusive, as I have been trying to indicate that it is, the problem of measuring growth is fearsome. Not only do we lack adequate data, but the qualitative and non-material aspects of growth are impossible to quantify. A confession of St. Augustine more than 1,500 years ago about the concept of time ought to be repeated daily by all who purport to measure economic growth: "For so it is, oh Lord my God, I measure it; but what it is that I measure I do not know."

Six of the most common gauges of economic growth are the percentage rates of increase in:

1. real Gross National Product, that is, GNP adjusted for price changes
2. real GNP per capita
3. industrial production
4. output per man-hour worked
5. output per unit of labor and capital combined
6. real disposable personal income per capita

Before considering what each of these gauges appears to show, let us consider certain major shortcomings that seriously limit what any of them really show. These ubiquitous flaws, which create troubles for anyone trying to compare growth rates between countries or between times for a given country, are:

1. deficiencies of data
2. vagaries of valuation
3. aberrations of averages
4. treacheries of timing

About the deficiencies of data I will say little, except that the basic figures on GNP or industrial production even for this country —and ours are the best in the world—involve liberal use of estimation and guesstimation, of interpolation and extrapolation, of approximation and adjustment. With respect to Russian data, I now know, and you too, that they are a lot better than I thought a month ago; but they are nevertheless hardly better than conjecture at many crucial points.

The valuation problem I have already alluded to. The list of things produced includes such heterogeneous products as apples, nuts, bolts, cloth, appendectomies, tractors, missiles, financial writing, and speeches. To measure the list by a single number it is necessary to put a value on each item. In a market economy, we can value most things by prices people voluntarily pay and accept. Even in our economy, however, a large and increasing share of output is governmental, and can be valued only in terms of things used up. But just using up something by no means guarantees that an equal value is created; sometimes it is more, too often it is less.

The magnitude of the valuation problem is shown by the comparatively simple problem of comparing Russian GNP with ours. The two lists of products must be valued by the same prices, otherwise the comparison will reflect differences in prices, not just differences in GNP. If Russian prices are applied to their output and to ours, our GNP is nearly four times theirs. If American prices are applied to the outputs of both countries, we are only twice their size. Russian GNP is commonly described as 40% of ours. This results from splitting the difference, but the difference that is split is not between two and four, which would give three, but between 27% and 53%, which are the two estimates of Russian GNP as a percentage of ours.

Averages can be tricky, and every one of the growth measures is an average of divergent rates of growth prevailing in different parts of the economy. It is possible, for example, for the over-all average to go up even if every separate part is constant or even declining. To see that this is possible, suppose that a country has half of its economy in agriculture, and that growth is slower in agriculture than in the other half of the economy (both these things are true of Russia). The average rate of growth for the whole economy will be halfway between the rate for agriculture and the rate for non-agriculture. Now suppose that the economy changes, and the non-agricultural segment is larger than the agricultural. Even if the rate of growth stays the same in both agriculture and nonagriculture, the new average rate of growth for the whole economy will be nearer the nonagricultural than the agricultural rate, and therefore higher than before. This kind of thing is in fact happening in Russia. In the United States, on the other hand, the opposite is happening. Agriculture here has an extraordinarily large rate of growth, so we are able to shift resources into things like services where growth is slower; and this pulls down the figures on our average rate of growth, even though the change is obviously a good thing. It would be possible for our rate of growth to be higher than the Russian rate in every part of the economy, yet for our average rate to be less than theirs.

Another affliction of our measures of growth is the problem of a proper time-span, whatever criterion is used. Like every kind of growth, economic growth proceeds at an uneven pace. Measurements must be made at times far enough apart to average out seasonal, cyclical, and erratic fluctuations. They must, for example, cover a full business cycle as an absolute minimum, and preferably several cycles. Measurements of growth must begin and end at comparable cyclical stages. A fictitiously high rate will result if we start at a cyclical trough and end at a peak, or a fictitiously low rate if we go from a peak to a trough. Peak to peak measurements are best, for peaks of successive cycles trace the course of economic growth in fairly smooth and regular fashion. For similar reasons, the periods used for measuring growth must not begin or end at the peak of a war boom or at the trough of a post-war reconversion.

These limitations on proper time periods prevent making—honestly—a number of comparisons in the period since the Second World War that would be interesting. In that period there have been only three peaks, 1948, 1953, and 1957, and the middle one, 1953, was the peak of the Korean War boom. Thus, there is one and only one period that meets the requirements for a meaningful measurement of growth, namely 1948 to 1957. While some politicians have presented comparisons of the growth rate from 1947 to 1953 with that from 1953 to 1959, this can only be described as unwary, unwise, or unscrupulous, for 1947 was a war reconversion trough, 1953 was both a war peak and a cyclical peak, and 1959 was a year of expansion but neither a trough nor a peak. Such unwise, unwary, or unscrupulous comparisons naturally invite other politicians to compare growth from 1945 to 1952 with growth from 1953 to 1960. On one basis, the rate of growth in real GNP is double in the earlier period; on the other basis, it is double in the later period. You pick your party, then you pick your periods; and so you "prove" that your party has done twice as well as the other party.

The treacheries of timing are especially hazardous in comparing growth rates of different countries. For the United States, 1948 to 1957 is a valid peak-to-peak period for measuring growth. For some other country, however, it may be a peak-to-trough or a trough-to-peak period. Comparisons covering the same period for two countries may, therefore, be misleading.

All these difficulties mean, not that measurements of growth are futile and fruitless, but that to interpret them requires considerable care, skill, judgment, objectivity, and sophistication about both economics and statistics. Since this audience has those qualities, let's proceed to survey the principal measures of growth, paying particular attention to the recent record in relation to the long-term record.

Real Gross National Product from 1909 to 1957 grew at an annual compound rate of 2.9% per year. The long-run growth trend has been fairly stable in spite of large departures above and below it. Between 1948 and 1957, the annual rate of growth in total real production was 3.8%, somewhat higher than the long-run rate.

Real GNP per capita. From 1909 to 1957 the annual rate of increase in real GNP per capita was 1.5%. From 1948 to 1957 the rate was 2.0% per year, again somewhat higher.

Industrial production, as measured by the Federal Reserve Board Index, increased from 1919 (when the index begins) to 1957 at an average annual rate of 3.7%. Between 1948 and 1957 the annual rate of increase was 4.4%, a little higher, but within the range of statistical variation that characterizes this series.

Real private output per man-hour worked increased from 1889 to 1957 at an average annual rate of 2.0%. From 1948 to 1957 the rate was 3.1%, or about 50% higher.

Real output per unit of labor and capital combined, useful as a measure of over-all efficiency, increased from 1889 to 1957 at an average annual rate of 1.7%. From 1948 to 1957 the annual rate of increase was 2.4%, about 40% higher.

Real disposable personal income per capita measures the income available to individuals, after taxes, to use as they please. The annual rate of increase from 1929 (when the data begin) to 1957 was 1.6%, a rate pulled down by depression and pushed up by war booms. From 1948 to 1957 the average annual rate of increase was 1.9%, despite high taxation and rapid population increase.

There are many other indicators of growth: length of the work week, or levels of education, for example. But the six indices that we have looked at suffice to illustrate the nature of the problems in answering the question: What is economic growth?

Even this brief look at the record shows the falsity of careless allegations that our economy is slowing down. The recent record, as best we are able to read it at such close range, is very good when judged by historical standards. Indeed, considering the great changes that have taken place and the major adjustments that the economy has made with flexibility and resiliency during the past 15 years, the record is one which should renew our faith in the vitality of our system. Perhaps we should, can, and will grow faster and better; but that is the "to be continued" part of our growth story.

Economic growth has been an important goal of our national policy since the founding of the Republic. It remains an important goal, in no way diminished by our remarkable progress. Indeed, economic growth has recently become a political rallying cry, accompanied sometimes by demands that the government revert to the mercantilist policies by which economic growth was sought in the 17th and 18th centuries.

The issue of economic growth has entered the arena of contemporary politics through a course which has characterized many issues in the past quarter of a century. That is that after we have gotten over the hill by private endeavors, and are on our way at a brisk pace, urgent demands arise that the government expedite and direct us.

Characteristically, individuals, private institutions, or general social forces break the paths and provide the initial momentum. Once the vision of an important goal gains currency, and once we are on our way toward attaining it, suddenly we become impatient for a magic carpet to put us there instantly. Our impatience is exploited by those promoting various political schemes. Some of these schemes have become as wilted and shabby as the proverbial saloon sandwich, as they are pushed decade after decade as means to reach whatever goals have most recently come over the horizon or are most rapidly being attained through private forces.

Much of the current emphasis on economic growth is of this character. All sorts of plans are put forth under the banner of growth, with little or no analysis of the way they might promote growth—except growth in Federal spending. The same spending plans, on the other hand, are often described as reasons for wanting growth. We could afford the spending, the argument runs, if we only had growth; and the implication is that those who paint these glowing pictures of what growth could do to expand Federal spending somehow have the key to growth.

The fact that too many of the considerations raised in discussions of growth cannot be taken seriously should not blind us to the fact that there are a number of important considerations that merit close examination.

The Soviet Threat is one of these.

The Soviet threat is real and has many points of thrust. It would be perilous to underestimate the danger. But how is it related to our own economic growth? Some people fear that the Russians will "catch up" to us someday and so fulfill the Khrushchev boast about burying us. Others fear that rapid Soviet growth will increase Russian military potential so greatly as to jeopardize the free world's defenses. Still others fear possible adverse "demonstration effects" of rapid Soviet development—that underdeveloped and uncommitted nations will turn to communism as a way of achieving national strength politically and economically. All these fears merit sober consideration—more consideration than can be given to them here.

First, it should be pointed out that we have a commanding lead over Russia in terms of both total and per capita output. Even if

Russian growth rates continue higher than ours, the absolute gap between us will continue to *increase* for some time to come.

Second, we don't know how large the gap really is—except that it is large. As was mentioned earlier, international comparisons, even if we had good data, are a difficult and unrewarding business. We don't know whether Russian GNP is one-half of ours or one-quarter of ours.

Third, international comparisons of rates of growth can be even more misleading than comparisons of levels of output. The Russians, starting from a lower economic base and in a period of postwar reconstruction, should be expected to have a fairly high percentage rate of expansion. Moreover, they are able to take over the accumulated technology already developed and exploited elsewhere. Furthermore, they are transferring masses of people out of low productivity employment in agriculture to industry with its more highly valued output per man-hour. They still have approximately 50% of their labor force in agriculture; we have only about 8%. Our employment is expanding in services, where improvements in output per man-hour are slow and limited. In other words, Russian growth is more rapid because they are still in the area where improvement is easy and the way has been shown, whereas we are more heavily involved in the difficult tasks of expanding productivity in medicine, journalism, education, engineering, and other services.

In short, there is no possibility that the Russian economy will overtake ours, at any time in the visible future—certainly not in this century. We should not begrudge the Russian people whatever rise they may achieve in their material levels of well-being in return for the privation and hardships they have suffered in the name of economic growth.

Even the "demonstration effects" of Russian economic expansion may be vastly overemphasized. While her 6% to 8% annual rate of growth in total production in recent years may seem impressive, other countries not under Communist domination have done and are doing better. The economic progress of West Germany, Japan, and Mexico, for example, is far more striking. As a matter of fact, Russia itself grew faster under the Czars during the decade before the First World War.

Unmet Social Needs is a slogan we hear these days as a call for accelerated growth. According to this argument, if we grow faster we will be better able to provide a greater variety of public services and to eliminate what we now regard as poverty.

One of the more pretentious versions of the "needs" argument is that we have shameful public squalor in the midst of vulgar private opulence. This argument has a strong authoritarian smell, an odor of desire to enforce the advocates' tastes on others through governmental machinery. It is reminiscent of groups abroad that used government power to burn other people's books, but our group wants to burn other people's tail fins. The argument about "public squalor" would be laughed out of court if confronted with the facts of the past decade on construction of schools, improvements in teachers' salaries, superhighways built, increases in the support of research, expansion in aid to the needy, diseases conquered, urban redevelopment, hospitals built, or indeed almost anything else. Growth in public services has been enormous in the past decade. The unmet-social-needers resort to pointing out plaintively that we don't yet have everything that they think we should want and to lamenting that private opulence dulls interest in social revolution.

The public squalor argument is, in fact, simply this decade's battlecry of socialism, which—intellectually bankrupt after more than a century of seeing one after another of its arguments for socializing the *means* of production demolished—now seeks to socialize the *results* of production.

Aiding the Economic Development of Other Nations is another reason often advanced for trying to accelerate our own rate of growth. This is a laudable and continuing goal of public policy. But it does not follow that increasing our own rate of growth and raising our own level of living will have much influence on the rate of economic progress elsewhere.

The problems of world economic development are formidable. The pressure of population on arable land, the extremes of ignorance in many underveloped countries, the diversity of languages, cultures, and political institutions—these and many other economic and social factors are far more important than the direct and indirect aid that we can give. This is not to underestimate the significant contribution that our foreign aid, investment, and technology can make to world development. But what we can achieve depends primarily upon how we allocate our resources to various ends, and on the kinds of international and domestic policies we pursue, rather than on variation in our own rate of growth. Our import and export policies, for example, are vastly more important to underdeveloped countries than whether our GNP grows at 2% or 5% per year.

The Real Growth Imperatives arise from the fact that a strong economy is a growing economy. An economy with a high per capita income such as ours generates a large volume of private saving which must flow into capital accumulation if the economy is to sustain itself. In other words, the continued vitality of the system requires growth.

But beyond such technical matters, we desire growth to promote our private ends and national purposes. It is that simple; we want growth because it enlarges the opportunities of our children, because it expands our capacities to pursue goals of our own choosing, because it increases the range of choices open to us, because it is a rewarding outlet for our creative energies and imagination, because achievement invigorates and stimulates. In short, through economic growth we lead richer and fuller lives.

Moreover, we desire growth for the preservation of our way of life. By continued growth we demonstrate to ourselves, and perhaps to the world, that our system of free enterprise and representative government is indeed strong and able to fulfill rising aspirations and to enhance the dignity of free men. We need to grow to demonstrate that our system is not headed for inevitable collapse, but will survive even in a world of oppression and hostility.

For a variety of reasons there is general agreement that economic growth is an important goal of economic policy. But there is disagreement over the relative importance of growth as compared with other goals and even more disagreement over the means by which growth should be pursued.

Growth is only one of several major goals of economic policy. Economic freedom, stability of employment, stability of the general price level, economic efficiency, and economic security all are important. Properly conceived and pursued, economic growth is compatible with all these other goals; but it becomes incompatible when pursued too ardently or by inappropriate means. Policies to promote growth or any other goal must reflect a compromise among competing goals.

Growth entails certain costs, and attempts to achieve greatly accelerated statistical growth rates may be costly in terms of human hardship. New machines may reduce prematurely not only the value of old machines but also the value of human skills acquired through long training and experience. New products may reduce the incomes of those producing old products. New industries in new locations may uproot homes and communities near old industries. Unless the costs of economic growth are equitably distributed, it is only reasonable to expect strong resistance to growth and its accompanying changes.

To get high rates of growth through more rapid capital accumulation means that people must save more, either voluntarily or by compulsion. In the Soviet Union people are forced to sacrifice current consumption and liberty to meet targets of capital formation imposed by the authorities. As much as Americans want economic growth, compulsions and depressed levels of consumption are costs which they would not willingly pay except in dire emergency.

A great variety of recipes for growth are in current vogue. Most of them are hackneyed antiques, spruced up a bit with new phrases and served under new names. In the main, these recipes represent two fundamentally different approaches: mercantilism and economic liberalism.

In many ways the debate about economic growth today is similar to the great debate two centuries ago over how best to promote the wealth of nations. The mercantilist approach of the 17th and 18th centuries was an engineering approach. The government by detailed design and elaborate regulation of economic life attempted to impose a coordinated plan of growth on society. Sumptuary laws to prevent frippery and waste, public monopolies to channel investment wisely, detailed regulation of labor and trade—all these were part of the scheme of things. Mercantilism gave way to economic liberalism—a biological approach to growth with the government cultivating growth, not imposing it.

The great success of the biological approach, especially in Great Britain and the United States, is a matter of historical record. It remains to be seen whether our basically liberal approach will give way to a rising tide of mercantilist reaction.

Today, one school of thought, the modern mercantilists, say that the government should create growth by massive increases in the quantity and diversity of government services and activity—in short, that government should force growth on the economy. This approach also involves forcing people to save more either through taxes or through inflation, in order to divert resources into collective use.

The opposite school of thought, the supporters of an open society, hold that the kinds and levels of public services should be determined on the basis of what we really want government to produce, that each governmental activity should be justified either on cost-benefit principles or on sound grounds of social responsibility, and that government can best promote growth by policies which release and give effect to the creative energies of private citizens.

While the factors that determine percentage rates of growth over a span of years are not fully understood, the success of past growth efforts and accumulated economic knowledge do tell us a good deal about the conditions of economic progress and how the government can best cultivate growth.

The underlying forces that promote national economic growth are basically the same as those that account for the economic progress of individuals. An individual's desire for a higher and more secure standard of living for himself and for his family is the basic stimulus. To this end he studies, plans, works, saves, and invests. He searches out new ways of doing things and develops new techniques and processes. Hence, one of the most effective means of stimulating economic growth—and at the same time one of our fundamental objectives in seeking economic growth—is to provide expanding opportunities for every individual to realize his own potentialities to the utmost and to open wider vistas for his children; to encourage initiative, independence, and integrity; to preserve and enlarge the moral worth of the individual; and to approach more closely to our ideals of personal freedom, justice, fair play, broad and equal opportunity, the rule of law, mutual respect, and charity.

Growth requires a flexible and adaptable economic system with freedom to experiment. New industries must spring up, and others must decline. New methods must be accepted and old ones discarded. Labor and capital must shift easily and cooperatively in response to economic rewards and penalties. The combination of an abundant flow of new ideas, a willingness to take risks, and the speedy adoption of successful new methods is a condition for a high rate of growth.

The translation of new ideas into practical processes is speeded by a high rate of saving, through which new equipment can be financed and put into use. Saving also contributes to growth even where new methods are not involved, since it makes possible a larger stock of plant and equipment, housing, and other physical capital, which add to our potential supply of goods and services. In this way, the prudence and responsible foresight of people in providing for future needs makes an essential contribution to our growth.

All of this requires an economic environment that can be brought about and maintained only by positive and progressive governmental actions. The government has a twofold function in promoting growth.

First, it must provide a legal and institutional climate conducive to private economic progress. Second, the government must provide various public services and facilities which, while valuable to the nation as a whole, do not offer sufficient rewards to induce private producers to provide them for sale, or do not offer sufficient direct benefits to induce private individuals to buy them.

Ten essentials of a positive government program for growth are as follows:

1. Orderly Government.   People must be free to pursue their private affairs—to work, save, invest, enter into contracts without fear of fraud, confiscation, or violence.

2. Equality of Opportunity.   Only when each individual has the opportunity to develop his potential to the fullest and to utilize his skills to the utmost will we obtain maximum growth. Public policy should be aimed at eliminating discrimination in education and employment, whether it results from color, religion, sex, birthplace, or social class. Our economy must be open to the ambitious and the able.

3. Price Level Stability.   Marked inflation or deflation destroys economic efficiency, distorts resource allocation, and retards growth. Monetary, budget, and debt policies should be conducted in such a manner as to promote reasonable stability of the general price level.

4. Stability of Employment and Income.   Occasional mild fluctuations in the level of economic activity are not yet avoidable, much as we all wish otherwise. In fact, the surest thing that can be said about our future growth rate is that it will fluctuate. But national policies must deal effectively with recessions so as to assure continuity of maximum employment opportunities and to alleviate the consequences of such involuntary unemployment as may occur. To achieve maximum sustainable growth, national policies must also prevent speculative excesses in boom periods.

5. Taxes.   Tax policy must serve several masters, and economic growth should be one of them. Taxes which penalize thrift, risk-bearing, and innovation have no place in a good tax system. Punitive rates applied to too narrow a base, a great hodgepodge of exemptions and exclusions, and discriminatory levies distort resource use and impede healthy growth. Tax reform should be directed toward improving the quantity and quality of investment, releasing incentives to personal effort, improving the cyclical flexibility of the tax system as a whole, and treating equally people in equal economic circumstances.

6. *Maintaining Competition.* Competition is the lifeblood of a free economy. To keep the system strong and growing the lines of entry into industry must be kept open, and monopolistic barriers to progress must be eliminated. A positive and vigorous antitrust program is essential to growth. Restrictive labor practices, likewise, need to be eliminated. Regulatory activities of government should be aimed at protecting the consumer and should not be allowed to stifle competition and prevent innovation in the regulated industries.

7. *International Trade.* International trade is a powerful ally of growth. By trade we can produce indirectly a greater quantity and variety of goods and services than by domestic production alone. The pressure of foreign competition also keeps our own industries more efficient. Continued efforts to reduce or eliminate trade barriers at home and abroad will pay large dividends in growth.

8. *Governmental Blocks to Growth.* Although economic growth is an avowed goal of policy, many governmental programs and activities tend to block growth. Growth involves change. When the government protects the status quo or insulates particular groups of business, labor, or consumers from the causes or effects of change, it retards growth. Many pernicious and unwarranted obstacles to growth are to be found in our agricultural policies, business subsidies, natural resource policies, regulation of industry, foreign trade policies, and grants-in-aid. If we are really serious about accelerating our growth, one of our first orders of business should be an attack on the whole structure of inefficiencies and impediments to growth induced by governments at all levels.

9. *Public Works.* Growth requires social as well as private investment. The government makes a genuine contribution to economic growth when it provides complementary public facilities and services desired by the community. But here strict cost-benefit principles should apply or growth will be retarded. Because public services are generally not valued in the market place, economic criteria

are difficult to apply. Realism and restraint are, therefore, of crucial importance in the use of public funds.

10. Maintenance and Development of the System.   Certain kinds of governmental expenditures to promote science, technology, health, and education also promote growth. Here again strict criteria should be applied, at least insofar as economic growth is to be served. Governmental activities should not supplant private activities and should be restricted to those areas where substantial benefits from governmental action are clearly apparent.

We are in the midst of a great national debate over economic growth. But until we understand what growth is, why it is an important policy goal, and how it can be achieved within a framework of economic and political freedom, the debate will range over many false and confused issues.

True growth in economic welfare involves both material and non-material benefits, widely diffused. True growth must conform to the values and aspirations of a free people. The "right" or optimum rate of growth is that rate which conforms to the voluntary choices of the people, rather than a rate obtained by coercion, compulsion, or excessive social costs. The rate of growth can be increased by improving the efficiency of the economic system and by pursuing wise public policies to create a favorable environment for growth.

The future chapters of our story of economic growth are still to be written. We can be confident that these chapters will be happy ones if we have the wit and wisdom to preserve and strengthen the forces of progress that have produced in America an abundant economy, a great nation, and a free people.

24

American Economic Power

NOT LONG AGO, when people thought about American economic power, they were thinking about the power of our economy to provide a better life for everyone, to provide higher material standards of living, and to provide a higher quality of life. Today when we think about American economic power we think in terms of national security.

What we require of our economy today, first and foremost, is the sinews of defense: supplies to strengthen our allies and materials with which to win friends and influence people all over the world.

That is an approach to economic power that Americans find distasteful. It was forced on us by the Nazis and the Japanese. As soon as we had disposed of them, we quickly disarmed and reverted to our peacetime economic goals, only to be brought up short by the Russians, who forced us back again to a goal of national security and economic power.

Most of us feel that approach to economic power is temporary. We don't like it and we are sure it will go away, but I think most of us really know better. We know it is here to stay and probably for generations.

Today, in this country, we are in the midst of a great national debate over appropriate policies for holding our economic power, or for economic growth, which is the popular phrase today. That debate in which we are engaged now is remarkably parallel, both in its

Presented before the American Power Conference in Chicago on 29 March 1960.

substance and its motivation, to a similar debate that took place two to three hundred years ago in England and in this country, too.

England, two hundred years ago, faced a mortal enemy dominating the continent of Europe and dedicated to the destruction of England and everything for which it stood. English economic policies of necessity attached paramount importance to national security. Exports and imports were all regulated by the government, with a view to maximizing England's strength while minimizing France's strength. Domestic production and prices were regulated in an attempt to see that only those things were produced which contributed to national security. There was elaborate legislation governing consumption in an attempt to prevent the affluent society of the 18th Century from dissipating its resources on uses which officials judged to have low social priority.

That 17th and 18th Century approach to economic power and economic growth is one that can be described by analogy as an engineering or architectural approach, that is, a design is drawn up at headquarters, specifications are written at headquarters, activities are planned and coordinated at headquarters, and a predetermined structure is supposed to be brought about in a predetermined way.

Toward the end of the 18th Century, a sharply contrasting approach to economic power attracted widespread support, an approach which I would describe again by analogy as a biological and agricultural approach. The essence of the biological or agricultural approach is to *cultivate* growth. It places emphasis on the conditions which will bring about growth, rather than on target shapes and sizes.

The outcome of the debate on economic growth two centuries ago was to drop the engineering approach and replace it with the agricultural approach; in other words, to specify the means we would use, rather than specify the ends.

Following that approach, England first, then the United States, reached a level of economic power that had not been dreamed of even by the people who advocated the approach. At the same time, they reached a level of national security that had not been equaled since the Roman Empire.

Now, it seems to me worth recalling that the present debate is one which we have been through before. It is the old debate of the 18th Century, between what was called liberalism and mercantilism. The alternatives that are being talked about today were thoroughly talked out and thoroughly tried out in the 18th Century.

At the end of the 18th Century, liberalism won a clean-cut victory. (In using the word "liberalism," I am not using it in its present perverted sense. Liberalism emphasized liberty and freedom of the individual to operate within a framework of rules of law.) Today, however, liberalism faces a powerful reactionary force which favors a return to something very much like the mercantile policy of the 16th, 17th, and 18th Centuries. Of course, mercantilism never disappeared completely. It diminished in importance, but it has been reviving for some time.

We have proposals today to regulate and limit private consumption and enlarge the role of Government in determining what will be consumed. We have proposals to limit credit to consumers for purposes which are judged unworthy and, at the same time, to subsidize credit for purposes or people judged to be meritorious. We have proposals today which look toward Government determination of wages and prices. We have proposals for limiting our imports and subsidizing our exports. As a matter of fact, all these things are not only proposals but, in some degree, actualities—and it is proposed that we go further in the same direction.

These proposals aren't really for just starting something new; they are for strengthening some mercantilist policies which already exist and for reducing the liberal policies which are still, on the whole, dominant. Now, in large part, of course, these proposals for a return to mercantilism are not related in any genuine way to the national security problem we face currently. On the contrary, they are policies that have been advocated for seventy-five years. The whole structure of policies has been jacked up and a new foundation is being run in underneath to support them.

Originally, these same policies were urged in the late 19th Century on the ground of justice, equity, and morality, as the existing system was judged to be unjust, inequitable, and immoral. With the passing of time the benefits of economic progress were widely dispersed to all classes of society.

With the dissemination of the benefits of economic welfare through the whole society, this argument for mercantilism or socialism on the basis of justice and equity began to disappear. But it was later argued that the economy would be more efficient if Government intervened extensively.

Some other countries adopted these policies and as their progress was watched and seen to be anything but efficient, and not to compare favorably with ours, or as parts of our economy that were operated by the Government were watched, this argument disappeared, too. Then the great depression came along, and the argument was that we should adopt these policies in order to prevent or eliminate severe depressions. So these policies were adopted during the 1930's to a much greater extent than at any time in our history; yet not until war came along did we get anything resembling a return to full employment and maximum growth.

These same policies were advocated, reasonably successfully, as necessary to prosecute the war successfully, although in the critical debate in the 18th Century the most decisive factor leading to the victory of liberalism was that England alone was providing supplies for the struggle against Napoleon, and the utmost economic efficiency was needed.

When the war ended, there was a period when people said, "We are bound to have a return to stagnation, deflation, and depression, and we should adopt all these mercantilistic policies immediately to prevent that." That didn't happen, but now the argument is that economic growth requires the same things that have been offered us as remedies for such a wide variety of different ailments. I am a little skeptical, when I see these policies being advocated for economic growth, as to whether the national security is the real reason.

What are the outstanding characteristics of the economy that was developed in this country and in England? The most obvious and by far the most widely noted is a very high level of economic output.

A second, scarcely less conspicuous feature, is the high record of economic growth. The material level of living of the average American has doubled approximately every generation, by which I mean every twenty or twenty-five years. Another way to put that is to say if exactly the same rate of growth continues into the future as has continued as far back as we have data available, we can expect our grandchildren to have an average family income of $25,000 a year— in current purchasing power.

The third feature of our economy is the extent to which its benefits have been shared by all parts of the population. As the Vice President told a Moscow television audience in 1959, we have become the nearest approach to a classless society.

A conception of economic possibilities similar to ours is stirring throughout the world today, in vast numbers of people in Asia, in Africa, and everywhere else. The spread of that happy economic vision is, unfortunately, a threat in the world today. It is a threat to the survival of society from which the vision sprang in the first place and in which alone it has become a reality. The reason there is danger now in the idea of attaining the same thing throughout the world is that people underestimate the time and effort required and misunderstand the means by which these things are acquired. There is a tendency to focus on the end, rather than the means, and even a tendency to feel that the fruits of economic growth now possessed by just a few hundred millions of people in the world could and should support billions of people.

The secret of American economic power lies, I suggest, in what has variously been called the market system, the price system, the free enterprise system, or the profit system. I prefer to talk about the price system. People think of prices in many different ways. They think of prices in terms of equity or justice or fairness or ability to pay, or profit and incentives, and so on. All these things are important, but they overlook what is by far the most vital role of prices: Prices are the organizing device of our society. The price system can be thought of as a great computer, far greater than any yet conceived by the business machine companies, which calculates instructions for the over-all efficiency of the economy and telegraphs its orders to participants, and even follows up and enforces those orders.

The key to our economic power, I suggest, is in this central organizing machinery of the price system. And in particular, in comparing ourselves with the Russians, our greatest economic advantage is in their lack of any such mechanism and the inherent difficulties encountered in introducing this into their economy.

Take the question of how much new steel capacity to build and where to build it and what combination of labor and capital and raw materials should be used in producing the steel. You have lots of choices between more or less capital versus more or less raw materials; more capital uses less labor, and more labor uses less capital. By having more small plants, you can save on transportation but by having fewer, bigger plants, you can gain efficiencies in production.

We have a system for making all of these calculations. Other economies, with very few exceptions, lack any such system; that, I think, is the real key to our economic power. It lies in the price system, not just in an incentive system. An incentive system gets people to do their jobs efficiently, but a price system insures that their jobs will be useful as well.

The Russians, as a matter of fact, are adopting our policies on incentive. The Russians value highly the role of incentives in getting people to do what they want done. Some of the Russians who were

over here recently were deriding us for our tax system and other devices that kill off incentives; they may be moving up abreast of us
there, or we may be moving down to them.

Even so, an incentive system leads only to optimization in the
small problems, but does not lead to solving the really basic one—
the fundamental problem of the allocation of resources—and I don't
see any immediate signs that they will overtake us there.

I don't expect to see the Russian economy approach ours, much
less overtake us. I think the chance of their doing that, even within
half a century, is negligible, unless we deliberately abandon the
policies that have made us strong and made us free at an even greater
rate than it seems to me we are doing, and unless they adopt them
at an even greater rate than they are doing.

I would summarize my views by quoting Vice President Nixon,
who said, in discussing the economic competition with Russia, that
"we can win that horse race, provided that we don't try to ride their
horse."

25

Automation and Unemployment

The Source of Innovation

A common view is that technological innovation, like the Mississippi, just goes rolling along, year in and year out, at a steady, sure pace, on an inevitable and predictable course.

This view has derived its most effective support from the late William F. Ogburn and his associate, S. C. Gilfillan, particularly from the former's *Social Change* (1933) and the latter's *Sociology of Invention* (1935). As the stream of culture flows on, generation after generation, it accumulates bits and pieces of knowledge and technique. These bits and pieces fit together into inventions or innovations. When the essential bits and pieces have come into existence through cultural evolution, it is inevitable that someone—in fact, often several people independently—will fit them together to form the innovation.

This innovation itself then moves along in the current of culture, becoming in its turn one of the bits and pieces destined in due course to be fitted into some other innovation. In this inexorable process, some inventions occur long before there is any social need for them; others fail to occur despite long and acute need, according to whether the times are right or wrong for them. Gilfillan has tried his hand, with some success, at predicting inventions in advance. One of his earliest attempts is one of the most fascinating, his article entitled "The Future Home Theater," *The Independent*, October

Prepared for The American Assembly at Harriman, New York, 3–6 May 1962.

17, 1912. This predicted television. There is little similarity technically between modern television and his forecasts, and his timing
was very much premature, but he made some penetrating forecasts
of the social consequences of television—as well as some that are
wide of the mark.

In sharp contrast to the view that innovations result from the
stream of culture just rolling along are the views that they result
from transcendent revelations, striking great geniuses like lightning,
or that they result from the industry, perseverance, and intelligence
of dedicated, self-reliant individuals. These views are as rare today
as the view that people who are unsuccessful or antisocial are responsible for their own shortcomings, not society.

A third view is that innovation results from social organization
for adapting what is possible to what is desirable. Our own social
organization provides for seeking innovations in diverse ways simultaneously: through the lone-wolf "ingenious Yankee," through the
scientific genius, through a corps of engineers and technicians,
through large scientific laboratories, through tightly organized,
closely programmed industrial organizations for research and development, through the vast informal network that has been dubbed
by Michael Polanyi "the republic of science." Social organization is
involved in making accessible to these diverse participants the ac-
cumulating knowledge and technology of society, in indicating to
them social needs and priorities, in providing them support, and in
giving them incentives to get the greatest yield in relation to resources spent. The process has been described by Richard Nelson as
"the interplay of moving frontiers of knowledge and growing need
upon the direction and likelihood of success of individual 'acts of
novelty.' "[1]

The third view of innovation is, of course, a special case of the
economist's general view of social economic organization.[2] This view,
in broad terms, is that the efforts of people as consumers to obtain as
much satisfaction as possible from their limited incomes, and the
efforts of the same people as producers to get as much income as
possible from their limited resources and capacities to work, interact
to set prices of consumers' goods and of productive services in such
a way that the relation between the prices of any two things measures their relative scarcity or abundance in terms of their ability to
satisfy wants. High prices tend to stimulate production of the high-
priced things, as a means of increasing the incomes of productive
services; at the same time, high prices tend to reduce the consump-

tion of the high-priced things, as a means of conserving the incomes of consumers for other uses. The social organization brought about through these price or market mechanisms governs what shall be produced, by whom, with what resources, and by what methods; and governs consumption similarly. It may be viewed as an elaborate mechanism for combining information on general, over-all priorities, with information on the specific circumstances of time and place; and at the same time as a mechanism for providing a powerful incentive to conform to the implications of the messages about what should be conserved and what may be used freely.

In such a view of the social economic organization, innovation is induced by complex relations among prices and costs, and more specifically by opportunities to change those relations in such a way that the change will redound to the benefit of the person making the change. This view does not imply that inventions can be ordered custom-fitted and delivered on schedule, nor that inventors are motivated exclusively by pecuniary gain. It does imply that technological developments are not autonomous, outside the influence of economic forces, but are influenced by economic forces just as they influence economic forces.

The development of textile machinery in the late eighteenth century can be interpreted, in this view, as the result of a major effort by the social organization. The earlier improvements in commerce and agriculture had made food and fibers more abundant and had created the possibility of transferring some people from agricultural production to other activities. Improved engineering technology made it possible to develop machines for handling cotton and wool. The combination of these circumstances presented eighteenth century society with a challenge and an opportunity, out of which sprang the industrial revolution.

A similar interpretation can be placed on the development of transportation in the early nineteenth century. Continued expansion of population and industry faced a serious constraint if transportation remained tied to waterways. If the vast land areas and resources of the United States were to attain economic value there had to be means of transportation over land. Faced with this barrier to its continued expansion, the social economic organization made a sustained and successful assault on the transportation problem.

The development and introduction of automation should be viewed in similar terms. To some extent the elements that make automation possible have come about through cultural evolution:

through achievements of science pursued for science's sake, through military developments, and through by-products of research and development on such problems as communication. Vigorous efforts to apply these elements to automation result from an acute social need to get as much output as possible in relation to the number of people employed. The precise magnitude and nature of such social needs, and of opportunities for meeting them, is communicated through prices—more precisely, through the relations of prices to one another. Prices also constitute a strong incentive to utilize the opportunities to meet the needs summarized by the messages, for this is the way to higher incomes.

Development and Introduction of Technological Change

In considering economic factors in technological innovation, including automation, a distinction should be made between the development of technology and its adoption. The factors influencing development differ in part from those influencing introduction.

There is a difference between the organizational arrangements by which our economy develops new techniques of production, and in particular techniques of automation, and the arrangements by which it develops new products. New products are developed mostly in laboratories serving a single firm whose main business is the production of such products, not research and development. New methods of production, however, are developed mostly in laboratories that serve all of industry. Since the outcome of research is uncertain, there is a substantial risk in new product development that any basic research will produce results whose value, if any, relates to products not made by the company. Consequently, research on new products tends to be confined to large companies with diverse product lines. (Results of research can, of course, be sold or licensed to other firms. This mitigates, but only partially, the drawbacks to a firm of supporting a laboratory whose results may not contribute to the firm's own product lines. Also, there are a few firms which specialize in developing new products for other firms to produce, but these are not a significant factor in developing new products.)

But for a firm engaged in producing automation equipment there is much greater assurance that any new discoveries it makes will fit its own business, since it does not expect to use the results itself but to sell them wherever they may have value in the production of a service or commodity. This difference in organization suggests the conjecture that automation may be the object of somewhat more intensive research and development than it otherwise would, in comparison with new products, simply because new discoveries in automation are more likely to redound to the direct benefit of the discovering firm.

Another factor working in the direction of disproportionate efforts to develop automation is the great need for automation in modern weapons systems. Many of the control devices developed for aircraft, ships, missiles, and space vehicles can be applied to, or modified for, the control of production processes. Perhaps more important, the basic science and technology that are created in developing weapons systems, and even more the scientists and technologists themselves, can be utilized in developing automation.

Technological progress is, presumably, directly related to the amount of industrial research. The amount invested in industrial research is directly related to the profits produced by research. From 1950 to 1960, annual expenditures on industrial research, adjusted for price changes, grew by 12 percent per year, a rate which implies doubling annual expenditures every six years. A principal reason for this extraordinarily rapid growth was that funds invested in research yielded a higher return than funds invested in other ways. The differential return on research over other investments appears to have diminished, and it has been estimated by Yale Brozen that expenditures on research in the 1960's will show only half the percentage rate of growth of the 1950's.[3] Perhaps, then, the 1960's will see a decline in this component of the forces tending toward disproportionate efforts to invent new automation methods.

The simple fact that capital is being accumulated faster than the labor force is growing tends to stimulate automation. The increasing amount of capital per worker means that the additional capital must, so to speak, be self-operating; that is, workers cannot be assigned to capital in the same ratio as formerly, and if the capital is to operate fully, each worker must be able to tend more of it. The process by which our social economic organization brings about this adjustment to the increasing ratio of capital to labor may be described, in the schematizations of economic analysis, as follows: As the amount of capital outstrips the labor force, a rise in wages comes about because owners of the additional capital, trying to find labor to operate it, attempt to "pirate" employees from other firms. The higher wages make it more profitable than formerly to develop labor-saving devices; or, to put it differently, some labor-saving devices which formerly would not have saved enough in wages to offset their own costs, hence were not developed, now save more than enough in wages to offset their costs, so are developed.

The analysis of the preceding paragraph applies to efforts to develop new automation techniques. Successful development of such techniques will bring greater rewards to the developer, now that the quantity of capital has increased relative to the quantity of labor, so more intensive efforts will be made (i.e., more costs will be incurred) in the effort to develop new techniques. But the analysis applies to the adoption of existing techniques, as well as to the development of new ones.

There are in existence at any time many labor-saving devices that are technically feasible but economically wasteful. Machinery for handling materials, for example, was introduced a decade or two earlier in the United States than in Great Britain. Materials handling techniques were, of course, known in Britain as soon as in the United States, if for no other reason than that technological communication between the two countries is virtually as free, fast, and fluid as within them. Britain's "lag" can be accounted for in large part by its lower ratio of labor costs to capital costs, and according to Seymour Melman, in *Dynamic Factors in Industrial Productivity*, when the introduction of machinery for handling materials came in Britain it was because the ratio of labor costs to capital costs had risen. Similarly, automation of an automobile assembly line was technically successful in the Morris plant in England in 1927, but was economically unsuccessful because the cost of the labor saved was less than the cost of saving it.

Wages

One step in the process described above, by which an increase in the quantity of capital stimulates automation, is an increase in wages. The increase in wages leads in turn to the development and introduction of labor-saving devices. An increase in wages will have this effect, whether it results from a larger amount of capital or from some other cause.

A particular industry which has experienced no increase, or even a decrease, in capital may find itself faced with a rise in wages because other industries are increasing in size and are successfully bidding labor away from it. This rise in wages will trigger the effort to introduce labor-saving techniques. Thus, even a declining industry may be forced to develop and introduce automation in order to raise its output per man-hour, and thus be able to meet higher wage rates prevailing in the rest of the economy.

There may be important differences, however, in how far the process of saving labor is carried, depending on the forces creating the rise in wages. In the case described above, where the rise in wages results from bidding among owners of capital whose capital would go untended (more precisely, under-tended), the process of automating to get along with less labor per unit of capital is self-limiting. As automation makes it possible for each worker to utilize more capital, the need to "pirate" labor declines, so the tendency for wages to rise disappears after they have gone up a certain amount. Thus, the displacement of labor by automation halts before it goes so far as to cause unemployment. (More accurately, this is what *would* happen if the ratio of capital to labor stabilized at a new, higher level. Actually, of course, the ratio is continuing to rise, so the upward pressure on wages is maintained. The introduction of labor-saving devices therefore continues. Nevertheless, it does not reach a rate leading to unemployment, for if it did the upward pressure on wages would halt and thereby halt the process of displacing labor.)

Where the rise in wages comes about through other forces it may induce an uneconomic degree of automation, that is, one that is wasteful because it goes so far as to displace labor for which there are not other employment opportunities as productive as those from which it is displaced. This effect will be most pronounced in industries where there are good technical possibilities of replacing labor by machines, as is often the case in industries which have long production runs on nearly identical items, for example, cigarettes or automobiles. It has been estimated by Stephen Sobotka (*Profile of Michigan*) that in the automobile industry a given small percentage rise in wages will lead to the introduction of enough labor-saving machinery to cause about three times as large a percentage decrease in employment. If, then, unions in the industry can raise wages 5 percent above what they otherwise would be, employment in the industry will be 15 percent below what it otherwise would be.

This 15 percent is not necessarily unemployed, to be sure; instead they are employed in other industries, where, by swelling the labor supply they have the effect of lowering wages, and where productivity tends to be lower because capital has been drawn away for the automobile industry. Thus, automation in the automobile industry may be carried to a point where it is uneconomic and wasteful in the twofold sense that too much capital is drawn into automobile production out of other uses, and that too much labor is forced out of automobile production into other uses. The fault, of course, lies not in automation itself, but in the forces which cause uneconomic automation in some industries by holding wage levels out of line with other industries.

Uneconomic automation can be induced also by forces that tend to lower artificially the cost of new equipment in comparison with the cost of old equipment. A special tax privilege for new equipment, for example, would lead to somewhat earlier scrapping of old equipment and replacement by new than accords with the amounts of resources consumed by the two pieces of equipment to get a given amount of output. In general, the availability of new machines requiring a smaller input of labor, power, and materials than is required to produce the same output on old machines does not necessarily mean that it is economically efficient to scrap the old machines. For the old machine to be scrapped, the saving of inputs by the new machine should be sufficient to compensate for the excess of the capital cost of the new machine over the salvage value of the old one. If the cost of the new machine is reduced by special tax privileges not accorded old machines, this necessary margin of advantage in the cost of inputs is less, and some automation will be profitable, and will be introduced, that would not have been introduced without the tax privilege. In short, the tax privilege can serve as an inducement to uneconomic displacement of labor, that is, displacement of labor before more productive alternative employment is available.

General Level of Employment

In considering the effects of automation on the general level of employment, it is important to recognize that building automation equipment, though it may reduce the total number of man-hours of work required over a long period, has the effect of redistributing the employment in time. Work that without automation would have been done in the future is, in effect, done now in building the machine. Suppose a pinsetting machine is being built for a bowling alley. When the machine is installed it will eliminate many man-hours of pinsetting labor. But during the period of its construction employment is actually increased, for more man-hours per day will be used during its construction than are being used to set pins. In fact, manual setting of pins will continue while the machine is being built, so the work on building the machine is a clear addition to the total volume of employment. Thus, in a sense, automation replaces a long trickle of employment by an initial splash.

This does not mean, either, that because of the initial splash of employment on building automation equipment a subsequent drought is in store. It sometimes happens—bowling may be a case in point—that automation leads, through price reductions or quality improvements, to so large an expansion in the industry that total employment is larger after automation is complete than it would be, even allowing for secular growth, without automation. This is not, however, typical.

A more general reason why doing the work of the future now does not mean future unemployment is that the total amount of work to be done in the future is infinite. Yale Brozen has estimated that it would require $2 trillion ($2 \times 10^{12}$) of net investment to automate all of American industry.[4] If the net supply of savings is $20 billion ($2 \times 10^{10}$) per year above what is needed to provide capital equipment for the growth of the labor force—and the figure is not likely to be higher in the near future—this would imply a century to get the job done. (It would not actually take that long, for the savings available would average more than $20 billion in a period as long as a century; but, on the other hand, new products and new technology will almost certainly push the required investment for total automation continually higher.)

In short, the problem of general unemployment from automation is a non-existent will-o'-the-wisp problem.

Dislocations

To the extent that there are real problems of unemployment associated with automation, they are problems of dislocation. Current construction, installation, and maintenance of pinsetting machines is creating more employment than if all existing bowling alleys were using pin boys; but it is not employment for the same kinds of people. Similarly, building, installing, and maintaining automatic elevators probably create more employment than if all elevators were still using operators and starters; but not for the same people. Even in industries where current construction of automated equipment employs fewer people than would be employed if the automated equipment were manual, it does not follow that automation has caused unemployment, but only that it has changed the occupational distribution of the labor force.

Even in very short periods when specific jobs are automated out of existence there may not be even temporary unemployment. If the economy is at "full" employment, other jobs will be available almost immediately for almost all displaced employees. When some of those automated out of their jobs do go through a period of unemployment, the explanation is almost always something other than automation: that the economy is not at "full" employment, for example, or that people are reluctant to move their homes. The situation of such unemployed is exactly the same as that of people left unemployed by a shift in consumer demand. The problem is not something special to automation, and measures for dealing with it should not be specialized to those who lost their last jobs because of automation.

Accounts of the amount of labor displaced by automation in specific situations are sometimes grossly exaggerated. A utility executive, to illustrate this, reported that in his company new automatic billing equipment and six employees are now doing a job that would require a hundred if it were done by hand. He added, however, that the job had not been done by hand since 1907. The new machines with their six people had replaced other machines with fourteen people. Furthermore, besides the six people now at work directly on billing, three had had to be added in other departments solely because of the billing machines. Thus, what at first sounded like a reduction in employment of ninety-four turned out to be a reduction of five. Finally, the executive added that of the eight displaced from the billing department, two had withdrawn from the labor force for other reasons, and the other six had been snapped up elsewhere in the same firm.

On the question of what actually happens in technological displacement—how many people are, as a matter of actual experience, unemployed, and for how long, because of automation—there is so little factual knowledge as to be essentially none. Talk about this seems to be, however, in inverse proportion to the amount of knowledge.

Automation and other labor-saving innovations, though they reflect such general cultural characteristics as the stream of technological and scientific progress, are substantially influenced by economic factors. Factors tending to stimulate a high rate of discovery and development of new methods of automation are:

1. Firms producing automation equipment serve all of industry. This means that they are likely to benefit from almost any results of research that they support; it thus leads them to support more research than would occur if production equipment were designed and produced in the same firms that use it—as are new products.
2. The development of modern weapons systems has created a great deal of new technology related to control systems, and a large corps of scientists and engineers capable of developing automation.
3. Industrial research grew at an extraordinarily high rate in the 1950's, thus tending to produce many new labor-saving devices. Probably industrial research will expand more slowly in the late 1960's.
4. The fact that the amount of capital available is growing faster than the labor force necessarily leads to the development of labor-saving techniques, that is, techniques by which each worker can handle a larger amount of equipment.

Many labor-saving devices that are known may be uneconomical, hence not in use. Any factor that raises the cost of labor relative to that of capital will lead to the introduction of some of the available labor-saving devices that previously were unused. How far the process will go depends on whether the upward pressure on wage rates is relieved as the process of automation approaches the point where labor would be forced into less productive occupations. When the upward pressure on wages is not relieved (that is, when growth in wages outstrips growth in productivity) automation may be carried to an uneconomic extreme, too much capital being drawn into certain industries and too much labor being forced out of them and into other industries. Automation may also be pushed to uneconomic extremes if special tax privileges are granted for new equipment but not old.

The construction of automation equipment tends to raise the over-all level of employment—to replace a long future period of employment by a shorter immediate period of higher employment. Opportunities for doing this will not be exhausted in the foreseeable future; indeed, it can be foreseen with considerable confidence that they never will be exhausted. There is, in short, no problem, nor any prospect of ever having a problem, of general unemployment due to automation.

Any problems of unemployment connected with automation are, like problems of unemployment connected with shifts in demand, problems of the distribution of the labor force.

26

Economic Statistics and
Economic Policy

THE FIELD OF STATISTICAL APPLICATION with which I have been most closely associated is economics. When I first studied economics, nearly thirty-five years ago, we were excited by the great things that were clearly within immediate reach to be grasped by the tools of statistics and mathematics. It is true that some of the books we read, like those of Irving Fisher, Pareto, Walras, Edgeworth, and Cournot, were not exactly hot off the press; Cournot's, in fact, was approaching its centennial, and the others mentioned were virtually all from the nineteenth century, though we also read Bowley and Evans and one or two others from the early twentieth century. Nevertheless, we had a feeling of excitement, of novelty, of innovation, and of imminent triumph. This is a feeling that I recognize in each new generation of economics graduate students as it comes on the scene. They are as convinced as we were that mathematics and statistics are the wave of the future for economics, the keys that will easily, speedily, and surely unlock all mysteries. They are, if anything, even more excited about the novelty of the mathematical approach. Some of this excitement and enthusiasm is even spilling over into psychology, sociology, and political science. Whether mathematics will make more substantial contributions to our understanding of the economy in the next thirty-five years than in the past thirty-five years is an open question. Its contributions, though not negligible, have by no means measured up to the enthusiastic expectations of thirty-five years ago.

Presidential Address presented before the American Statistical Association in Philadelphia on 9 September 1965.

For statistics, however, the story is different. Its contributions to economics may not have been exactly the ones we expected, but they have exceeded rather than disappointed our expectations.

Statistics and economics are intertwined in at least three distinct ways:

First, economic theory and statistical theory have borrowed profitably from one another. Statistical decision theory, for example, made an important gain when Abraham Wald's basis of the loss function was changed by Jimmie Savage from absolute cost to what economic theorists had long known as "alternative cost" or "opportunity cost." Economic theory, in turn, made a significant advance based on decision theory when von Neumann and Morgenstern restored the concept of utility to the foundations of economics, from which it had been drummed out in disgrace a dozen years earlier.

The second way in which economics and statistics are intertwined is that our factual knowledge of the economy rests largely on statistical investigations. The most notable of these were initiated by Wesley Mitchell at the beginning of the century, carried on since the First World War at the National Bureau of Economic Research, and in many cases eventually picked up by government bureaus. It is as a result of Mitchell's work and that of his associates and followers at the National Bureau that economists know the facts about business cycles; about national income and its distribution; about gross national product; about consumer prices; about productivity; and about several other important aspects of the economy. (Mitchell, by the way, was President of this Association in 1918.)

Third, economic policy is to a certain extent guided by and evaluated by statistical measurements. (More precisely, policy is guided by statistics to an uncertain extent.) Our monetary authorities, for example, are responsible for the Index of Industrial Production, which they initiated and have repeatedly improved because of its importance in fulfilling their responsibilities for the stability of the economy.

I propose to devote the rest of my time this evening to some remarks about economic statistics and economic policy. Five or six years ago I had occasion, as the Chairman of tonight's session has told you, to look into this rather closely, particularly in regard to prices, employment, and economic growth.

In my observation, differences on economic policy do not arise, for the most part, from differences in the results desired from economic policy. Nor do they arise, except indirectly, from differences about economic theory, for example between Keynesian and quantity theorists. They arise in large measure from different pictures of what the world is like; that is to say, from different notions of what the facts are. Even the differences in theory are in large part rooted in the same source; thus, those who attribute more importance to fiscal than to monetary policy usually are not familiar with the empirical study made for the Committee on Economic Development's Commission on Monetary Policy by Friedman and Meiselman,[1] or in a few cases presumably are familiar with it but do not accept it as competent work.

I suggest that our national economic policies in the 1950's were misguided by statistics which were properly enough interpreted had they been accurate, but were not sufficiently accurate; and that our policies in the 1960's are being misguided by statistics that are accurate enough but are being misinterpreted. I refer particularly to price statistics in the 1950's and to unemployment statistics in the 1960's. To avoid misunderstanding, perhaps I should say not "misguided" but "less than optimal," for the record of our economy during the past twenty years hardly leaves room for the term "misguided" except in that sense.

It is often suggested that prices have always risen. Frequently a speaker or writer remarks that prices have doubled in the past twenty-five years, and then slips in a reference to "this continuous rise in prices." Others profess that the behavior of prices since the Second World War has been unprecedented, and proceed to attribute this to special causes, usually monopoly in labor or in business.

Indexes of United States prices have been constructed back to 1720 for wholesale prices and back to 1800 for retail prices. Only the broadest kind of interpretation can be based on the early data because of their limitations; and it has to be kept in mind that at the Revolutionary War there was a complete rupture in the series, of which the phrase "not worth a Continental" is a reminder.

In the broadest sweep, however, the series show near-constancy in the basic trend of average prices over the whole 245 years. There is, in fact, an upward movement averaging, speaking very roughly, one-half of 1 per cent per year.

A second striking characteristic of the 245-year sweep is that high, sharp peaks occur intermittently. Each peak, of course, is associated with a war. Conversely, each of our wars except the Mexican and the Spanish is marked by a peak. If we sort the 245 years into two groups, according to whether the country was at war or at peace, we find that during years of war prices have risen something like an average of 10 per cent per year, and that during years of peace the rate has been minus one-half of 1 per cent per year. This slight decline in years of peace represents gradual recoveries from the wartime peaks; in fact, after each war except the Second World War prices eventually regained, or practically regained, at least momentarily, their pre-war level.

A third striking feature of the 245-year series is that there are long tidal movements: periods of two and three decades in which the prevailing movement was upward or downward. The period from 1865 to 1895, for instance, was one of creeping deflation, in which retail prices fell by nearly half and wholesale prices by nearly two-thirds.

A fourth feature of our price history is recurrent short waves. These are associated with business cycles. Typically price levels are steady as recovery commences, and remain so until the late stages of expansion. They then begin to rise. They continue rising as the peak is reached and recession sets in, but stabilize in the latter part of the recession. Only in severe recessions do price levels actually fall to an appreciable extent. Thus the long-run rise of half a per cent per year represents a cumulation of rises in normal business cycles, offset every so often by a fall during a severe recession.

Here we see a possibility of a real change in the behavior of price levels: If severe depressions have been eliminated, as is believed now even more widely than it was believed in the 1920's, we may have something like a gradual, ratchet-like upward movement in the price index. If that were the case—I shall indicate later that I doubt that it is—it might be more important than previously for our economic policy makers to be vigilant to prevent even small rises in price levels. We might have a situation like that in medicine, where progress has given enlarged importance to problems which formerly seemed minor compared with many overwhelming problems that now have almost disappeared.

Price levels have behaved much the same in the business cycles since the Second World War as in comparable cycles before. Nevertheless, each recession sees numerous economic commentators assuming that prices naturally fall when business falls, and writing that the continued rise represents something unnatural, unprecedented, and disastrous. Special explanations are then offered.

Apart from the fact that there has been no special behavior to require, or even permit, special explanations, the explanations that are offered most frequently—union wage policies or business price policies, depending on whose ox the commentator wishes to gore—would not account for inflation anyway. Monopolistic practices might account for prices being higher than they otherwise would be (though even this is dubious when applied to an average of prices for the whole economy) but inflation is a matter not of high prices but of rising prices. If monopolies are causing rising prices, the extent of monopoly must be rising. Although many people believe this to be true for both labor and business, statistical studies suggest that it is not true for either.

Although the Consumer Price Index has more than doubled since 1940, over seventy per cent of that rise had occurred by 1952. Beginning with 1952, the Consumer Price Index has risen an average of about one and one-quarter per cent per year. Nineteen fifty-two was the year after the "accord" between the Treasury and the Federal Reserve, terminating the pegging of interest rates on government bonds; it was also the year after the end of heavy fighting in Korea; and it was the year before the change of party in Washington.

In a period of prosperity such as has prevailed since 1941, the index has a definite upward bias, arising not only from improvements in the quality of goods, which some economists have recently recognized as causing a problem of measurement, but also from quite a number of other sources.[2] The magnitude of the upward bias cannot be appraised accurately, but it may well account for all, or even a little more than all, of the upward movement of the index since 1952. If this is true, as I personally am inclined to guess that it is, we need not take seriously the danger I mentioned earlier of a cumulative, ratchet-like price rise resulting from the apparent disappearance of major depressions.

Nevertheless, throughout the 1950's the administrations and—more important—the Federal Reserve were fighting inflation. The rise in the index due to statistical biases intensified a sensitivity to inflation that resulted partly from the great inflation of the Second World War and the lesser inflation of the Korean War,[3] but partly from the fact that some of the worst consequences of those inflations did not occur until after they were over—for example, when people retired to find that, in real value, about half of what they had set aside before the war for retirement had been confiscated for the war.

Because of this sensitivity to the dangers of inflation, the rise in the index, slight as it was, probably caused the monetary authorities to be too restrictive and too quick to curtail or limit expansion in the economy.

There are other instances in which economic policy has been misguided by statistics that were inadequate for the reliance put on them. I will turn briefly, however, to an example, unemployment statistics, in which the fault is not so much in the statistics as in the interpretations of them.

Discussions of employment are still heavily conditioned by the traumatic experience of the 1930's. For the ten years 1931 through 1940, the median rate of unemployment was eighteen per cent of the civilian labor force, and twenty-five per cent of the non-farm civilian labor force. This median of eighteen per cent was approximately the rate that prevailed in 1938 (nineteen per cent) and 1939 (seventeen per cent). The lowest rate for any year in the decade was fourteen per cent, in 1937. During the other fifty-five years of this century there has been no year in which the rate was as high as the lowest rate in the decade 1931 to 1940.

Outside that decade, the highest rate was twelve per cent in 1921, the second highest was ten per cent in 1915, and the third highest was nine per cent in 1930. In contrast to the median of eighteen per cent in the decade 1931–1940, the median for the preceding thirty years was four and four-tenths per cent, and the median for the decade 1951 to 1960 was four and two-tenths per cent. Here again we see a basic similarity, at least in broad outline, between our experience since the war and our previous experience.

Various economists have at one time or another purported to see an upward trend in unemployment figures in the past fifteen years. In general, those who see such a trend are those who favor public policies that they think would have a greater chance of adoption if there were such a trend; and those who fail to see such a trend are those who favor policies more likely to prevail if there were no such trend.

One evidence of a trend is that at the business peak of 1953 unemployment had gotten down to three per cent, at the 1957 peak to four per cent, and at the 1960 peak to five per cent. It must be noted, however, that if three unequal numbers are arranged at random, there is one chance in three that they will ascend or descend monotonically. Also, the 1953 peak was associated with war, which almost always brings abnormally full or over-employment; but if we ignore 1953, as we should for this purpose, we have only one observation on the direction of change. If we look back to the 1948 peak, we find four per cent unemployment, which destroys the monotonicity; and if we look ahead to the next peak we see that the figure is already down nearly to four per cent, also destroying the monotonicity.

Although a superficial analysis such as that just sketched can not be taken seriously, whichever conclusion is drawn from it, an analysis of the unemployment figures shows that an upward trend is built into them, at least for the time being, by the fact that they are not standardized.

The general unemployment rate may be regarded as an average of the rates prevailing for various parts of the labor force. Unemployment rates vary considerably from one part of the labor force to another: they vary, for example, with age, sex, race, education, occupation, and marital status. The relative size of the various parts of the labor force is shifting; the proportion of the labor force that is female, for example, has doubled, approximately, in this century. New entrants in the labor force are, by American definition, unemployed from the moment they enter until they get their first jobs, and the proportion of new entrants is rising.

About five years ago I had a rough calculation made of the rise that could be expected in figures on unemployment during the next five years if the actual rates of unemployment stayed exactly the same for all parts of the labor force. This calculation showed, in other words, the effect to be expected from demographic changes alone. It turned out that the over-all unemployment figure would rise nearly ten per cent in five years if unemployment rates were unchanged—that is, by about one-half of a percentage point.[4]

A standardized average—one in which the rates for the various parts of the labor force are always represented in the over-all average with weights representing a labor force of standard composition, regardless of changes in their actual representation in the labor force —would avoid the changes due not to employment changes but to demographic changes. This is not to say, however, that the unemployment figure, if there is to be a single number that is *the* unemployment figure, should be a standardized average. Whether a standardized average should be used depends on the decisions which the figure is to guide. For some purposes, changes in the aggregate number unemployed are important regardless of whether the cause is changes in unemployment rates or changes in the composition of the labor force. This is true in judging the welfare requirements or the political consequences of unemployment. For other purposes, changes in the unemployment rates per se are important and should be abstracted from demographic changes. This is true in judging policies affecting the over-all level of economic activity.

An index of unemployment—that is, a standardized average expressed as a percentage of some base figure—would have another advantage, namely to focus attention on changes in the level of unemployment instead of on the absolute level. The absolute level is an ambiguous concept, not really subject to meaningful measurement. The definition of an unemployed person used by the Bureau of the Census is a person who did not work at all during the calendar week and either was looking for work or would have been looking had he not been sick, or already expecting recall from a layoff, or convinced that no work was available in his line. This definition is certainly vulnerable to criticisms made of it from time to time, and so is the treatment of part-time workers and holders of two jobs. It seems to me unlikely, however, that other definitions can be evolved that are subject to substantially less criticism, even though the criticisms might be different.[5] Most of the objections are eliminated, or at least greatly vitiated, when attention is focused on changes in unemployment instead of on the absolute level. An index would also eliminate international comparisons, which generally are fallacious.

Unemployment statistics, like price statistics or any other statistics, are subject to error; and unemployment statistics, like price statistics, are subjected to burdens that their precision does not justify. Our unemployment statistics do include valid measures of sampling error, which our price statistics do not. But the problem of seasonal variation and the margin of sampling error are such that differences of a tenth of a percentage point do not support the conclusions sometimes based on them by publicists, politicians, and a few economists. Similarly, the figures for geographic areas or other subdivisions of the total labor force are not accurate enough for some of the important economic policies based on them, for example, aid to depressed areas, or extending the duration of unemployment benefits.

For guiding the over-all rate of economic activity, unemployment statistics need to be complemented by statistics on job vacancies. This is difficult to measure, or even to define rigorously; but substantial and significant efforts are at last under way and—judging by reports at one of the sessions of this Annual Meeting—seem to afford some prospect of success.

The moral I extract from the two foregoing examples, and others with which I will not burden you, is that, while in principle economic statistics can be of enormous value in economic policy, in practice they often lead to errors in economic policy. One kind of error arises when figures are not sufficiently accurate, and mislead policy makers who interpret them at face value. A second type of error arises when figures are accurate enough, but are interpreted erroneously. To reduce the incidence of the first kind of error, it is incumbent upon statisticians to develop better techniques, to teach better techniques to those who are or will become practitioners, and to inculcate—and themselves adhere to—the highest standards of objectivity and technical competence. To reduce the incidence of the second type of error it is incumbent upon us to extend and improve the statistical education of all economists—not just those who will be compiling and analyzing statistics, but all who will have a role in interpreting statistics and influencing action based on them. Great strides have been made and are being made in both these tasks, yet it is not clear that we are keeping up with the needs.

27

Taxes

You have asked me to discuss the effect of taxes on economic growth. I really need to say only one word to summarize the effect: *bad*. I can't just sit down and leave it at that, however, because the implied prescription—abolish all taxes—does not seem feasible right now. Two facts that we might as well face are (1) just about every tax is bad for economic growth, and (2) we are going to be paying lots of taxes as long as we live.

Talking about the relation of taxes to economic growth just now is a little bit like discussing the relationships of the British upper classes to their wives. Everybody is talking about the relationships of the British upper classes—but not just to their wives. Similarly, everybody is talking about the effects of taxes—but not just on economic growth.

On the plane this afternoon I read the text of the nationwide television speech that President Kennedy gave last night on taxes. He claimed that the tax bill he favors will stimulate economic growth. But growth isn't the only claim he made. Here's a list of 13 *other* things he said the tax bill will do:

- prevent recessions
- create prosperity
- perhaps abolish business cycles
- increase the standard of living
- reduce unemployment

Presented before the Public Expenditure Survey of Wisconsin in Milwaukee on 19 September 1963.

- reduce juvenile delinquency
- reduce racial injustice
- reduce the automation problem
- create new markets
- balance the Federal budget
- solve the balance of payments problem
- encourage freedom in other countries
- eliminate depressed areas

The President did not claim, however, that the tax bill is an economic panacea. In fact, he said explicitly: "I do not say it will solve all of our economic problems"—and the next sentence lists some spending programs needed for that.

The spending programs were listed under three headings, which he described in the following words—the third interests me the most: first, "education and job retraining"; second, "area redevelopment and youth employment"; third, "and the rest."

Taxes can be discussed from the point of view of their effects on

1. raising the revenues to pay for government expeditures
2. counteracting business cycles
3. equalizing the rich and the poor
4. rewarding merit and punishing demerit
5. promoting efficiency and growth

What you decide would be the best tax policy for one of these goals may not be the one you recommend, because it may impede another goal. For example, even if you know that all taxes are bad for growth, you won't recommend abolishing all taxes, because that would not be good for 1, 2, 3, or 4. The problem of practical tax policy is to find taxes that compromise among all these objectives and are politically acceptable as well. But that is *not* my subject tonight, thank goodness.

In order to discuss the effect of taxes on growth I shall have to discuss the causes of economic growth, then discuss the relation of taxes to those causes. But before I do that let me expand a little on my two opening remarks (1) that practically every tax is bad for growth and (2) that we are going to continue to pay lots of taxes.

Why is practically every tax bad for growth? Practically every tax is related to the amount of some economic activity—to the amount of something produced, the amount bought, the amount shipped; or else it is related to the effects of economic activities—to the income earned, or the gross amount of money received, or the value of things accumulated. About the only exception I can think of is a head-tax—a tax for just existing, regardless of your activities or their consequences.

Now, saying that a tax is related to an activity is another way of saying that how much tax you pay is related to the amount of that activity you carry on. So when you decide what activities to engage in, or how much of them to carry on, you are going to consider the tax consequences. That means, in general, that you will carry on less activity than if there weren't any taxes, since the incentive is reduced. Furthermore, the taxes on different activities will not strike you as the same—some are on activities you were already disposed to avoid, whereas others are on activities that you would carry on even with no reward. So the effect of taxes is not only to reduce your total input into the economy, but also to change your pattern of activity.

It is a *logical* possibility, of course, that the changes in the pattern of economic activity will promote growth. In fact, that logical possibility always has great appeal to economic theorists; it is a challenge to try to conjure up ingenious tax gimmicks which might improve the efficiency of the economy according to one pet criterion or another. But, for practical purposes, the effect will almost surely be adverse. Why that is so is a question to which I shall return.

My other remark, besides the one that all taxes are bad for growth, was that we are going to continue to pay lots of taxes.

Why? My answer will surprise you, and may seem unrealistic. It is because of the temper of the times—the ideology, if you like, or the current patterns of our group thought.

The explanation is not primarily in the objective facts of the times—not Russia, automation, urbanization, increased population, or all the other things so often mentioned. Some of these, especially defense, *are* reasons why government spending cannot be eliminated or reduced to nominal amounts.

But mostly these are not the things that account for the rapid growth of government spending. What accounts for a major part of that growth are the so-called welfare activities. One of the most rapidly growing fields of Federal expenditure is Federal aid to state and local governments. People can escape the compulsion, force, and confiscation of local governments by living in other localities; and they tend to do this when a local government tries to impose taxes that exceed the value the citizens place on the public services rendered. Escaping the Federal government is a more difficult matter. Much of the transfer of services to the Federal government is at bottom a device for bringing to bear compulsions that people will not tolerate when they can make direct comparisons of benefits and costs. Federal benefits seem largely costless, and Federal taxes seem largely benefitless, because the two cannot be even remotely compared.

Many of these activities financed by government could even be carried out better through private channels were it not for the general spirit of the times. The root of the great growth in government expenditures is the great growth in the political art of bidding for votes with tax dollars. As this degeneration of democracy into demagoguery proceeds, expenditures are likely to rise, not fall. And expenditures are likely to be covered primarily by taxes, not by debt or currency issue.

It may surprise you that I say expenditures are likely to be covered by taxes. The fact is, however, that from mid-1947 to mid-1961 the Federal government actually took in over $4 billion more in cash than it paid out. True, this $4 billion surplus becomes a sizable deficit if we add the past two years; but we should not expect—or want—to balance cash receipts and expenditures except over three- or four-year periods.

The reason we are likely to continue to cover expenditures by taxes is what was recently referred to as the persistence of the Puritan ethic: People just don't believe in government debt or monetary inflation. I may say I agree with them. I understand and accept the sophisticated economic arguments that national debt per se won't bankrupt the country or cause inflation. But I am also aware of the limiting effects on expenditures when costs are brought into the open and met from current income, instead of being concealed. Those who aren't aware of this should study South America—say, Brazil. Without the limit on public expenditure derived from the Puritan ethic, there would be no limit at all.

The economic climate most conducive to national economic growth is one where the many individuals in the economy are co-ordinated through free markets. When individuals enter freely into transactions with others, the result is to approximate the maximum of over-all economic efficiency. The freedom that is important is the freedom to compete, to hire away your competitors' raw materials and employees, to bid away their customers. Under such a system each unit of labor, land, equipment, and natural resources tends to go to the use where it adds most to the national output, as judged by what people will pay voluntarily for various products. The reason resources flow to their best use in a free market is that they get the highest rewards there.

But taxes distort this allocation of resources, thereby reducing economic efficiency and growth.

1. Taxes reduce total input by reducing net pay.

2. Taxes push economic activity out of the market, since market activities can be taxed easily. This impedes the division of labor and specialization on which economic growth and efficiency depend.

3. Taxes tend to reduce the competitiveness of the economy. New businesses are handicapped; for example, they have no past profits from which to claim tax refunds for the losses they often experience in their initial years, and they may not make enough in the time allowed to offset fully these initial losses. Big firms enjoy certain advantages; for example, the sum of the taxes for individual firms is higher than if all are consolidated, for then losses offset profits. Capital can be obtained cheaper by reinvestment than through markets, for paying out earnings subjects them to the personal as well as the corporate income tax.

4. Taxes tend to produce a bias against risk-taking. The progressive feature of personal taxes reduces the gains from success, but not the loss from failure. Again, equity financing is handicapped relative to debt because interest is considered a cost but dividends are not.

5. Taxes encourage overdevelopment of some industries, for example extractive industries, at the expense of others.

6. Taxes dissipate a good deal of economic potential just through the costs of compliance and the cost of legal avoidance.

7. Taxes tend to accumulate over the years a variety of special gimmicks, exemptions, etc., which with time lose whatever merit they may have had.

In conclusion, let me note that small taxes have small effects on growth. Our tax system grew up when taxes were low, and their effects on growth were neglected because they were trivial. Now, however, tax rates are high, and not only their total magnitude but also their crazy-quilt pattern hinders growth.

Two things need to be done to stimulate growth: (1) Lower taxes, and (2) reform the tax structure.

The only practical time to get reform is when lowering the total tax burden. In theory, we might suggest lowering some taxes while raising others. In practical politics, we are likely to go further: lowering all taxes, but some more than others. Real opportunities for tax reform are few and far between. We face such an opportunity now —indeed perhaps the best opportunity in the whole fifty-year history of the Federal income tax. It would be sad if that opportunity for reform were to go down the drain in a frantic scramble for tax reduction at any cost. As between the two, tax reform is likely to make a more lasting contribution to economic growth than tax reduction—if only because it is likely to be longer lived.

28

Fiscal Policy

OUR TOPIC IS FISCAL POLICY and what it can do and has done toward
eliminating the ups and downs of business activity that are called
"business cycles."

What do we mean by the term "fiscal policy"? The word *fisc*
in Latin meant the public treasury of Rome. Now the word *fiscal*
is an adjective meaning relating to the treasury of a government.
When we discuss fiscal policy we refer to the Federal Government,
not a state or local government.

Policy, a more familiar word, means a systematic course of action
or, sometimes, the principles underlying a course of action.

So, in discussing fiscal policy today, we are discussing the principles guiding the actions of the Federal treasury. More specifically,
we are talking mainly about the total amount of money taken in
by the Federal Government from taxes and other sources, and only
to a lesser extent about the exact form of these taxes and who pays
them. And we are talking mainly about the total amount of money
spent by the Federal Government but only secondarily about what
that money is spent for, or who gets it.

Most pointedly, when we discuss fiscal policy, we talk about the
relation between the Government's receipts and its expenditures—
about the surplus or deficit—rather than about the actual levels of
receipts or expenditures.

*Notes preparatory to video-taping a lecture in Pittsburgh on 26 November
1962 for the national Television series "The American Economy" of the "College of the Air."*

A surplus means, of course, that the Government takes in more than it pays out. A deficit means that it pays out more than it takes in. So, in talking about fiscal policy we talk mainly about the amount of surplus or deficit that the Federal Government experiences—or, rather, about the principles guiding the Government's actions to control its surplus or deficit.

The reason there is so much interest in the Federal surplus or deficit is, of course, that many people, and practically all economists, believe that an increase in the deficit, or a reduction in the surplus, has an expansionary effect on the economy—that is, causes an increase in employment and production, and therefore in wages and profits.

Correspondingly, it is believed by nearly all economists that a decrease in the Federal deficit, or an increase in the surplus, tends to check economic activity.

It is not our purpose today to examine the validity of this widely held theory. Let me just remark that it *is* merely a theory. It *is* just hypothesis, opinion, speculation, or plausible conjecture. It cannot be proved by logic alone, like a proposition in geometry. A logical analysis only tells us that we cannot tell what effect a deficit or surplus will have on economic activity except by looking at the facts.

And there is no factual evidence to confirm the theory. There is even a little factual evidence that casts doubt upon it. One of the foremost economists—Professor Milton Friedman of the University of Chicago—has concluded from extensive scientific studies of the factual evidence and careful analysis of the theoretical reasoning that the theory is, as he put it, "part of economic mythology, not the demonstrated conclusions of economic analysis or quantitative studies."

The fact is that we just don't know what relation there is, if any, between Government surplus or deficit and the level of economic activity. As another famous economist, Professor Frank H. Knight, likes to say, quoting a 19th Century humorist, "What you don't know doesn't hurt you—what hurts you is knowing so danged much that isn't true."

In this state of ignorance it is enlightening to review the recent history of economists' opinions on the subject. Until about 30 years ago, virtually all economists argued that the Federal budget should be in balance all the time. In the 1932 presidential campaign, at the bottom of the Great Depression, Mr. Hoover and Mr. Roosevelt outdid one another promising to reduce Government expenditure.

And when President Roosevelt took office in 1933 he actually did reduce some expenditures for a few months, even halting construction on some partly finished buildings, like the Department of Commerce Building in Washington.

It should be noted that it is impossible to balance the budget every year, or even to balance it exactly in any one year. Government receipts decline in a recession. This is especially true of income taxes, but it is also true of postal receipts, transaction and excise taxes, tariff receipts, and nearly all others. And even where tax obligations stay the same—as real estate taxes do—defaults rise. So Government receipts are bound to fall in a recession.

Expenses will not fall as much, because a reduced volume of work requires nearly as many people; defense and law enforcement needs are just as great as before; and projects and programs cannot be curtailed instantly. Welfare payments, like unemployment benefits, actually rise.

So, balancing the budget every year is impossible, even if it were desirable.

But even if it were possible, why balance by years? Why not balance every quarter, every month, every day? Even if by years, why calendar years from January through December? Why not March through February, or July through June?

What we have to mean if we are to talk sense about balancing the budget, is balancing it not in one cycle of the earth around the sun, but in one cycle of economic activity. Even here, if we try to be very precise and not fuzzy, we must have a notion of balancing on the average. Otherwise some may take balancing over the business cycle to mean balancing from one peak to the next; others, from one recession to the next.

I don't want to get bogged down in technical details here, though in a way I'm glad I got into that one—if only to illustrate the kind of precision and quasi-mathematical analysis that is required for clear thought and analysis in economics.

About 30 years ago, the universal idea that budgets should always be balanced gave way to a theory of Government spending called "pump-priming." The idea was that if Government would spend some money this would start the economy on the upgrade. Later, when pump-priming expenditures failed to eliminate the unemployment, the pump-priming theory was dropped and a new one, called "permanent stagnation," was introduced to support the same conclusion, namely, that government spending would stimulate the economy. The permanent stagnation theory held—preposterous as it seems today—that there were no more good opportunities for investment, that everything had already been invented, and that all the necessary production equipment had been built.

In the past 20 years, when the economy has been operating at a high level and growing rapidly, in complete contradiction of the permanent stagnation theory, still another theory leading to the conclusion that the Government should run a deficit has been put forth. This one is labeled "compensatory fiscal policy." It holds that Government spending should be changed to offset changes in private spending, thus keeping the total level of spending constant. This theory of compensatory fiscal policy is the one I referred to in the beginning, which virtually all economists accept today, but for which there is no real evidence.

The reason evidence is so hard to get is that the effect of Government spending depends on where the Government gets the money. If it is really additional money that was not in existence before, then we are in the field of monetary policy. The quantity of money can be increased without the Government's running a deficit or even when the Government is running a surplus. The effect of a deficit itself can only be analyzed when the stock of money is fixed. But if the stock of money does not increase, the Government's deficit comes out of somebody else's funds, and that may have a depressing effect, offsetting the expansionary effect of the deficit.

But let's examine the practical performance of Federal fiscal policy since the Second World War to see whether it has helped to stabilize the economy, according to the theory of compensatory deficits and surpluses.

What we find is that Federal spending, far from being a stabilizing force, has actually been the most unstable of all the major components of national income. It has been more unstable than spending on nondurable goods, on services, on consumer durables, on producer durables, or even on home building. And fluctuations in Federal spending have not had any systematic relation to fluctuations in the business cycle. The upshot is that Federal spending has simply been a large and very erratic factor, perturbing the economy, not stabilizing it.

One of the main reasons for this is, of course, that Federal spending has been dominated by international considerations, and also by such factors as farm policy and domestic welfare measures—urban redevelopment, aid to dependent children, depressed areas programs, etc.

For example, the largest peacetime deficit in our history was in the fiscal year 1959, which began three months after the recovery from the 1957–58 recession started. This deficit was $13.5 billion; but $6 billion—nearly half of this—was due to matters unrelated to the recession, especially defense and farm prices supports. Of the other $7.5 billion, $6 billion, or 80%, was due to automatic stabilizers, and only about $1.5 billion was due to what are called discretionary measures—measures taken especially for that recession.

This leads me into the final point I want to make: the difference between automatic stabilizers and discretionary ones. By an automatic stabilizer we mean an arrangement whereby Government receipts are tied to the level of economic activity in such a way that a decline in receipts is caused automatically when economic activity declines without any administrative or legislative body's having to exercise judgment.

The most important automatic stabilizer in the Federal budget is the corporate income tax. Corporation profits fluctuate widely with business conditions, and over half these profits are taken by the Government. So even a mild recession curtails this source of funds sharply. (Corporation profits, especially corporation-retained earnings, are an important automatic stabilizer in themselves, though not a governmental one.)

Another important automatic stabilizer is unemployment benefits. As unemployment rises, these payments rise. Similarly, the personal income tax is an important automatic stabilizer. Automatic stabilizers go into action promptly and adjust their magnitude to the magnitude of the recession. They reverse automatically as recession changes to recovery. They account for about 80% of actual compensatory changes in the Government budget. In short, they have done a pretty good job.

Discretionary changes—that is, changes in tax *rates*, not just in tax yields under given rates—or new spending programs take so long to conceive, legislate, and execute that they often come into effect only after the need for them has vanished. In other words, their effects are often perverse rather than stabilizing. (This points up the need for forecasting beyond the range now possible.) Discretionary changes or new programs have only a small effect during any one cycle. And they don't go away after the need has passed. The permanence of such temporary measures is one of the factors accounting for the steady growth of Federal expenditures.

To appreciate the practical difficulties of discretionary fiscal actions aimed at stabilizing the business cycle, let's consider the possibility of improving on the automatic action of taxes by changing the rates instead of relying on the changes in tax receipts that occur with fixed rates as incomes fluctuate.

Let's look at the recession of 1960. We now know by hindsight that May, 1960, was the peak month, and that there was a decline in economic activity from then until February, 1961, which was the low month. The June, 1960, figures were the first to show a decline, but they were not available until July or August, and the decline was small. Furthermore, not all of the figures declined. Some were up.

Even in July, the industrial production figures were above the May ones. And not until September did unemployment figures take a turn up. So it would have been November or later before a cut in tax rates would have been considered.

That it would have been November or later is supported by two facts:

1. The National Bureau of Economic Research, the source of accepted dates of business turning points, never dates a turn until at least six months after it has occurred.
2. In January, 1961, a committee appointed by the President-elect to recommend measures for dealing with the recession recommended that a tax cut not be considered until spring.

Thus, the cut in rates would almost surely not have been made until after February, 1961. We know now that recovery began then, although we did not know this until late in the summer of 1961.

This discussion has left out political considerations. With the election in November, the administration, if it had had the power, would have been under strong pressure to cut tax rates for political gain. And the opposition party would have been under even stronger pressure to promise that, if elected, it would cut tax rates.

In summary, I have made four main points:

First: Economists are almost unanimous in believing that fiscal policy can help stabilize business cycles. There is no more evidence for this opinion, however, than there is for other and contradictory opinions that have been held almost unanimously by economists in the not too distant past.

Second: The actually performance of Federal fiscal policy in the past 20 years has been a major destabilizing factor.

Third: The automatic stabilizers have performed well and are likely to continue to do so.

Fourth: Discretionary measures have performed poorly, even perversely, and are likely to continue to do so.

V

Welfare

29

Neomercantilism and the
Unmet Social Need-ers

THAT A SYMPOSIUM SHOULD BE HELD on the subject "The Private Versus the Public Sector" is a tribute to the power and pervasiveness of propaganda. For the phrase represents no specific substantive issues. Its frequent occurrence in discussions of economic and social policy reflects the susceptibility of intellectuals to hidden persuasion by phrasemakers who seek status and affluence in our society or aspire to overpower the elite through flamboyant, imaginative, entertaining, and "gliberal" glowering.[1]

When I say that no specific substantive issues are involved, I mean two things. First, the facts are not as they are portrayed. Second, even if the facts were as they are portrayed, the implications and significance of those facts would not be as represented. I would concede readily, of course, that attempts to discuss the phrase seriously should lead directly to age-old questions of great moment about relations between the individual and the state.

The discussions, written and oral, of the public versus the private sector that have drawn attention to this issue—or, rather, that have created the impression that there is a specific issue here—picture a society in which expenditures on schools, sanitation, care of the indigent, public health, highways, communication systems, churches, science, and the higher forms of art, music, drama, and literature, are in squalid decline as a consequence of serious reductions in the funds available. The facts are just the opposite. There has been tremendous acceleration in the past decade in building schools, in-

Prepared for a private symposium in Sea Island, Georgia, in September 1961.

creasing teachers' salaries, building superhighways, supporting science, aiding the needy, conquering disease, clearing slums, constructing hospitals, building churches, publishing books, performances by symphony orchestras, attendance at art galleries, and innumerable other worthwhile public activities. The growth of public expenditures since the Korean War has been great, and that growth has been almost entirely in public services—in the "welfare state," not in national security.

Part of the misrepresentation is achieved by statistical prestidigitation. I will not comment on outright prevarication and downright error, except to say that both are considerably more common than prevailing canons of good taste permit one to recognize publicly.

What is the distinction between a "public" service and a "private" service? Included in the list that I have just given, of areas in which spending is alleged to have declined but actually has increased, are a number of items that those who argue about the "public" versus "private" issue would ordinarily not class as "public." The classification is generally made, not according to whether the facilities are available to the public, but according to whether the costs are paid by the public through governmental agencies using money raised by compulsion. However, the division between "public" and "private" ought to be made on the basis of who has access to the facilities, not by reference to who paid for them. Medical research supported by the Rockefeller Foundation is in the public sector just as much as medical research supported by the National Institutes of Health. The telephone system is just as much a public facility in the United States as in England or as the post office in the United States. Care of orphans is as much a public service when provided by a private charity as when provided by a government agency.

Goods and services that are produced privately and provided to the public on a sort of "common carrier" basis—that is, to anyone who pays an announced price—are, of course, not available to those without money or credit. This is not, however, a distinction between the public and private sectors. Many private services are available on the basis of need, without regard to ability to pay; National Merit Scholarships are an example. On the other hand, many public services are available only on an ability-to-pay basis; admission to Yellowstone Park, a room at Old Faithful Inn, or delivery of a letter are examples. Public provision of goods and services need not mean public production of those goods and services; college education under the GI Bill is an example.

Those who argue that the public sector should be increased often define the public sector implicitly, not even as everything that is paid for by the government, but as only that part that is provided directly by the government through government employees using government-owned facilities. They are thus arguing in effect that the provision of certain services should be transferred from private to public hands. Churches are a good example of a public facility that in this country is provided exclusively by private funds. Even the most ardent advocates of transferring the financing and control of public facilities from private to public hands stop short of advocating this transfer with respect to churches, presumably because of an ingrained belief in separation of church and state. Private institutions of higher learning are another case in point. In this instance, perhaps the principal reason that the "unmet social need-ers" usually stop short of advocating transfer to public control is that many of the most imaginative of them are employed by private universities, and their most valuable economic freedom is academic freedom. (It should be noted, however, that public financing of political parties is occasionally advocated; and this would be more dangerous to our political liberty than public financing of religion would be to religious liberty, or than public financing of higher education is to academic freedom.)

Indeed, the "public squalor argument is," as I have said on another occasion, "simply this decade's battle cry of socialism, which —intellectually bankrupt after more than a century of seeing one after another of its arguments for socializing the *means* of production demolished—now seeks to socialize the *results* of production."

The statistical prestidigitation used to misrepresent trends in the public and private sectors is sometimes a tribute to the authors' ingenuity—or perhaps only to the assiduity with which they have absorbed Darrell Huff's masterful little book telling *How to Lie with Statistics*. Their shifts from absolute numbers to per capita figures, to percentages of one base or another, and back again, sometimes involve footwork fancier than that of Eliza crossing the ice. A particularly meretricious device is to express some public expenditure as a percentage of gross national product—or of national income or of consumer income or of consumer expenditures on tail fins—and then interpret a decline in this percentage as a decline in the public sector. Some of the more pretentious statistical efforts project astronomical growth in needs over the next decade—or generation—and then project microscopic rates of expansion, and thus display an awesome portrait of an increasing gap and impending disaster.[2]

A last resort, when the more homely statistical contrivances fail, is Russia. Comparisons with the Russians can be made in absolute terms, in per capita terms, in absolute rates of change, in percentage rates of change, in lead and lag times, and in various other ways—most of which are spiced with a generous dash of imagination and speculation as to what Russian data, and sometimes our own, really mean. A couple of summers ago the newspapers reported an impending lag in women's gymnastics. According to the reports, the proportion of Russian women engaging in organized gymnastics—gymnastics through the public sector, that is—is far greater than the proportion of American women. Worse still, the Russian lead is steadily widening. "A country that doesn't do better than we do [at training engineers, at foreign language training, at turning out steam engines, at research in entomology, at women's gymnastics, or whatever the subject may be] perhaps does not deserve to survive," is frequently the somber conclusion of these comparisons.

Another approach to the "public" versus "private" sector discussion makes little or no use of statistical or factual argument, but relies on an analysis through the apparatus of theoretical economics. This approach starts with the recognition that we have a "mixed" economy. That is, some economic functions are carried out through private enterprise, some through government, some through the family, and some through eleemosynary institutions. The proper proportions for this mix, it is implied, are to be determined on the principles of marginal analysis, just as are the proportions between the production of automobiles and the production of moving pictures. But governmental decisions are not the resultant of independent, voluntary decisions by individuals, and so are not amenable to marginal analysis. The decisions are, in fact, often of an all-or-none character, though they may be determined by the marginal voter.[3]

Even in the private sector, choices are not made among great aggregates like recreation and transportation. On the contrary, choices are made among comparatively small units that may contribute to a number of different kinds of service, as when a consumer's purchase of an automobile contributes both to his recreation and to his transportation to his work or even in his work. Furthermore, the ratios among various types of expenditures are not chosen for all people, but are simply the results of aggregating individual choices.

Another feature of analytical approaches to the public-sector vs. private-sector discussion is that they frequently profess, and apparently with pride, to be "pragmatic." It is seldom clear what "pragmatic" means in this context. Often it seems to mean not that the test of a policy is how it works, but whether it can be "put across." Also, the label "pragmatism" often seems to conceal neglect of long-run or indirect consequences, for analysis of these is necessarily theoretical.

De Tocqueville pointed out in 1840 that democracy in America seems to cause the pressures to solve a problem to mount as the problem itself dwindles. He applied this particularly to inequality:

> The hatred which men bear to privilege increases in proportion as privileges become fewer and less considerable, so that democratic passions would seem to burn most fiercely just when they have least fuel. I have already given the reason of this phenomenon. When all conditions are unequal, no inequality is so great as to offend the eye; whereas the slightest dissimilarity is odious in the midst of general uniformity: the more complete this uniformity is, the more insupportable does the sight of such a difference become. Hence it is natural that the love of equality should constantly increase together with equality itself, and that it should grow by what it feeds on.[4]

This burning-most-fiercely-when-the-fuel-is-least seems to operate in much of our social spending on welfare measures. Only after substantial success was beginning to be achieved in providing retirement income, through individual insurance and private pension plans, did pressure for public provision of retirement income build up to the point of compulsory federal provision of funds for old age. As the problem of medical care for the aged has steadily diminished, partly because of improved health of the aged, partly because of higher per capita income, which has made it easier for people to provide their own resources for old age and to care for their aged relatives, and partly because of the wide increase in organized saving for retirement, pressure for some form of governmental program has increased. Similarly, in the case of race relations, only after rapid progress finally began to occur through private means did serious pressures grow for governmental compulsion. There are many other examples of the same kind.

De Tocqueville makes two other remarks that are particularly helpful in understanding the current pressures for expanding collective action and diminishing individual action:

> As conditions of men become equal amongst a people, individuals seem of less, and society of greater importance; or rather, every citizen, being assimilated to all the rest, is lost in the crowd, and nothing stands conspicuous but the great and imposing image of the people at large. This naturally gives the men of democratic periods a lofty opinion of the privileges of society, and a very humble notion of the rights of individuals; they are ready to admit that the interests of the former are everything, and those of the latter nothing. They are willing to acknowledge that the power which represents the community has far more information and wisdom than any of the members of that community; and that it is the duty, as well as the right, of that power, to guide as well as govern each private citizen.[5]
>
> Every central power, which follows its natural tendencies, courts and encourages the principle of equality; for equality singularly facilitates, extends, and secures the influence of a central power.
>
> In like manner, it may be said that every central government worships uniformity: uniformity relieves it from inquiry into an infinity of details, which must be attended to if rules have to be adapted to different men, instead of indiscriminately subjecting all men to the same rule.... The faults of the government are pardoned for the sake of its tastes; public confidence is only reluctantly withdrawn in the midst even of its excesses and its errors; and it is restored at the first call.[6]

In addition to the points made by De Tocqueville, two other factors seem to me to contribute to the growth of collective action.

The first of these is failure to diagnose a problem and failure to analyze the consequences of a proposed solution, or else wrong diagnosis and wrong analysis. The provision of retirement income through a federal social security program, for example, began shortly after the Great Depression, and it may well be that hardships of the aged that were in fact due to that depression were attributed to inadequate provision for old age. Similarly, since the Korean War, financial hardships entailed in medical care for the aged are in fact due largely to the transitory inflations of the Second World War and the Korean War which, in effect, confiscated large fractions of the savings of many who are now retired; but the hardships (or alleged hardships) are misdiagnosed as due to persistent forces that will continue to affect all retired people.

Instead of myself discussing the neglect of long-run consequences, I should like to quote from the Federal Reserve Bank of Chicago's *Business Conditions* bulletin of June, 1961. Under the title "Depressed Areas—Some Lessons from the Past," the bulletin says:

> In the course of wide debate, economists and public policy makers have often overlooked the fact that depressed areas have been a recurring aspect of the economic development of this country. American history includes many accounts of the rise and fall of communities and whole regions owing to changes in technology, exploitation and exhaustion of natural resources, changes in demand and the migration of industry to other parts of the country in response to the pull of new markets—the same factors cited as contributing to chronic unemployment in today's depressed areas. . . .
>
> There is, of course, an inherent danger that some attempts at solving the problem may backfire and only prolong the process of readjustment as well as contribute to an inefficient allocation of the nation's resources. . . .
>
> Thus, the experience of economic readjustment to the decline of the lumbering industry in the northern counties of the Lake states has emphasized . . . that there is always the risk that some attempts to solve the problem of depressed areas may not work at all and may only complicate and delay the adjustment process. Witness the collapse of the campaign to promote farming on the cutover lands despite vigorous backing from the state governments, the railroads, lumber companies, local businessmen and even "experts" from the agricultural colleges.

I have the impression that good examples could be drawn from European history of the great costs that may be incurred by neglecting long-run consequences when adopting policies that seem to provide some hope of temporary relief of symptoms. For the United States, it is probably not a great distortion to say that most of the worst economic problems that we face today have been created by the long-run ill effects of policies adopted in the past to deal with some much smaller problem.

The other force that I think must be added to De Tocqueville's in explaining the contemporary movement toward larger federal spending, for which the "unmet social needs" argument has provided buttressing, is a rather profound change in our political processes since his day. The expansion of the federal government's welfare activities has led to a great increase in the importance of pressure groups. Many of the programs for expansion of the public sector get their effective backing, not from those who would receive the service, but from those who would sell it to the government. While this is strikingly true in the case of education, medicine may seem to be a counterexample; but in the case of medicine, the opposition to expanded government activity comes from those who are now selling the service and who visualize others selling it or themselves selling it on less advantageous terms if the government expands its activity.

As a matter of fact, as government welfare programs have fallen more and more under the control of pressure groups, the real problems have tended to be neglected. The consideration of depressed-areas relief illustrates this. There is not *a* depressed-areas problem, but many different problems, with varied causes. Some of the most serious of these problems are in the so-called "hillbilly" areas—the mountain regions of certain Southern and border states. These groups for the most part lack sufficient voting strength to attract any substantial federal funds. Federal funds flow instead to areas where breakdown of law and order, lack of even justice in the courts and administrative agencies, demoralization of the labor force, and exploitation by state and local governments have driven industry away. Federal funds tend to subsidize and perpetuate the causes of the difficulty. In the "hillbilly" areas, on the other hand, there would be some prospect for success of efforts to improve the level of education and skills, knowledge about opportunities elsewhere, and mobility.

In conclusion, let me remark that it is perhaps a mistake to call the position of the "unmet social need-ers" socialism, even though their position represents, as I pointed out earlier, a gradual evolution from the socialist position of a century ago and is its contemporary counterpart in the United States. Socialism has traditionally been associated with government ownership of land and capital. The modern movement would continue a large measure of private ownership and private enterprise, but seeks to elaborate and to extend control of private activities and to confiscate a large and growing part of private products. This is carried on partly in the name of unmet social needs at home, and partly in the name of national security. It is in many respects on all fours with mercantilism, the economic policy followed by England and other European countries in the seventeenth and eighteenth centuries, which was a major cause of the American Revolution. Indeed, the movement to enlarge the "public sector" represents perhaps the most powerful reactionary force that has arisen since the departure of mercantilism from this country with the adoption of the Constitution in 1789.[7]

30

Political Entrepreneurship
and the Welfare Explosion

REMARKABLE AS IS THE SPEED at which the prosperity and well-being of Americans are growing, this rate of growth is far surpassed by the rate of growth of governmental "welfare" and "antipoverty" programs.

Expenditures on social welfare programs designed to deal with individual welfare (not including such community services as city planning and urban renewal, parks, recreation, water and sewer works, and so forth) increased by 14 percent from 1964–65 to 1965–66 and by another 14 percent from 1965–66 to 1966–67. Since the Second World War such expenditures have grown roughly 10 percent per year.[1]

For government spending on welfare to increase when income per capita is increasing would seem natural *if* nongovernmental spending on welfare were declining, or if inequality among families were increasing; but in each instance the facts are the opposite: Private charity is increasing, and inequality is decreasing. Even if private charity were falling and inequality were rising, their rates of change would have to be very sharp indeed to offset the dramatic rise in real income per capita, which has doubled approximately every generation for at least a century.

Poverty has been diminishing rapidly by any reasonable definition of poverty except one that defines the poor as those in the lowest *x* percent of the income distribution. A definition of that sort—the

Presented before the American Enterprise Institute for Public Policy Research in Washington, D.C., on 1 March 1968.

bottom third, for example, or the bottom tenth—seems to be implicit in much public discussion of poverty. That definition, as far as I can see, has only one merit—that the growing number of people who are growing prosperous in the poverty game need not fear a reduction in the market for their services.

What then are some explanations of this paradox, that welfare expenditures are rising, perhaps even at an accelerating rate, while poverty is diminishing?

One possible reason why governmental welfare activities are increasing as poverty is declining is that because of urbanization the poor now are more dependent on governments than formerly. In a rural area there are, for example, opportunities for the poor to produce income in kind, by repairing their houses, foraging for their fuel, raising their food, or even carrying their water. In a rural and less mobile society there may be more mutual aid among relatives, friends, fellow workers, church members, neighbors, and other groups.

Another explanation may be an increased awareness of what economists call "neighborhood effects." Just as a contagious disease is dangerous to others than the immediate sufferers, or an unsightly junkyard causes displeasure to nearby residents, or a smoking chimney bothers people besides those who own it, so poverty may impose hardship on others than the poor. People may fear that the poor will commit crimes, riot, vote foolishly, spread disease, or otherwise be objectionable. Thus it may be argued that, although poverty is declining, our awareness of its direct harm to us has grown, so we are more willing than formerly to pay to eliminate it. This increased liking for welfare activities is reinforced by increased ability, as incomes rise, to pay for what we like.

Some might argue that consciences are more refined today, so people recognize more strongly their moral obligations to their fellow human beings in misfortune. Others might argue that consciences are blunter today, so people have fewer compunctions about using force to impose their views of charity or self-interest on others. Either argument could help explain growth in government welfare expenditures even when poverty is diminishing.

The foregoing rationalization of what has happened—and no doubt many more could be and have been contrived—reflect a rationalistic approach to political economy that is more in vogue among economists than among political scientists. Many political scientists would analyze the situation in terms of power and apply

analyses like the foregoing to groups within the power structure
rather than to the whole society.

More than half a century ago, discussing the effects of universal
suffrage in England, Dicey wrote:

> It has, in the first place, made known and called attention to the
> real or supposed wishes or wants of the poorer electors.
>
> It has, in the second place, increased the power of any well or-
> ganised Parliamentary faction or group, which is wholly devoted to
> the attainment of some definite political or social object, whether
> the object be the passing of socialistic legislation or the obtaining
> of Parliamentary votes for women. For such a group may certainly
> come to command a vote in Parliament sufficient to determine
> which of the two leading parties, say, speaking broadly, of Con-
> servative or Radicals, shall hold office. In such circumstances one
> of these two parties is almost certain to form an alliance with a
> faction strong enough to decide the result of the great party game.
> Hence it may well happen that socialists may for a time obtain the
> active aid, and to a certain extent the sympathy, of a great party
> whose members have no natural inclination towards socialism.
> This possible tyranny of minorities is a phenomenon which was
> hardly recognized either by the statesmen or by the thinkers of
> 1860 or 1870, but it is a fact to which in the twentieth century no
> reasonable man can shut his eyes.
>
> The course of events, in the third place, and above all the com-
> petition for office which is the bane of the party system, have at last
> revealed to the electorate the extent of their power, and has taught
> them that political authority can easily be used for the immediate
> advantage, not of the country, but of a class. Collectivism or
> socialism promises unlimited benefits to the poor. Voters who are
> poor, naturally enough adopt some form of socialism.[2]

Certainly any serious attempts to analyze contemporary American welfare measures must concentrate on politics. A major part
of the explanation for the welfare explosion of the past four years
surely lies in the directions pointed out by Dicey fifty-four years ago.
During the 1950s Negro citizens began to vote in appreciable numbers for the first time since the 1870s. The two civil rights bills of
the Eisenhower Administration, though their provisions regarding
voting were seriously weakened in Congress before the bill was
enacted,[3] nevertheless were followed by a rapid increase in the proportion of southern Negroes voting. An even more important factor
in the enfranchisement of Negroes was their large migration to the
north, which began during the Second World War. In the north they

encountered fewer obstacles to voting and soon became one of the blocs with which northern politicians reckoned in considering how hard to press for civil rights legislation—first within the northern states, then in Congress.

With Negroes enfranchised to a significant and growing degree and prepared to vote as a bloc on measures supposed to benefit Negroes (as the "poor," the "disadvantaged," "minority groups," or whatever term might be used), the political forces described by Dicey have operated strongly.

Dicey's suggestion that welfare measures result from the votes of the poor may not have been correct for the United States before the recent enfranchisement of Negroes. Most of the welfare measures enacted in the past—and some serious students of the subject say *all* such programs—have the actual effects of injuring the poor but helping the middle classes. Thus, the farm program helps land owners, not farm laborers or tenant farmers; the minimum wage law helps skilled labor but hurts unskilled labor; social security pensions benefit whites more than Negroes (because whites live longer on the average), but cost Negroes more (because they begin to work and therefore to pay social security taxes, younger and retire older); urban redevelopment has aggravated the housing problem of the poor but helped middle- and even high-income groups.

Now it is possible, of course, that the middle class supported these laws out of ignorance and misunderstanding, thinking that their only effect was to help the poor and not realizing that they actually helped the middle class. At least as plausible a possibility,[4] however, is that support for these measures is not independent of the fact that in practice their principal effects are to provide benefits to the large middle class at the expense of the poor, particularly by handicapping them in the market place, and to some extent at the expense of high-income taxpayers. Still another consideration is that, as Milton Friedman points out in relation to public housing, "the general interest that motivated many to favor instituting the program is diffuse and transitory. Once the program was adopted, it was bound to be dominated by the special interest groups that it could serve."[5]

Another possible explanation of a political character for the welfare explosion of the past four years, besides the Negro enfranchisement, lies in the nature of American political parties.

There really is no such thing in our country as a national party in the sense that British, French, German, Scandinavian, Canadian, and Australian parties are national, because there is no effective party discipline here. The Democratic and Republican parties somewhat resemble the Howard Johnson, Holiday Inn, TraveLodge, and other systems of motels: They are franchise operations which license one or another group in various states, counties, and cities to use the name. Indeed, Howard Johnson has rather more control over its franchise operators than do the national Republican and Democratic parties over their local organizations; a motel would lose its franchise and the right to the name if it were to follow a policy deviating in important respects from the national policy.

A national party is not without influence on its local organizations, but its influence works mostly through offering such inducements as jobs on the public payroll, federal funds for local purposes, or consideration for constituents in their relations with federal agencies. The national party can sometimes be outbid by other individuals or organizations with more compelling inducements, especially substantial influence in local elections.

The national parties are in large measure federations of strong local organizations, and these local organizations are able, when they are sufficiently concerned, to bring about exceptions to, or even reversals in, national policies which they find offensive. The relation is not unlike that between the monarch and his barons in the days of feudalism.

The poverty programs of the past three years could strengthen the hand of the monarch at the expense of the barons. That is, they could bring about a truly national political party, capable of taking national stands and holding them against the opposition of local party "machines." Local machines are based, of course, on the ability to deliver votes. That ability is based in large part on their ability to deliver, or appear to deliver, to their voters the services those voters want. Before the first world war, it is said, the "boss" in a poor district ("poor" then meant "immigrant") kept track of his constituents' problems. When they were unemployed, he saw that they got a sack of potatoes. When one of the children got into trouble with the truant officer, he saw that the matter was minimized. When a scholarship was awarded by a public university, he visited the family to deliver the good tidings and the first congratulations. In short, he rendered useful personal services to his constituents, and they heeded his advice about voting.

The poverty program has brought about a great opportunity to create for the first time a truly national party, independent of local party bosses. Its programs are being administered—or, to put it another way, its large number of well-paid positions are being filled—by a national organization controlled in Washington rather than by officials of local governments or local party organizations. Correspondingly, its benefits are being conferred directly on the poor through organizations reporting to Washington, not through organizations controlled by the local political apparatus. Thus, it is delivering the services that should win the gratitude of the voters. The implications of this are not lost on local politicians. Hence the "war on poverty" has been accompanied by a noisy and bitter war among politicians in almost every city, with the local "bosses" arrayed against what they consider "usurpers" backed by Washington.

Doubtless all the forces and tendencies so far described have played roles of varying magnitudes in one or another welfare program. No one of them is the key to understanding all programs. Doubtless, too, there are welfare programs that have not been influenced in any significant degree by any of the forces I have described.

I propose to devote most of the rest of this essay to another force, one which I shall call *political entrepreneurship*.[6] I do not think that political entrepreneurship is the full explanation of government welfare activities, or that it plays a role in all of them. I do think that it is an important factor in many programs, and that some of the phenomena associated with it are interesting and important.

Politicians, I suggest, do not simply respond to needs and desires expressed by voters, weighing the support to be gained or lost by advancing one cause or another. They do that, of course, just as businessmen do it in deciding which consumer demands to serve. But just as business entrepreneurs also seek new products and services that will please consumers, even though consumers have not thought of the products themselves and therefore are not actively seeking them, so political entrepreneurs actively seek new programs to put before the public, even though no appreciable part of the public is demanding them.

Unlike the businessman, however, the politician almost never can introduce a truly new program. The businessman who is convinced that the public will find electric forks desirable in conjunction with electric carving knives does not have to persuade the public of the merits of electric forks in order to be allowed to offer them. If he believes in electric forks, he makes the investment to produce and distribute them. Then, by demonstrations, advertising, or free samples, he directs attention to the forks. People who thought the idea was silly—as many thought silly the idea of an electric knife, an electric toothbrush, an electric can opener, an electric blanket, an electric razor, an electric pencil sharpener, an electric wastebasket, or an electric letter opener—may, in fact, find merit in an electric fork when they actually try one, just as many have with the other gadgets I mentioned. If they do find merit in the new product, *they* are better off because of the entrepreneur's innovation, and *he* is better off because of his profits from their patronage. If the public does not buy the gadget, the public has lost nothing, but the entrepreneur has lost his investment—and probably his job.

The political entrepreneur cannot bring his constituents a truly new program because he has to persuade them before he can give them a demonstration. He has to persuade his clients to take the risk that a business entrepreneur would take. If what the political entrepreneur offers is something that his constituents have not experienced before, it is exceedingly hard to convince a sufficient number to agree to assigning government money to the project. Thus, for the business enterpreneur the test of a new product is not whether the public is actively seeking it but whether, when it is actually introduced, the public will prize it enough to confer their support on the man or firm who made the innovation. For the political entrepreneur, the test is whether the proposal sounds attractive enough *in advance* to win the public's support for the man or party who proposes the innovation.

Now the kind of innovation that meets the test of the political entrepreneur usually is not one that promises the voters a new service with which they are unfamiliar, but one which brings them a service with which they are already familiar. The innovations of political entrepreneurs consist, therefore, not in new services to the public, but in large part of offers to have the government pay costs that the voters are now paying personally for existing services.

The government's assumption of responsibility for education in the nineteenth century seems to have been a good example of the way in which a government welfare program may simply transfer costs from an individual to a collective basis without increasing appreciably the amount of the service. This was true both in England and the United States.

In 1833, when the government of England first began to subsidize schools, at least two-thirds of the youth of the working class were literate, and the school population had doubled in a decade—although until then the government had deliberately hindered the spread of literacy to the "lower orders" because it feared the consequences of printed propaganda. By the time of the Education Act of 1870, which first introduced freedom from fees and compulsion to attend, nearly all young people were literate. This literacy had been obtained mostly in schools which charged fees. James Mill wrote in 1813:

> From observation and inquiry assiduously directed to that object, we can ourselves speak decidedly as to the rapid progress which the love of education is making among the lower orders in England. Even around London, in a circle of fifty miles radius, which is far from the most instructed and virtuous part of the kingdom, there is hardly a village that has not something of a school; and not many children of either sex who are not taught more or less, reading and writing. We have met with families in which, for weeks together, not an article of sustenance but potatoes had been used; yet for every child the hard-earned sum was provided to send them to school.

Thus, public education in England affords an illustration of government welfare services which did not result in new or improved services, but simply transferred the cost from individuals to the government. In England, since the tax system was regressive, there were not even the benefits of redistributing the costs to those best able to pay.[7]

It seems to have been true in the United States also that the government began to provide "free" schooling only after schooling had become nearly universal.

In New York, a commission appointed in 1811 to consider establishing Common Schools found that schooling was already widespread except in thinly populated areas. "In populous cities, and the parts of the country thickly settled," the commission reported, "schools are generally established by individual exertion." The commission recommended state subsidies to schools, but curiously—curiously, that is, if one thinks in terms of needs for public assistance and not in terms of votes—granted the subsidies uniformly on a per capita basis, rather than giving special help to sparsely populated areas.

By 1821, schooling was all but universal—90 percent of all children between five and sixteen years of age were in school. While the schools were now subsidized, education was free only to those who could not afford to pay. Not until 1867 was schooling made free, and not until 1874 was it made compulsory. Both of these steps were taken at the instigation of teachers, not parents.[8]

Another example of a welfare measure whose principal effect has been to transfer costs from individuals to the government, rather than to bring new services that people were not previously receiving, is the recent federal program to provide medical care for the elderly.

After the passage of the medicare bill and as its effective date approached, a state of near panic began to infect many hospital administrators. Nightmares were conjured up of hordes of the elderly besieging hospitals, far beyond their capacity. That nothing of the kind would occur could have been foreseen from several studies made in the 1950s of the number of older people needing but not receiving medical care.

Perhaps the best of these studies was the one done in 1957 by the National Opinion Research Center at the University of Chicago. It found that:

> About one person in twenty in the older population [aged sixty-five years or older] reported that he was doing without needed medical care because he lacked money for such care. . . .
> In general, the "very sick" group in the older population seemed the least able to pay for medical care. Many of these persons were already receiving substantial free care and services.[9]

This study was consistent with several others showing that surprisingly few of the elderly lacked medical care for financial reasons. So medicare's removal of financial barriers should not have been expected to create a sudden rush. In time, no doubt, the fact that medical care is nearly free will, as with all commodities and services, change people's notions of how much they need—contrast the amounts of water people "need" when it is essentially free with their need when it is expensive in money or effort.

It is interesting to note that when medicaid was enacted a considerable majority of the population already had private health insurance. By the end of 1959 the proportion for civilians was 72 percent and growing rapidly, having almost doubled in the preceding decade and quadrupled in the preceding 15 years.[10]

The task of the political entrepreneur, then, is to identify services which are being purchased by substantial and identifiable blocs of his electorate and to devise means by which the cost of these services will be transferred to the public. Successful innovation lies not in getting something done that was not being done before, but in transferring the costs to the public at large. Only if fairly large numbers of voters are already paying for the service will the offer to relieve them of the cost be likely to influence their votes.

While relieving the beneficiary of a service of its cost will ordinarily be welcome, most of the other consequences of political entrepreneurship are likely to be less welcome.

Among the consequences are that genuine hardship cases—people who are helpless, who have no one at all to whom they can turn, who are therefore utterly dependent on social welfare—may be neglected. These people, the desperately poor, usually are not sufficiently numerous to carry influence through their own votes, and they do not purchase the services for which the political entrepreneur offers to have the government pay the bills. While they can share in these services once the government assumes the bill, such services are not the ones they need the most. Political enterpreneurs, for example, do not—at least they do not yet—bid for votes by offering to have the government pay family food bills. (Government programs of food distribution are, for the most part, undertaken for the benefit of food producers.)

Appalachia, and "hill-billy" country in general, was a case in point—at least until the lightning of Washington's attention happened to strike it a few years ago.

A responsible group of physicians who recently visited Mississippi reported (and in reasonably calm language, considering the substance of the report) seeing children literally starving: drinking contaminated water; eating one meal a day, and that meal inadequate in vitamins, minerals, and proteins; suffering from chronic sores and chronic diarrhea; and receiving nothing from the government or from anyone else. "Malnutrition is not quite what we found," they remarked, "the boys and girls we saw were hungry—weak, in pain, sick; their lives are being shortened; they are, in fact, visibly and predictably losing their health, their energy, their spirits. They are suffering from hunger and disease and directly or indirectly they are dying from them—which is exactly what 'starvation' means."[11]

"Our antipoverty programs have bypassed the rural poor. Rural poverty is not as apparent as urban poverty. The rural poor, especially the white rural poor, are not well organized, and have few spokesmen for bringing the nation's attention to their problems. . . . Rural people have been shortchanged in public programs."[12] I would add to that that Indians have been shortchanged too. George Wallace, the former governor of Alabama, is reported to have taken satisfaction in pointing out, when questioned at the University of Minnesota in 1964 about the poverty of Negroes in his state, that he had never seen Negroes in Alabama in as dire poverty as the Indians he had seen in Minnesota—adding that the condition of the Alabama Negroes is being ameliorated faster than that of the Minnesota Indians.

Even residents of the most prosperous and enlightened cities are likely to have their civic pride dampened by finding out what provision their city makes for the widows and children of policemen and firemen killed in line of duty. The kind of people who populate a city's prisons—mostly alcoholics and derelicts, not rapists, arsonists, robbers, or murderers—and the treatment they receive will further depress civic pride.[13] So will the treatment of the senile and the insane:

> Comfortless, nameless, hopeless save
> In the dark prospect of the yawning grave.[14]

Those who advocate having the government provide a service which people have been providing for themselves, such as education or medical care, often assume that the result will be a substantial increase in total expenditures on the service. The government, having access to compulsion, can easily obtain huge sums quickly for any purpose it chooses, and it appears far easier to obtain funds that way than through millions of individuals, each evaluating the worth of the service to himself in comparison with other uses for his limited income.

In fact, however, the consequence of the government's participating heavily in a welfare program often is a sharp deceleration in the rate of growth of total spending on the service.

Usually, of course, total expenditure continues to grow, so there is a certain amount of conjecture in determining whether it grew as fast as it would have without the government take-over. The data for personal health care in the United States after the introduction of medicare and medicaid are, however, so striking as to verge on the incredible. For the fiscal year 1966–67, total per capita expenditures (public and private), measured in constant dollars, failed for the first time since the depth of the Great Depression, thirty-five years ago, to register an appreciable gain. Public expenditures made their biggest recorded jump by far, nearly 50 percent or about $4 billion. Private expenditures fell by \$3.3 billion, although they had been doubling (in current dollars) approximately every decade for the previous thirty years (a 7 percent annual rate of growth). The total in current dollars increased just enough to match the increase in population and prices, so that the per capita total, in constant dollars, showed essentially no increase. The previous year there was a rise of about 5 percent, a rate fairly typical of the past decade or longer.[15]

For education, E. G. West gives data and analyses suggesting strongly that growth in total expenditures, in both England and New York, was substantially decelerated after the government began to provide education free, and that the total amounts now being spent are considerably below what they would have been if the governments had provided only for those unable to pay.

After analyzing the experience of the National Health Service in Great Britain, D. S. Lees concludes that, "far from being extravagant, expenditure on NHS has been less than consumers would probably have chosen to spend in a free market. The record of hospital building in particular has been deplorable."[16]

One of the principal reasons why total spending on a service is less under a government welfare program than when individuals pay for the service themselves (the government providing only for the needy) relates to the economics of consumer choice. A second principal reason relates to the politics of collective choice.

Suppose that there is no public school system, and that each family has one child in school and is paying tuition of \$500 per year. Now suppose a public school is started. The public school charges no tuition, but does levy additional taxes of \$500 per year on each family. Obviously the change has made no practical difference.

(More realistic assumptions—in particular, varying the number of children and hence the tuition from family to family when the school is private, and varying the amount of additional taxes from one family to another when the school becomes public—would be appropriate for some problems but are needless complications for the point being made here.)

As time goes by, however, the shift from tuition to taxation begins to make a difference. Consumer incomes rise—in the United States they double every generation. Education, also, rises in value. Both factors cause families to wish to improve the quality of their children's education, perhaps, to a level costing \$600. Since the public schools are providing a \$500 education, a family may consider transferring its child to a private school charging $600. This family finds, however, that it cannot make the $100 increase, but must make a $600 increase, to an expenditure level of $1,100, because it will still have to pay the $500 tax even if its child no longer attends the public school.

Small, manageable increments in expenditures on education are thus closed. All families but a few of the richest will have to leave their children in the public school. If the public school were to stand pat permanently on its $500 education, then after a long enough time a considerable number of families would be able to manage the total outlay of $1,100.

Probably, however, the public school will not have stood pat at the $500 level. Parents who desire $600 educations, but are precluded from sending their children to $600 private schools because their total cost would then be $1,100, will try to get the public school to improve its level to $600.

If a sufficient number of parents desire this, and desire it enough so that it becomes the dominating factor in their voting, some increase will be obtained. If a majority of voters desire the $100 increase *and* are prepared to make this the exclusive consideration in their voting, the full $100 increase will be obtained. Except under such extreme conditions, the increase is almost sure to be less.

Many voters who desire the increase of $100 in expenditures per pupil will, in practical politics, oppose a $100 increase in taxes. They realize that only a small part of a $100 increase in taxes will go to schools, the rest being divided among public purposes of greater interest to others.

Migration from large cities to their suburbs is in some instances motivated partly by desires to focus tax dollars more nearly the way they could be focused through consumer choice in the market. People paying taxes of a few hundred dollars in the city may move to a suburb where their taxes are five times as high, because city taxes plus tuition at a private school exceed taxes in a suburb where public schools are as good as the private ones in the city. Suburbs may even specialize: some have excellent schools, while others provide for the retired.

The services chosen by political entrepreneurs for handling by the government tend to be those on which the expenditures of individuals are rising rapidly. The successful political entrepreneur is the one who first senses what services have grown to the point where offering to have the government pay the bills will be attractive to voters. This point is likely to come after a substantial number is obtaining the service, but while expenditures on it are still growing fast enough for people to have problems in adapting their budgets. Thus, just when expenditures are growing rapidly under consumer choice, a good political entrepreneur is likely to get them transferred to the machinery of collective choice, and that machinery brings about a slowdown in the rate of growth.

If the level of government expenditures on a service falls, under the politics of collective choice, too far behind the level that would prevail under the economics of individual choice, an entire new private system may grow up.

A fascinating example of this is occurring in England, where private health insurance is growing rapidly because the services rendered by the National Health Service fall so far short of what many people want and can afford through insurance. The British United Provident Association now provides protection something like that of Blue Cross in America for hospital bills and Blue Shield for doctors' bills.[17] About 1,500,000 people are covered, and the number is growing about 10 percent per year. We may conjecture that some day enough people will be spending enough money on this service to attract the eye of an alert political entrepreneur, who will offer to have the government pay the premiums.

An interesting example in some American cities is the rapid growth of private patrol services supplementing the public police. For Minneapolis and St. Paul, one informal estimate is that at least 300 patrolmen and guards (not including private detectives and in-side security staffs) from four private firms provide supplemental police services to residential and business subscribers. The public police forces number 1,400 to 1,500. Thus the private effort equals about 20 percent of the public.

In discussing the development of public schools in New York I mentioned that the instigation for making education free and compulsory came from teachers, not parents. This reflects the principle that

> . . . those individuals who work in a service which is provided by government can afford to bring greater than average influence to bear upon government policy since their incomes will be particularly responsive to it. In contrast, the consumers, having interests which are spread over many products and services, cannot so afford to buy influence over the supply of only one of them. In particular, they will not be able to afford the information necessary to evalu-

ate the full implications of government policy such as, for example, the true incidence of taxation necessary to pay for "free" services or the eventual effects of a "free" service upon consumer choices.[18]

Generally, as a service is taken over by the government, it is increasingly responsive to the interests of the professionals who staff it, and decreasingly responsive to the preferences of the clients. This tendency is likely to be accentuated by the present growth of unions of government employees.

Thus, while the desire to shift the cost of services may make voters responsive to offers by political entrepreneurs, subsequent developments are likely to lead to dissatisfaction with the service: There is not as much of it as the public would be willing to pay for, and it is run with major emphasis on pleasing the professionals who run it instead of pleasing the clients who use it.

Summary and Conclusion

One of the ways politicians compete for votes is by offering to have the government provide new services. For an offer of a new service to have substantial electoral impact, the service ordinarily must be one that a large number of voters is familiar with, and in fact already use. The most effective innovations for a political entrepreneur to offer, therefore, are those whose effect is to transfer from individuals to the government the costs of services which are already in existence, not to alter appreciably the amount of the service reaching the people. There may be, to be sure, some shifting among individuals in the ultimate incidence of the cost, but these shifts are at least as likely to be to the disadvantage of the poor as to be to their advantage.

An important result of transferring a service from the economics of individual choice to the politics of collective choice is to reduce the total amount of resources devoted to the service—that is, to reduce it below what it would have been under individual choice. One reason for this is that, under collective choice, consumers ordinarily find it difficult to make small, continuous upward changes in the amounts they spend on the service, because they are not relieved of the taxes they pay for the public service when they replace it with a more expensive service. Another reason is that the public may— quite rationally—resist the tax increases necessary to support increases in the particular services they want, because they know that the increases would be spent only to a small extent on those particular services.

Other ways in which the public is likely to be disappointed in the consequences of collectivizing a service arise from the professionalization of the service, which leads to its being run according to the notions and interests of the employees, and from the deterioration in quality that results when the demands for the service outrun the funds to support it.

With the passage of time, if the amounts people would be willing to spend individually on the service greatly exceed the amounts being provided collectively, private systems may begin to flourish again. The depressing effect on individual expenditures of the taxes being paid for the collective service becomes less controlling as incomes rise or the value of the service rises. The collective service may then become a second-class service largely confined to the poor.

A basic implication of my remarks is to reject the whole framework in which most public discussion of welfare measures is set. Even though it is known that public opinion data have been used in computers to help a presidential candidate decide what stands to take, the public—including Washington journalists who pride themselves on their sophistication—continues to discuss issues largely in rationalistic and philosophical terms. If a bill is introduced in Congress, and if the preamble to the bill, the speeches of its advocates, and the propaganda of the executive agencies which would administer it all say there is a dire need that is not being met, that the bill would meet the need, and that those who oppose the bill are evil enemies of the poor and selfish friends of the rich, then the whole public discussion runs in these terms. The journalists let the issues be set for them in these terms, and they write about it for the public in these terms. They treat alike those who oppose the bill because they favor its stated objectives and those who oppose the bill because they oppose its stated objectives.

My suggestion is that a very different framework—call it "realistic" if you agree with it, "cynical" if you do not—is necessary to understand the adoption, financing, and operation of welfare programs. This framework includes entrepreneurial politics, which I have emphasized here. It also includes the theory of majoritarian democracy, the operations of legislative bodies and their committees, and other aspects of "the new political science." And finally it includes many facets that I have not touched on—for example, the use of "pseudo-events" to manipulate the public opinion that will affect the calculations of political entrepreneurs. Rejection of the old framework is, I think, bound to distress those who realize how many of their pet beliefs and methods of approach to issues of public policy will be left stranded by the rejection.

31

Social Security

FEW PEOPLE UNDERSTAND that Social Security is on a pay-as-you-go basis. Most people think that the taxes paid by them and their employers, for which the government uses the euphemism "contributions," result in funds being accumulated to their individual accounts, from which their benefits eventually will be paid. In fact, the so-called contributions are a special tax earmarked for certain specific governmental expenditures, in much the same way that the federal tax on gasoline is earmarked for specific purposes.

Social Security taxes when received by the government are not set aside for the person who paid them nor credited to an account in his name. Instead, they are paid out immediately to someone who is already drawing benefits. Social Security taxes are imposed for the benefit of those already on the rolls, not for the benefit of those who pay them. Correspondingly, when a person is drawing benefits, they are not a return of money he and his employers paid in earlier, but taxes collected for his benefit from those still working and their employers.

Much confusion and concern about the future of Social Security would be dispelled if the public understood that the purpose of Social Security taxes is to provide benefits now to those who already have retired or otherwise qualified for benefits, and that the source of funds for benefits is taxation of those still working and their employers.

Presented before the Subcommittee on Social Security of the Committee on Ways and Means of the House of Representatives of the U.S. Congress in Washington, D.C., on 14 May 1975.

Once this is understood, it is clear that whether one will get his Social Security benefits when he qualifies is simply a question of whether enough taxes will be levied and collected at that time. The availability of funds to pay benefits has almost no relation to what was paid in and little relation to the trust funds. The trust funds simply represent working balances needed because income and outgo are not equal day-by-day, week-by-week, month-by-month, or even year-by-year. How large the trust funds need to be depends on how great are the short-run imbalances between income and outgo, and how long it would take Congress to enact remedial legislation to correct a long-run imbalance. Once the pay-as-you-go nature of the system is understood, it is easy to see that the short-run and long-run financial problems of Social Security are entirely different.

For the rest of this century, the main problem is that the present level of taxes is insufficient to cover the present level of benefits. An important part of the deficiency results from the method used to adjust benefits for inflation. The adjustment is made in a way that under current conditions will overadjust benefits as prices rise. This can be corrected in a straightforward way.

Beginning in the early part of the next century, the problem will be that there will be many more old people in proportion to people still working. Whereas there are now 30 people to be supported by each 100 working people, there will eventually be 45 to be supported by each 100. The "baby boom" of 1940–65 will result in a retirement boom from 2005 to 2030. The "birth dearth" since 1965 means that beginning about 1985 and lasting until at least 1995—and as much longer as the birth dearth continues after 1975—there will be a drop in the ratio of working people to retired people. Thus, if benefits are maintained, taxes will have to rise about 50 per cent.

Social Security benefits should continue to be related to earnings. Benefits should continue to be financed entirely from a tax on earnings rather than partly from general taxes. In order to protect the principle of financing earnings-related benefits by earnings-related taxes, some present benefits which are not related to earnings ought no longer to be financed from payroll taxes. Of the several benefits that would be removed from payroll-tax financing under this principle, the most significant is Medicare. The 1.8 per cent payroll tax now collected for Medicare would, if released for earnings-related Social Security benefits, be sufficient, after correcting the method of adjusting benefits for inflation, to balance income and outgo for some time to come.

There should be a comprehensive study by a non-Government body of such fundamental issues as full reserve funding vs. current cost financing; the effects of Social Security on productivity, capital formation, and private savings; the relationship between private pensions and Social Security; the appropriate size of the trust funds; and other basic issues.

The Social Security System has never, so far as I know, been subjected to a totally independent, detailed scrutiny of all of its actuarial, statistical, and technical assumptions and procedures. The trustees' reports and the reports of Advisory Councils have relied ultimately on the data and analyses of present or former members of the Social Security staff. No one else is competent enough, and the Trustees and Councils do not have enough time for completely fresh people to develop competence comparable with that of those who have had long experience with Social Security.

This is not to impugn in the slightest the competence, integrity, and dedication of the Social Security staff. But a review or audit needs to be *independent,* for truly independent reviews and audits have a value that cannot be attained without total independence.

The situation is in some ways like that with data on the Russian economy 20 years ago. There were numerous American experts working at different institutions and reaching generally consistent conclusions. The then chairman of the Council of Economic Advisers noticed, however, that all the experts had been trained alike and had been closely associated. He therefore arranged for a foundation grant to a private institution which had never studied the Russian economy, in order to bring in an outstanding economist who had never studied the Russian economy and to start from scratch to study the Russian economy. The resulting findings, while they took more time than would have been needed by those already in the field, brought about important revisions in our understanding of the Russian economy.

In the next few years Congress and the public will focus more attention on Social Security than it has ever received before. It is important that completely independent evaluations and analyses be available, and this is by no stretch of the imagination a reflection on the present small group of Social Security experts. In addition, many basic issues should be studied that are outside the scope and competence of the Social Security Administration. The System is now 40 years old, and it is urgent that there be an independent, detailed, thorough, objective, non-Governmental review.

32

Demagogues and Loopholes

SOME 75 MILLION AMERICANS have just filled out forms—and checks
—for the Federal income tax, which will extract close to $150 billion
from individuals and businesses in the government's fiscal year beginning July 1. Payments in the 1974 fiscal year will be double those
of 1965.

Against that background, misinformed, demagogic, and even
fraudulent criticisms of the income tax easily find audiences and
readers which will add to their authors' incomes or votes.

Irresponsible and incompetent charges are especially reprehensible because they draw attention away from the many real faults
and inequities that permeate the tax system.

In the 60 years since the income tax began in 1913, thousands of
changes have been made in it. Continuing re-examination of the tax
laws and constructive criticism are needed. Honest observers will
disagree over what is "right." On the other hand, shallow, dishonest
criticism beclouds the real issues, and can stand in the way of efforts
to improve the tax system.

Consider the strident use of the term "loophole." "Loophole"
used to refer to something that crept into the tax law by mistake.
Perhaps in trying to anticipate all possible situations, some possibilities would be overlooked and escape taxation. Perhaps special
provisions would be made to alleviate hardship, but ingenious taxpayers for whom the provisions were not intended would devise
legal ways to take advantage of them. Many of these loopholes were
simple mistakes, but some were suggested by people clever enough

Written for the Rochester Democrat and Chronicle of 23 April 1973.

to anticipate their effects better than the Congressmen did. However these loopholes arose, Congress, with advice from the Internal Revenue Service, worked hard at rooting them out.

Nowadays, however, the word "loophole" is applied to provisions of the tax laws intentionally put in by Congress after lengthy consideration. The purpose of these provisions generally has been to make the income tax a little less burdensome, to make it less of a handicap to economic activity, or to encourage people to support voluntarily various worthy activities, such as religion, charity, and education, which are in the public interest.

One of the charges against tax loopholes is that they benefit the rich primarily. A recent Treasury Department listing of what it loses by tax provisions sometimes called loopholes reveals that the largest losses are generally from those loopholes that benefit middle- and low-income taxpayers, not just the rich. For example, the deductibility of state and local taxes costs the treasury about $8.3 billion per year, over 40 percent of which goes to taxpayers with incomes below $20,000. Exclusion from income of pension contributions costs the Treasury $3.65 billion, over 70 percent of it going to taxpayers below $20,000. Provisions relating to the aged, blind, and disabled cost $3.26 billion, 90 percent of which goes to those below $20,000.

Recent revisions in the tax laws have been concentrated on providing tax relief for individuals, especially the poor, at the expense of corporations, especially large corporations. For the four calendar years 1969–1972, tax changes made effective since 1969 have *increased* corporate income taxes by an aggregate of $4.9 billion, but *decreased* individual income taxes by $18.9 billion. Excise taxes on autos and telephones, mostly affecting individuals, also have decreased by $3.5 billion.

A great deal of demagoguery has centered around the fact that in 1970 112 people of the 15,323 who reported incomes over $200,000, including 3 of the 624 with incomes over $1,000,000, paid no tax. On investigation, it turned out that some of these had paid high taxes to foreign countries, having earned the incomes there; foreign taxes, of course, are credited against the U.S. tax to avoid double taxation. Some of these people had far higher incomes in 1969, and the state income taxes they paid in 1970 on those 1969 incomes exceeded their 1970 incomes, leaving them no tax liability. Some had high deductions for interest they had paid. Some simply had expenses in earning their incomes that exceeded the incomes— under realistic accounting they would have reported losses, not incomes—so they were not truly high-income people at all. All of these facts appear in the public record of hearings last July by the Joint Economic Committee of the Congress, though newspapers, magazines, radios, and television gave them nothing like the prominent coverage they had given—and continue to give—the original charges. For authors, journalists, and politicians to continue to insinuate that many high-income taxpayers are getting off scot-free is sheer mendacious prevarication.

Dishonest as are many of the widely publicized criticisms, the fact remains that the income tax is shot through with inequities. We like to think that two people in equivalent economic circumstances owe about the same taxes, yet that is far from true. It is shameful that invalid, simplistic criticisms have drawn attention away from criticisms that are valid but often complicated. Is it mere coincidence that several of the most publicized of the false critics are themselves in high brackets through inherited wealth? One leading economist summarized some of his criticisms of the income tax by saying that as it stands it is not a tax on being rich so much as a tax on getting rich.

Responsible criticism of the tax laws should begin with a reexamination of the purposes for which particular provisions have been enacted. Should married couples receive the tax benefits of income splitting, at estimated "costs" to other taxpayers of $22 billion annually? Should homeowners receive almost $10 billion in reduced taxes, at the expense of renters? Should employee benefits—available to some but not all employed people—escape tax to the tune of some $6 billion annually? Are the provisions allowing some $1.3 billion in tax relief in connection with oil and gas depletion (including exploration and development costs) in the best interest of the nation (especially now when we face fuel shortages)? Are the advantages of giving preferential treatment to capital gains sufficient to offset the inequities that arise because some ordinary income, but by no means all, can easily be converted to capital gains and thereby gain the preferential tax treatment?

The list could be extended to include many, many more examples of provisions of the law which can be taken advantage of by some, but not all, taxpayers. There is room for honest differences of opinion as to whether each of these types of "preferential" tax treatment is "fair" or "equitable." The test should be, does it benefit the nation?

33

The Pace of Change

MANY OF OUR CONTEMPORARIES are awe-struck by the furious pace of change to which we are being subjected. They feel that at last, after all these millennia, it is we who face unrelieved, terrifying, incomprehensible novelty, such as no human ever faced before. History is divided into two exhaustive and mutually exclusive epochs: from the Beginning to Us, and Us.

But from an important point of view the changes going on in the 20th century are small compared to those in the 19th century—more specifically, the 99 years from Waterloo to Sarajevo. From the beginning of that century to its close, the great majority of educated people in the Western world underwent a radical transformation in their notions of God, man, society, nature, government, and morality —"the eternal verities." This had gotten under way, of course, during the Enlightenment, and indeed can be traced back to the Renaissance.

At the beginning of the century, the story in Genesis was generally accepted; by the end of the century, Darwinism was coming to prevail. At the beginning of the century, human nature was understood by the concepts of the Bible, Aristotle, Hobbes, or Rousseau; at the end of the century, by the concepts of James, Pavlov, Freud, or Dewey. At the beginning of the century, no person or message had ever traveled faster than by wind, gravity, or muscle; at the end of the century, the steamship, railroad, automobile, air-

Presented before the American Statistical Association at Detroit on 27 December 1970.

plane, telegraph, telephone, and wireless were common. At the beginning of the century, energy could be transmitted only as far as gears, shafts, and belts would carry it; by the end of the century electrification was well under way. At the beginning of the century, physics was scarcely more than mechanics, but by the end of the century, quantum physics was well established. At the beginning of the century, it was accepted almost without question that 90 per cent of humanity must be cold, hungry, diseased, superstitious, brutish, and vermin-ridden; by the end of the century, a new conception was deeply rooted that these miseries need not exist, and more progress had been made toward eradicating them than in any two previous centuries. At the beginning of the century, the ability to read was uncommon; at the end of the century, it was well on the way to becoming universal. At the beginning of the century, democracy was scarcely more than an idea; by the end of the century, the suffrage was approaching universality. Slavery was common at the beginning of the century, gone by the end. At the beginning of the century, there was almost no control of infectious diseases; by the end of the century, bacteria had been discovered, their role in spreading disease was understood, and the idea of eventual prevention was well accepted. The thing that impressed Sir William Osler (1849–1919) most about the change in medicine during the 19th century was the introduction of anesthetics in surgery.

It may be that scientific literature is now doubling every ten years, that the number of patents is doubling every few years, that the number of new products is growing exponentially, as we hear so often, but it is intellectual, ideological, spiritual, moral, and social revolutions that constitute real change in human beings—not just substituting plastics for metals or metals for wood, not just substituting jets for propellers, not just adding color to photography and television, not just supplementing sulfa drugs with penicillin. Changes in the 20th century do not compare for radical impact on humanity with the 19th century's shattering of the eternal verities. We have not recovered yet; and it is not clear that we will ever recover.

34

Modern Communication

WHATEVER THE TECHNICAL possibilities of communicating *any*thing, not *every*thing can be communicated to everyone, for both the technical channels for sending information and the human channels for receiving it are limited. Just as it has been said that formerly we knew an edited version of the past, so it could be said that now we get edited versions of tiny fractions of the present. Each individual gets pretty much the same edited versions of the same tiny fractions, so there may actually be less information in the population at large than when not so much was going out, but different people were getting different information. Far from our seeing the complexity of reality, which would happen if different people knew about different things, and different ones of those knowing about any one thing knew different things about it, it is more nearly true that everyone knows the same few facets of the same few subjects. Furthermore, the group of people doing the selecting and editing—the journalists, and more generally the "intellectuals" (in the sense of middlemen who purvey the ideas of scholars, scientists, and philosophers to laymen) tend to be homogeneous in outlook and point of view ("Agnew's Complaint"). We must distinguish between an enormous number of more or less *identical* communications being received by the population and a smaller number of *different* communications being received. As is so often the case with social phenomena, what is true for the individual (that he is receiving more information) may be the opposite for society as a whole (it may be receiving less).

Presented before the American Statistical Association in Detroit on 27 December 1970.

Notes

The Faltering Economy (pages 11–24)

1. I am indebted to Burnett Anderson, Milton Friedman, Charles Moeller, Jr., Harold C. Passer, Ezra Solomon, and George J. Stigler for suggesting changes that I consider improvements.
2. In 1947 the Consumer Price Index rose 14 percent, but this represented, in large part, the index coming back into line with reality after having been unrealistically low during the Second World War.
3. GNP in current dollars for the first quarter of 1975 showed a decline from the previous quarter. The data were not available, however, until two days after this lecture.
4. Milton Friedman tells me that a paper by Michael Darby, soon to be published in the *Journal of Political Economy*, shows that this and other widely accepted figures on unemployment during the 1930's would be substantially reduced if they were based on the definition of unemployment that is used in current figures.

What Can We Do About It? (pages 25–31)

1. William H. Riker, in Robert C. Blattberg, ed., *The Economy in Disarray*.
2. For a thorough factual analysis of the causes of the Great Depression of the 1930's, see Milton Friedman and Anna Jacobson Schwartz, *The Great Contraction, 1929–33* (Princeton, N.J.: Princeton University Press, 1965). This is a reprint, with certain additions to make it self-contained, of Chapter 7 (pp. 299–419) of *idem, A Monetary History of the United States, 1867–1960* (Princeton, N.J.: Princeton University Press, 1963).

What Do We Really Want from Our Economy? (pages 77–82)

1. Richard M. Nixon, then Vice President, was Chairman of the Cabinet Committee on Price Stability for Economic Growth. I was then a

Special Assistant to the President and Executive Vice Chairman of the Committee. The other members of the Committee were Robert B. Anderson, Secretary of the Treasury; Ezra Taft Benson, Secretary of Agriculture; James P. Mitchell, Secretary of Labor; Frederick H. Mueller, Secretary of Commerce; Raymond J. Saulnier, Chairman of the Council of Economic Advisers; and Arthur E. Summerfield, Postmaster General.

The Price System (pages 107–110)

1. For superb explanations of the fundamental role of prices in a free economy I recommend the following two references, which are, in fact, principal sources of my remarks here:

Frank H. Knight, *The Economic Organization* (New York: Augustus M. Kelley, Inc., 1951). This small book was written in the late 1920's, but until the early 1950's was availably only in limited editions, which were used extensively in teaching economics at the University of Chicago, and occasionally at a few other colleges and universities. The framework which Knight introduced here has influenced writers of several widely used textbooks in economics.

F. A. Hayek, "The Use of Knowledge in Society," *American Economic Review* 35:519–30 (September 1945). Though written for a more technical audience than was the author's famous book of about the same date, *The Road to Serfdom*, this short article is equally lucid and important.

Wages, Productivity, and Prices (pages 111–119)

1. This paper was prepared for President Eisenhower's Cabinet Committee on Price Stability for Economic Growth. The work of many people, inside and outside the government, was drawn on freely and extensively without keeping records of their contributions. George P. Shultz and Albert Rees had a major part in its preparation, as also did Walter D. Fackler, Herbert Stein, John Kendrick, and Martin J. Bailey, and no doubt others of the many who gave generously of their advice and assistance in the work of the Cabinet Committee. The members of the Cabinet Committee are listed in the footnote to Chapter 11.

The version given here was presented before the American Institute of Industrial Engineers in Rochester on 11 November 1971. The only significant change from the original version is the addition of the first three paragraphs.

Guidelines (pages 145–162)

1. I am indebted to William H. Meckling, Dean of the Graduate School of Management of the University of Rochester, for extensive and intensive assistance, especially with the second and third sections of this paper. Indeed, he should be listed as co-author, except that the faults of the paper cannot fairly be held against him.
2. "Wages, Productivity, and Prices," Chapter 16 above.

Economic Growth (pages 175–190)

1. This paper was prepared for President Eisenhower's Cabinet Committee on Price Stability for Economic Growth. The work of many people, inside and outside the government, was drawn on freely and extensively without keeping records of their contributions. Walter D. Fackler had a major part in its preparation, as did Herbert Stein, Edward Dennison, John Kendrick, Martin J. Bailey, and no doubt others. The members of the Cabinet Committee are listed in the footnote to Chapter 11.

Automation and Unemployment (pages 197–208)

1. Richard Nelson, "The Economics of Unemployment," *Journal of Business,* 1959.
2. F. A. Hayek, "The Use of Knowledge in Society," *American Economic Review* 35:519–30 (September 1945); and Frank H. Knight, *The Economic Organization* (New York: Augustus M. Kelley, Inc., 1951).
3. Yale Brozen, "The Future of Industrial Research," *Journal of Business,* 1961.
4. Yale Brozen, in Howard B. Jacobson and Joseph S. Roucek, eds., *Automation and Society* (Westport, Conn.: Greenwood, 1959).

Economic Statistics and Economic Policy (pages 209–217)

1. Milton Friedman and David Meiselman, "The Relative Stability of Monetary Velocity and the Investment Multiplier in the United States 1897–1958," in Commission on Money and Credit, *Stabilization Policies* (Englewood Cliffs, N.J.: Prentice-Hall, 1963).

2. Price Statistics Review Committee (George J. Stigler, chairman), *The Price Statistics of the Federal Government* (New York: National Bureau of Economic Research, 1961).

3. The price index makes it appear that a great deal of inflation occurred just after the Second World War. This was in fact largely a matter of the index's getting back in touch with reality after having had its head held in the sand during the war.

4. This calculation was made in 1960 by Walter D. Fackler, now at the University of Chicago Graduate School of Business. He used forecasts published in 1959 by the Bureau of Labor Statistics (BLS) of the composition of the labor force in 1965. In testimony before the Joint Economic Committee on January 29, 1964, Fackler presented a revised calculation, based on the BLS's 1963 forecasts of the 1965 labor force. The revised calculation showed essentially the same ten per cent rise mentioned here. On the other hand, Albert Rees, of the University of Chicago Department of Economics, tells me that (in contrast with Fackler's procedure of averaging rates from 1959 or 1957 weighted according to the composition of the labor force in 1965) he, Gertrude Bancroft of the BLS, and the President's Council of Economic Advisers have all made calculations in which current rates were weighted according to the composition of the labor force in 1955 or 1957. In all three of these calculations the effect of changes in the composition of the labor force was only about half as great as in Fackler's calculation, and in one case the direction was reversed. This does not affect the point made in the text, but it does warn against uncritical acceptance of the specific figures used for illustration.

5. During the Annual Meeting at which this Presidential Address was delivered, Robert Stein of the Bureau of Labor Statistics reported on current experimental work with improved definitions. His report perhaps justifies more optimism than I have expressed here about the consequences of improved definitions.

Neomercantilism and the Unmet Social Need-ers (pages 233–241)

1. See Vance Packard, *The Hidden Persauders*, *The Waste Makers*, and *The Status Seekers*; J. Kenneth Galbraith, *The Affluent Society* and *The Liberal Hour*; C. Wright Mills, *The Power Elite*; and almost any issue of such magazines as *Harper's*, *Atlantic*, *Saturday Review*, *Reporter*, *New Republic*, *Nation*, etc.

2. Mark Twain anticipated some of our contemporaries nearly ninety years ago in his *Life on the Mississippi*: "In the space of one hundred

and seventy-six years the Lower Mississippi has shortened itself two hundred and forty-two miles. That is an average of a trifle over one mile and a third per year. Therefore, any calm person, who is not blind or idiotic, can see that in the Old Oölitic Silurian Period, just a million years ago next November, the Lower Mississippi River was upward of one million three hundred thousand miles long, and stuck out over the Gulf of Mexico like a fishing rod. And by the same token any person can see that seven hundred and forty-two years from now the Lower Mississippi will be only a mile and three-quarters long, and Cairo and New Orleans will have joined their streets together, and be plodding comfortably along under a single mayor and a mutual board of aldermen. There is something fascinating about science. One gets such wholesale returns of conjecture out of such a trifling investment of fact."

3. This is not to minimize the importance of Milliman's points about the relevance of marginal analysis to choices among various projects within the public sector. The point here is that the diversion of the national income between the public and the private sectors is not the sum of individual balances between the expenditures through the public and private sectors. The public-private division is political, not economic.

4. Alexis de Tocqueville, *Democracy in America*, Mentor edition, p. 294.

5. *Ibid.*, p. 291.

6. *Ibid.*, p. 295.

7. W. H. Ferry says in the January 1962 issue of the *Bulletin* of the Center for the Study of Democratic Institutions: "Modern mercantilism will remove the economic machine from the middle of the landscape to one side, where, under planning by inducement, its ever more efficient automata will provide the goods and services required by the general welfare. . . .

   "This is the promise of modern mercantilism, and if the time is not yet, it is yet a time worth striving for."

Political Entrepreneurship and the Welfare Explosion
(pages 242–258)

1. Ida C. Merriam, "Social Welfare Expenditures, 1929–67," *Social Security Bulletin*, December, 1967.

2. A. V. Dicey, *The Relation Between Law and Public Opinion in England during the Nineteenth Century* (2d edition; London: Macmillan and Co., Limited, 1914). Introduction to the Second Edition, pp. lxiv–lxv.

3. The Senate majority leader at the time, who played a major part in weakening the bills, is now President, and in his present office assumes much the same stance on these issues as have all of his predecessors of the past quarter-century.

4. Suggested to me by George J. Stigler, who said that Aaron Director suggested it to him.

5. Milton Friedman, "Social Welfare Measures," Chap. XI in his *Capitalism and Freedom* (Chicago: University of Chicago Press, 1962), p. 179.

6. The ideas presented here came to my mind mainly as a result of reading E. G. West's *Education and the State* (London: Institute of Economic Affairs, 1965).

   Gordon Tullock, in *Entrepreneurial Politics* (Charlottesville: University of Virginia, Thomas Jefferson Center for Studies in Political Economy, 1962), p. 21, has used the terms "entrepreneurial politics" and "political entrepreneur":

   > An individual may run for some office, offering a platform of some specific measures. Then he is a political entrepreneur. If, on the other hand, he unites with a number of other candidates, to present jointly a uniform program to the voters, then the "party" is the entrepreneur.

   Tullock's emphasis is on the analogy between profit maximizing and vote maximizing, while mine in the present paper is on the innovative or new-product aspects of entrepreneurship.

7. These facts and the quotation are from West, *op. cit.*

8. The quotation and the other information about the development of public education in New York is from E. G. West, "The Political Economy of American Public School Legislation," *Journal of Law and Economics,* Vol. 10, 1967, pp. 101–28.

9. Ethel Shanas, *The Health of Older People* (Cambridge: Harvard University Press, 1962), p. 92.

   There would be a case for raising the ratio "one person in twenty," or 5 percent, in the first sentence quoted to one person in 12, or 8 percent. When people who reported that they had been ill but had not seen a doctor were asked why not, 5.6 percent said they could not afford a doctor; hence the figure in the quotation. At another point in the interview, however, "after detailed discussion of finances and the problems which older people faced in living on a limited income, all respondents were asked: 'Are there any things you especially need that you've had to do without because you don't have enough money?' . . . Only eight of every one hundred persons in the older population specifically said that they needed medical or dental care."

10. Rita R. Campbell and W. Glenn Campbell, *Voluntary Health Insurance in the United States* (Washington: American Enterprise Institute, 1960), p. 1.

11. Joseph Brenner, Robert Coles, Alan Mermann, Milton J. E. Senn, Cyril Walwyn, and Raymond Wheeler, "Children in Mississippi," in *Hungry Children*, a Special Report of the Southern Regional Council (5 Forsyth Street, N.W., Atlanta, Georgia), undated but apparently 1967, pp. 5–6.

12. *The People Left Behind*, a report by the President's National Advisory Commission on Rural Poverty (Washington: Government Printing Office, 1967), p. 11.

13. Center for Governmental Research, Inc. (Rochester, New York): *The Monroe County Penitentiary*, March 1964; *Justice Detained: A Pilot Study of Defendants Confined in the Monroe County Jail*, October, 1967.

14. From the translation by William Mackworth Praed of Sophocles' *Chorus from Ajax*.

15. Basic data from "Public and Private Expenditures for Health and Medical Care, Fiscal Years 1929–67," Research Note #21, Division of Health Insurance Studies, Social Security Administration, November 20, 1967.

    Public expenditures in millions of 1967 dollars rose from $8,645 in 1965–66 to $12,640 in 1966–67, while private fell from $30,743 to $27,360, raising the total from $39,388 to $40,000. Per capita, the total was $198.16 in 1965–66 and $198.99 in 1966–67, while 1964–65 was $188.45. The 1966–67 data are preliminary estimates.

    Although I had predicted—or, more accurately, suggested tentatively in conversations with a few medical administrators—that the medicare and medicaid programs would cause a slowdown in the growth of funds available for medical care, I nevertheless consider that the preliminary estimate for 1966–67 must be substantially below the correct value. It does not seem possible that expenditures that had been growing so fast for so long could have come to such a screeching halt as these data indicate.

16. D. S. Lees, "Health Through Choice: An Economic Study of the British National Health Service," *Freedom or Free-for-all?* (Ralph Harris, ed.) (London: Institute of Economic Affairs, 1961), p. 76.

17. A B.U.P.A. brochure dated January, 1968, for which I am indebted to Marion B. Folsom, who called my attention to B.U.P.A., asserts that four major advantages are associated with private treatment in illness:

    1. Arrangements can usually be made quickly and conveniently.
    2. Freedom to have the specialist you and your doctor choose. . . .

3. A private room. . . .

4. Privacy and . . . greater freedom of visiting hours.

These are followed by a reference to "a warm and human service."

18. West, "The Political Economy of American Public School Legislation," *op. cit.*

Index

Academic freedom, 235
Academic–journalistic complex, 5, 29
Accounting, 81, 121, 206, 263–264
Acton, Lord, 10
Ad hoc explanations, 124
Administered prices, 124, 125
Administrators, 128, 129
Adriamycin, 21
Advertising, 27, 96, 248
Affirmative action, 9
Affluent society, 89, 192
Africa, 69
Age, 215
Aged, 263
Agnew, Spiro, 267
Agriculture, 114, 179, 183, 189, 192, 199
Agriculture, Department of, 270
Aid to dependent children, 228
Airplanes, 84, 201, 265–266
Alabama, 252
Alaska, 20
Alaska pipeline, 22
Alcoholics, 252
Allocation of capital, 20
Allocation of products, 23, 133
Aluminum, 160
"America the Beautiful," 45
American Assembly, 197n
American Bankers Association, 145n
American Economic Association, 93, 97, 127
American Economic Review, 129, 131n, 270, 271
American Enterprise Institute, 30–31, 242n, 275
American Federation of Labor–Congress of Industrial Organizations (AFL–CIO), 168
American Indians, 19, 252

American Institute of Industrial Engineers, 270
American Legion, 43n
American Petroleum Institute, 22
American Power Conference, 191n
American Revolution, 45, 211, 241
American Statistical Association, 210, 265n, 267n
"America's sixty families," 89
Anderson, Burnett, 269
Anderson, Jack, 66
Anderson, Robert B., 270
Anesthetics, 266
Anthropology, 95
Antitrust cases, 24
Antitrust Division, 151
Antitrust law, 24
Antitrust program, 189
Appalachia, 251
Appendectomies, 178
Apples, 178
Arbitrage, 140
Architecture, 172
Argonne offensive, 43
Aristotle, 265
Armistice, 43–44
Army, 48–51, 108
Art, 95, 233, 234
Asia, 69
Asians, 19
Atlantic Monthly, 272
Audits, 261
Australia, 246
Austria, 44
Authoritarianism, 26, 59, 67, 177, 184
Authors, 264
Automatic stabilizers, 228, 230
Automation, 98, 197–208, 219, 220
Automobile safety, 6

Automobiles, 6, 7, 20, 72, 100, 116, 129,
    131, 139, 141, 177, 202, 203, 236,
    237, 263, 265
Averages, 178, 179
Awns, 11

Baby boom, 260
Bacteria, 17, 266
Bailey, Martin J., 270, 271
Balance of payments, 121, 152–155,
    159–160, 219
Balance of trade, 153
Bancroft, Gertrude, 272
Bankers, 97, 153, 158, 159
Banks, 19, 137, 153
Barber shops, 116
Beef, 133
Beer, 146
Belts, 266
Benson, Ezra Taft, 270
Berrigan, Daniel, 60, 63, 66
Berrigan, Philip F., 60, 63, 66
Bicycles, 131
Big business, 100
Bill of Rights, 61
Billing, 206
Biology, 95, 192
Birth dearth, 260
Black Panthers, 60
Blacks, 14, 19, 40, 50, 244–245, 252
Blankets, electric, 248
Blattberg, Robert C., 269
Blind, the, 263
Block, Joseph, 103
Blough, Roger, 103
Blue Cross, 255
Blue Shield, 255
Bolts, 178
Bonds, 80, 120, 137, 138, 159, 213
Book burning, 184
Borrowing, 156
Boston, Massachusetts, 23
Bowley, Arthur L., 209
Bowling, 204
Brazil, 221
Brenner, Joseph, 275
British United Provident Association,
    255, 275

Brookings Institution, 30
Brozen, Yale, 30, 205, 271
Brunner, Karl, 170
Buchwald, Art, 11
Building, 227
Building materials, 142
Bureau of the Census, 216
Bureau of Internal Revenue, 62
Bureau of Labor Statistics, 126, 272
Bureaucracy, 17–18, 24, 64, 164
Burke, Edmund, 9
Burns, Arthur F., 146, 168, 169, 261
Business, 85, 89–93, 100, 104, 128, 148,
    168
  cycles, 114, 123, 147, 167, 179, 210,
    212, 218, 219, 224, 226, 227, 229
  decisions, 121
  indicators, 30
  leaders, 85
Business Council, 25n
Businessmen, 26–27, 86, 153, 247–248
Butchers, 133
Butter, 130
Buying power: see Purchasing power

Cabinet Committee on Price Stability
    for Economic Growth, 77n, 269–
    271
Cairo, Illinois, 273
California, 13, 33
California Institute of Technology, 104
Cameras, 99
Campaign rhetoric, 4
Campbell, Rita R., 275
Campbell, W. Glenn, 275
Can openers, electric, 248
Canada, 99, 104, 153, 156, 245–246
Canadian Stock Exchange, 156
Cancer, 104, 125
Cannon balls, 177
Canute, King, 41
Capital, 23, 107, 108, 112, 115–116, 119,
    121, 152, 187, 195, 201, 203–204,
    207, 222
  accumulation, 185, 186
  allocation, 20
  formation, 261
  markets, 156

Carving knives, electric, 247
Caste, 108
Catalogues, 165
Center for Governmental Research, 275
Center for the Study of Democratic Institutions, 273
Centralized economy, 177
Ceylon, 19
Champerty corporations, 18, 23–24
Chappaquiddick affair, 65
Charity, 77, 187, 234, 242, 263
Chemistry, 95
Chicanos, 19
Churches, 233, 234, 235
City planning, 242
Civil liberties, 9, 52, 161, 165
Civil rights, 24, 245
Civil Service System, 39
Civil War, 45
Co-trimaxazole, 21–22
Coal mining, 22
Coalitions, 33, 244
Coercion, 109, 161, 190
Coffee, 135–136
Coles, Robert, 275
Collective bargaining, 17, 58, 118, 119
Collective choice, 253, 255–257
Collective control, 25
Collectivism, 28, 38–42, 67, 88, 244
"College of the Air," 224n
Colleges, 38, 64, 235
Columbia University, 92
Columnists, 29, 64
Commentators, 29, 64
Commerce, 199
Commerce, Department of, 157, 226
Commission on Monetary Policy, 211
Commission on Money and Credit, 271
Committee for Economic Development (CED), 168, 169, 211
Common carrier, 234
Common Cause, 5
Common cold, 125
Common law, 25
Communication, 4, 42, 109–110, 115, 200, 233, 267
Communism, 182
Communist Party, 55–56

Comparative advantage, 99
Compensatory fiscal policy, 227
Competition, 33, 96, 109, 115, 119, 189, 221, 222
Compulsion, 109, 161, 190, 252
Concentrated industry, 100, 125
Concentrations of power, 118–119
Congress, 5, 6–7, 20, 21, 26–28, 33–34, 46, 64, 58, 68, 104, 109, 130, 160, 164, 168, 169, 171, 244, 245, 257, 259n, 260, 263, 264
Connor, John T., 157
Conscience, 243
Conscription, 43–51, 62
Consolidated Edison Company, 19
Constitution of the United States, 4, 25, 34, 39, 58, 61, 77, 97, 241
Construction, 126, 142
Consumer choice, 253, 254
Consumer Price Index, 159, 166, 269
Consumers, 27, 148, 198, 247
Consumers' goods, 131–144
Consumption, 79, 135, 136, 137, 186, 192, 193, 198–199
  rationing, 139
  taxes, 136–138, 142
Contracts, 165
Controller of the Currency, 19
Coplon, Judith, 66
Copper, 160
Copyrights, 24
Corporations, 23–24, 42, 103–104, 153, 228, 263
Corruption, 69
Cost of government, 4
Cost of Living Council, 22, 171
Costs, 152, 185
Cotton, 199
Council of Economic Advisers, 145, 150–152, 261, 270, 272
Cournot, Antoine A., 209
Courts, 5, 7, 10, 25, 68
Cox, Archibald, 56
Crafts, 85
Creativity, 175, 185, 187
Credit, 140, 147, 149, 153
Criminal law, 8
Crime, 243

Cromolyn, 21
Culture, 26, 78, 175, 184, 197
Customs, 28, 108
Cutover lands, 239
Czars, 183

Darby, Michael, 269
Darwin, Charles, 265
DDT, 19
Debt, 121, 143, 222
Declaration of Independence, 61
Defense, 28, 182, 220, 226
Defense, Department of, 6, 155
Deficiencies of data, 178
Deficit spending, 4
Deflation, 54, 123, 149, 188, 212
Delegation of power, 7
Demagoguery, 7, 10, 221, 263
Demand, 148, 149, 152, 154, 164
Democracy, 40–42, 70, 237, 238, 257, 266
Democratic Party, 96, 246
Demography, 260
Demoralization, 18
Dennison, Edward, 271
Dentistry, 274
Depletion, 264
Depressed areas, 104, 228, 239, 240
Depression, 29, 81, 84, 90, 102, 123, 125,
    194, 212, 238, 252, 269; see also
    Recession
Derelicts, 252
Detergents, 20
Devaluation, 154–155
Development, 184, 200
Dewey, John, 265
DiBona, Charles, 22
Dicey, Albert Venn, 38–42, 244, 245, 273
Differential earnings, 137
Dignity, 77
Direct election, 10
Direct primary, 39
Director, Aaron, 274
Disabled, 263
Disarmament, 44
Discretionary measures, 228
Discrimination, 7, 188
Disease, 125, 176, 184, 234, 243, 266

Dishes, 140
Dislocations, 205–208
Distributions, 23, 37, 54–55, 129, 144, 177
Dividends, 222
Division of labor, 222
Doctors, 71–73
Domestic reforms, 65
Draft, the, 43–51, 62
Drama, 233
Dramatists, 29
Drugs lag, 21–22
Due process, 58, 72, 161
Durable goods, 143

Earnings: see Income
Eavesdropping, 66
Economic analysis, 145–146, 225
Economic control, 157
Economic development, 184
Economic education, 59, 94–104
Economic freedom, 79–80
Economic growth, 20, 78–79, 82, 114,
    121, 125–126, 175–192, 194, 195, 210
    measurement of, 79, 176–181
    taxes and, 218–223
Economic hardship, 126
Economic mobilization, 133
Economic policy, 77–78, 172, 209–217
Economic power, 191–196
Economic progress, 187, 193
Economic stability, 101
Economic Stabilization Act, 22
Economic system, 59
Economic theorists, 220
Economics, 104, 108, 168, 180, 209, 210
Economists, 26–27, 64, 97, 128, 146, 225,
    243
Economy, 12
Economy of abundance, 89
Edgeworth, Francis Y., 209
Editorial writers, 64
Education, 4, 5, 26, 31, 59, 78, 79, 84, 85,
    94–104, 114, 132, 175, 181, 183, 190,
    215, 219, 235, 240, 248–250, 252–
    255, 263
Education Act of 1870, 249
Effective demand, 148, 149, 154, 164

Efficiency, 56, 81, 113, 119, 121, 147, 149, 164–165, 169, 171, 185, 188, 190, 194, 219, 221, 222
Ehrlichman, John D., 64–65
Eighteenth century, 29, 42, 61, 181, 186, 192–194, 199, 240
Eisenhower, Dwight D., 77n, 244, 270, 271
Election proceedings, 5
Electricity, 97–98, 142, 266
Elevators, 205
Ellsberg, Daniel, 60, 66
Emergency Petroleum Allocation Act of 1973, 22
Employees, 256, 259
Employers, 259
Employment, 78, 79–80, 82, 98, 112, 118, 125–126, 163, 172, 185, 188, 203–205, 210, 225; see also Unemployment
full, 12, 80, 126, 167, 194, 206
Employment Act of 1946, 124, 125
Ends and means, 192, 195
Energy, 7, 266
Energy crisis, 22
Engineering, 90, 183, 186, 192, 199
Engineers, 198, 236
Engines, 236
England: see Great Britain
Enlightenment, 265
Entomology, 236
Enterprise, 81
Entrepreneurial politics, 247–258, 274
Environment, 118–119, 128, 135, 187, 190
Environmental Protection Act, 6
Environmental Protection Agency, 18, 21
Environmental suits, 24
Equal sacrifice, 131
Equality, 35, 69, 134, 193, 195, 238
Equity financing, 222
Ethics, 26, 64
Europe, 29, 240; see also names of countries
Evans, Griffith C., 209
Excise taxes, 23, 226, 259
Expectations, 166

Expenditure rationing, 133–134
Expenditures: see Government expenditures
Exploration, 264
Exports, 121, 155–156, 160, 184, 192, 193
Extractive industries, 222

Fabricant, Solomon, 84
Fackler, Walter D., 30, 270, 271, 272
Fair play, 77, 80, 187
Faltering, 11, 16
Fanaticism, 40
Farm Board, 4
Farm Foundation, 120n
Farm policy, 228
Farm program, 92–93, 245
Farming, 4
Fear, 161
Federal Communications Commission, 19
Federal Energy Administration, 23
Federal government: see Government
Federal Reserve Bank of Chicago, 239
Federal Reserve Bank of St. Louis, 103
Federal Reserve Board, 54, 93, 101–102, 148–149, 152, 153, 159, 166, 168, 170, 181, 210, 213–214
Federal Trade Commission, 9
Federalist papers, 7
Feldstein, Martin, 13
Ferry, W. H., 273
Feudalism, 246
Fibers, 199
Fields, W. C., 11
Financial flows, 30
Financial writing, 178
Finished products, 147
Firemen, 252
First World War, 39, 43–45, 47, 66, 101, 183, 210, 246
Fiscal policy, 224–230, 252
Fixed incomes, 120
Fixed interest rates, 159
Floating exchange rates, 158, 159, 163
Folsom, Marion B., 275–276
Food, 134–135, 199, 243, 251
Food and Drug Administration, 21
Food stamp program, 20

Ford, George H., 50
Ford, Gerald R., 20
Foreign aid, 153, 154, 184
Foreign exchange, 154, 158
Foreign-flag ships, 20
Foreign investments, 153, 155–156
Foreign languages, 95
Foreign loans, 153
Foreign policy, 16, 28
Foreign taxes, 263
Foreign trade, 81, 99, 104, 145, 152–159, 163, 184, 189
Forks, electric, 247–248
Forward commitments, 165
Founding Fathers, 7, 34
France, 40, 44, 66, 69, 86, 154, 245–246
Franchises, 246
Free economy, 59
Free enterprise, 30, 185, 195
Free markets, 31, 52, 56, 159, 164
Free society, 30
Free speech, 5
Freedom, 25, 26, 32, 35, 39, 41, 58, 70, 77, 79–80, 88, 96, 104, 109, 118, 161, 164, 165, 169, 171, 185, 187, 190, 193, 219, 221, 235
Fresno, California, 43
Freud, Sigmund, 265
Friedman, Milton, 3, 12, 30, 102, 111, 245, 269, 271, 274
Fringe benefits, 112, 119
Fuel, 129, 131, 243, 264
Full employment, 12, 80, 126, 167, 194, 206
Fuller, Buckminster, 11
Furniture, 140
Future, 16–24

Galbraith, John Kenneth, 169, 272
Gallup poll, 57
Gasoline, 129, 131
Gasoline excise tax, 23, 259
Gears, 266
General Motors Corporation, 36, 37–38, 63
General scarcity, 142
Genesis, 265
Geniuses, 198

Geology, 95
German Empire, 39–40
Germany, 43, 44–45, 69, 129, 183, 245–246
GI Bill, 235
Gilfillan, S. C., 197–198
Gilman, Harry, 49
Goals, 107
Gold, 152, 153, 154, 158
Goldberg, Arthur, 53
Goldwater, Barry, 4
Goodwill, 109, 118
Government, 5, 7, 34, 61, 85, 148–149, 161, 188, 220, 224, 265
    authorities, 27
    bonds, 120, 137, 138, 159, 213
    borrowing, 132
    changes in, 4
    control, 96, 143
    debt, 221
    deficit, 149, 166, 170
    employees, 256
    expenditures, 12, 14, 16, 182, 219–221, 224–228, 234, 259
    intervention, 16–25, 39, 56, 63–64, 91–93
    limited, 30
    loans, 20, 33
    local, 220
    monopoly, 100
    powers, 59, 62, 68–70
    regulation, 22, 23, 127, 189
Graduate students, 209
Gray markets, 119, 148, 154
Great Britain, 29, 44, 66, 69, 86, 99, 133–134, 154, 186, 192, 194, 202, 218, 234, 244–246, 248–249, 253, 255
Great Campus Craze, 67
Great Depression, 29, 238, 252, 269
Greece, 50, 176
Gross National Product, 15, 30, 178–180, 183, 210, 269
Guaranteed loans, 20
Guidelines, 59, 145–162
Gulliver, 17
Guns, 130
Gymnastics, 236

Haldeman, H. R., 64–65
Happiness, 23, 26
Harassment, 157
Harbors, 115
Hardship, 126, 251
Hardware, 140
Harper's, 272
Harris, Ralph, 275
Harvard University, 13, 30–31, 56
Hatfield, Mark, 51
Hayek, F. A., 29, 270, 271
Health, 4, 23, 26, 39, 69, 71, 72, 78, 114,
    161, 190, 233, 252
Health, Education, and Welfare, De-
    partment of, 6, 19
Health insurance, 250, 255
Heart disease, 125
Heavyweight boxing champion, 36–37,
    47–48
Hershey, Louis B., 49
High schools, 64
Highways, 184, 233, 234
Historians, 89
History, 15, 64, 95, 96, 265
Hitler, Adolf, 44–45, 60, 66
Hoarding, 132
Hobbes, Thomas, 265
Holiday Inn, 246
Holidays, 113
Homeowners, 264
Hoover, Herbert, 4, 225
Hoover Research Institute, 30–31
Hospitals, 184, 234, 253
Hotels, 140
Housman, A. E., 50
Housing, 143, 245
Howard Johnson Motels, 246
Huff, Darrell, 235
Human nature, 92
Hummel, 11

Idealism, 78
Ideals, 77, 82
Ideology, 87–88, 220
Ignorance, 176, 184, 225, 245
Illegal credit, 140
Immigration, 35–36, 45, 246
Imports, 121, 136, 160, 184, 192

Incentives, 115, 128, 135, 147, 195–196
Income, 30, 32, 69, 90, 112, 120, 178, 181,
    188, 198, 210, 227, 273
Income distributions, 30, 132, 137, 242
Income taxes, 5, 13, 58, 62, 137, 138,
    144, 223, 226, 228, 262–264
Incomes policy, 164
Independence, 77, 187
Independent, The, 197–198
Individual choice, 255–257
Individual differences, 93
Individual freedom, 96
Individualism, 28, 30, 35, 41, 88
Inducement, 109, 110
Industrial production, 178, 181, 229
Industrial Revolution, 90, 199
Industry, 100, 114, 116, 125, 183, 185–
    186, 199, 222
Inefficiency, 26, 121, 161
Inequality, 237, 242
Infant mortality, 125
Inflation, 111–112, 119, 123, 157, 170,
    221, 260
    Federal Reserve Board and, 148–149,
        152, 153, 159, 213–214
    harmful effects of, 120–121, 188
    inflationary gap, 130, 132, 138
    price controls and, 132, 133, 143, 146,
        148–150, 164–167, 171, 172
    steel prices and, 53, 54, 57
    unemployment and, 12, 13, 165, 166
    unions and, 100–101, 125, 148
Information, 109–110, 121, 147, 199, 267
Ingenuity, 128
Inheritance, 264
Initiative, 39, 77, 187
Injustice, 133, 149
Innovation, 21, 115, 197–200, 250–251
Installment credit, 102
Institute of Economic Affairs, 275
Insurance, 80, 121, 143, 250, 255
Integrity, 77
Intellectuals, 29–30, 31, 165, 233, 267
Intelligence, 198
Interdependence, 32, 39
Interest, 159, 166, 213, 222
Interest groups, 5, 7, 64, 245
Internal Revenue Service, 5–6, 171

International monetary system, 158
International relations, 156, 159–161
International trade: *see* Foreign trade
Interventionism, 29
Interwar period, 91
Inventions, 197, 199
Investments, 7, 19, 137, 153–156, 184, 186, 189, 201, 227, 248
Ireland, 69
Isolationism, 28
Italy, 69, 86, 176

Jacobson, Howard B., 271
James, William, 265
Japan, 127, 153, 183, 191
Job opportunities, 78
Job vacancies, 216–217
Johnson, Lyndon B., 96, 157, 274
Joint Economic Committee, 264, 272
Jones, Homer, 3
Journal of Business, 97, 271
Journal of Law and Economics, 274
Journal of Political Economy, 269
Journalism, 183
Journalists, 29, 40, 62, 63, 64, 89, 96, 146, 257, 264, 267
Judges, 10
Justice, 28, 35, 62, 69, 77, 80, 187, 193, 195
Justice, Department of, 62
Juvenile delinquency, 219

Kendrick, John, 270, 271
Kennedy, Edward, 65
Kennedy, John F., 53, 56–59, 96, 218–219, 229
Keynes, John Maynard, 211
Khrushchev, Nikita, 55–56, 182
Kierans, Eric, 156
Knight, Frank H., 3, 30, 92, 271
Knives, electric, 248
Knowledge, 114–115, 119, 128, 197, 198
Korean War, 123, 180, 213, 234, 238–239
Ku Klux Klan, 62

Labor, 23, 112, 116, 147, 149, 168, 187, 195, 201–204, 221–222
    contracts, 165

law, 24
    negotiations, 59
    relations, 27–28
    surpluses, 117
Labor, Department of, 270
Labor force, 13–14, 114, 215
Labor unions: *see* Unions
Laissez-faire, 41
Land, 20, 221–222
Land owners, 245
Language, 28, 95, 109, 184, 236
Las Vegas, Nevada, 36
Laughlin, Lawrence, 30
Laundry machines, 69
Law enforcement, 5, 226
Law schools, 71
Lawsuits, 8, 24
Lawyers, 32, 71–72, 98, 129
League of Nations, 44
Leases, 165
Lees, D. S., 253, 275
Legal expenses, 23–24
Legislators, 26–27; *see also* Congress
Leisure, 175, 177
Letter openers, electric, 248
Leukemia, 104
Liberal education, 21
Liberalism, 28, 62
Liberty, 39, 88, 95–96, 186
Licensing, 20
Lilliputians, 17, 84
Limited government, 30
Linen, 140
Lippmann, Walter, viii, 25, 33, 34, 63, 67, 170
Liquidation, 137, 140–141
Literacy, 249
Literature, 233, 266
Lithium carbonate, 21
Litigation explosion, 8, 23–24, 62
Lizards, 12
Local governments, 220; *see also* Government
Loeb Awards to Business and Financial Journalists, 175n
Logic, 91, 92
Long cycles, 212
Loopholes, 262–264

Lorie, James H., 30
Losses, 152
Lottery, 48
Low-income groups, 120–121
Lumbering, 239
Lyricists, 29

Magazines, 264
Malnutrition, 251
Man-hours paid, 113–117
Man-hours worked, 113–117, 152, 178, 181
Management, 79, 115, 116, 119, 152
Managerial revolution, 90
Manners, 28
Manufacturing, 114
Margin requirements, 160
Marginal analysis, 236, 273
Marijuana, 69, 72
Marital status, 215
Market economy, 30, 178
Market power, 53
Market system, 23, 195
Markets, 2, 31, 52, 56, 119, 148, 154, 156, 159, 164, 199, 219
Massachusetts, 13
Materialism, 78
Mathematics, 91, 96, 209
McCracken, Paul, 167
Meany, George, 168, 169
Meat, 129, 133–134
Meckling, William H., 271
Medicaid, 250, 252, 275
Medicare, 237, 250, 252, 260, 275
Medicine, 90, 125, 132, 142, 183, 212, 238, 252, 266, 274
Medicines, 7, 71, 79
Meiselman, David, 211, 271
Melman, Seymour, 202
Mercantilism, 42, 61, 88, 181, 186, 193, 194, 240–241, 273
Mercenaries, 49, 50
Mermann, Alan, 275
Merriam, Ida C., 273
Metals, 266
Methodology, 91
Mexican War, 45, 211
Mexico, 183

Michigan, 203
Middle-income groups, 120–121, 245
Migration, 254
Militarism, 45
Military expenditures, 153, 154
Mill, James, 249
Milliman, Jerome W., 273
Mills, C. Wright, 272
Mills, Wilbur, 6
Milwaukee Society, The, 3n
Minerals, 251
Minimum wages, 14, 98, 104, 245
Ministers, 29, 89, 96
Minneapolis, Minnesota, 255
Minnesota, 252
Minorities, 14, 17, 244; see also Blacks
Minority rule, 33, 40–41, 42
Mints, Lloyd, 3
Missiles, 104, 177, 178, 201
Mississippi, 251, 272–273, 275
Mississippi River, 197
Mitchell, James P., 270
Mitchell, Wesley C., 210
Mobility, 240
Mobilization, 132
Moeller, Charles, Jr., 269
Monetary policies, 146, 149, 166–167, 171, 188, 227
Monetizing debt, 170
Money, 14, 108
Money supply, 14–15, 30, 54, 101, 103, 149, 166, 167
Monopoly, 56, 90, 99–100, 124, 125, 186, 213
Monroe County, New York, 103, 275
Montreal Stock Exchange, 156
Morality, 69, 77, 85, 187, 193, 265
Morgenstern, Oskar, 210
Mortgages, 137
Moscow, 55, 176, 194
Motivation, 37
Moving pictures, 236
Mueller, Frederick H., 270
Music, 95, 233
Mutual respect, 187

Nader, Ralph, 5, 63
Napoleon Bonaparte, 194

Napoleonic wars, 39, 44
Nation, The, 92, 272
National Advisory Commission on Rural Poverty, 275
National Bureau of Economic Research, 30, 102, 210, 229, 272
National Commission on Productivity, 168
National defense, 28, 182, 220, 226
National Health Service, 253, 255
National income, 30, 210, 227, 273
National Industrial Conference Board, 111n
National Institutes of Health, 234
National interest, 128
National Merit Scholarships, 234
National Opinion Research Center, 94, 250
National output, 118
National policy, 181–182
National security, 78, 191, 192, 193, 240
Nationalism, 39–40
Natural gas, 20, 22
Natural resources: *see* Resources
Nature, 265
Nazis, 127, 191
Need, 132
Neighborhood effects, 243
Nelson, Richard, 198, 271
Neomercantilism, 233–241
New Deal, 97
New Left, 42
New Orleans, Louisiana, 273
New products, 185, 200, 205, 266
New Republic, The, 58–59, 92, 272
New York, 13, 20, 23, 33, 249, 253, 255
New York Times, The, 55–56, 128
Newspaper writers: *see* Journalists
Newspapers, 65, 168, 169, 264
Nineteenth century, 28, 29, 38, 40, 61–62, 63, 92, 193, 199, 209, 225, 248, 265–266
Nixon, Richard M., 46, 53, 60n, 64–65, 163, 167–169, 172, 175, 194, 269
Nondurable goods, 227
Novelists, 29, 40, 89, 96
Nuclear power, 22

Nuts, 178
Nutter, Warren, 8–9, 10, 261

Objectivity, 96–97
Occupational Safety and Health Act, 6
Occupations, 32, 151, 215
Office of Price Administration, 127–130, 137
Offshore drilling, 22
Ogburn, William F., 197
Oi, Walter, 51
Oil, 264
Old Faithful Inn, 234
Open society, 35–42, 186–187
Opinion polls, 8, 68, 120, 168
Opinion Research Corporation, 94
Opportunity, 35, 77, 113, 117, 118, 150, 175, 185, 187, 188, 240
Orchestras, 234
Organization, 79, 108–110, 115, 119, 198
Orphans, 234
Orwell, George, 9, 63, 157
Osler, William, 266
Output, 118, 152, 177
    per man-hour paid, 113–117
    per man-hour worked, 113–117, 152, 178, 181
    per unit of labor and capital, 113, 178
"Oxford pledge," 44

"Pa–and–Ma" stores, 54
Pacific Northwest, 19
Pacifism, 28
Packard, Vance, 272
Pareto, Vilfredo, 209
Parks, 242
Part-time workers, 216
Passer, Harold C., 269
Passports, 58
Patents, 24, 266
Patriotism, 35, 109, 135
Pavlov, Ivan Petrovich, 265
Pay Board, 167, 171
Peace, 35, 40, 45–46, 69, 122–123, 212
Pearl Harbor, 46
Pencil sharpeners, electric, 248
Penicillin, 266
Pennsylvania, 36

Pensions, 237, 261, 263
Perkins, Frances, 4–5
Permanent stagnation, 226–227
Perseverance, 198
Personal freedom, 165
Personal income, 178, 181
Petroleum industry, 22–23
Pharmaceuticals, 21–22
Philanthropists, 40
Philosophers, 267
Phosphates, 20
Photography, 266
Physics, 95, 266
Pilgrims, 122
Pittsburgh, Pennsylvania, 52
Plastics, 266
Playwrights, 96
Plumbing, 140
Pluralism, 35
Poets, 29
Poland, 44
Polanyi, Michael, 198
Policemen, 252
Political action, 24
Political entrepreneurship, 247–258,
    274
Political institutions, 33, 184
Political parties, 96, 245–246
Political processes, 34, 177, 239–240
Political science, 64, 95, 209, 257
Political scientists, 89, 243–244
Political thought, 61
Politicians, 62, 157, 216, 264
Politics, 109, 181–182, 229, 255–257
Pollution, 17, 20
Population, 42, 79, 179, 184, 199, 220,
    260
Pornography, 69, 72
Post office, 234, 270
Potatoes, 249
Poverty, 176, 183, 242–243, 263
Poverty programs, 246–247, 251–252
Power, 63, 67, 68–70, 118–119, 191–196
Praed, William Mackworth, 275
Pragmatism, 237
Preachers, 40
Presidential election of 1936, 4
Pressure groups, 240, 244

Prestidigitation, 235
Prevarication, 234
Price(s), 116, 118, 178, 192, 198, 210
    administered, 124, 125
    control, 14, 19, 23, 56–57, 93, 121–122,
        133–138, 143, 145–152, 163–172, 193
    fixing, 153–154, 159
    flexibility, 121
    guidelines, 145–152
    history, 122–123
    level, 111, 118, 137, 188
    relative, 135–136, 141, 143
    retail, 211
    stability, 12, 14, 78, 80–81, 82, 121–
        126, 147, 149, 167, 185, 188
    statistics, 216
    system, 52, 54, 56, 107–110, 128–129,
        132,147, 195, 199–200
    wholesale, 122, 211
Price Commission, 166–167, 171
*Price Statistics of the Federal Govern-
    ment, The*, 272
Price Statistics Review Committee, 272
Priorities, 107
Prisons, 8
Private police, 255
Private property, 30
Private sector, 233–238
Producers, 198
Production, 112, 172, 192, 201, 210, 225
Production workers, 113
Productivity, 15, 30, 79, 111–119, 151,
    163, 167, 203–204, 210, 261
Professional standards, 72
Professions, 85
Professors, 29, 97, 99
Profit maximizing, 274
Profits, 15, 95–96, 149, 152, 167, 195, 201,
    222, 225, 248
Progress, 28, 35, 62, 69, 81, 176, 187, 188,
    193, 266
Propaganda, 233, 249
Proportional representation, 39
Propranolol, 22
Prosperity, 35, 69, 80, 119, 213, 218, 242
Proteins, 251
Prussia, 44
Pseudo-events, 258

Pseudo-facts, 91
Psychology, 209
Public debt, 170
Public education, 249
Public expenditures: *see* Government, expenditures
Public facilities, 78
Public interest, 118–119, 147–150, 152, 157, 165
Public interest law firms; *see* Champerty corporations
Public opinion, 28–31, 38–39, 61–62, 64, 70, 89, 96, 257, 258
Public policy, 27, 28
Public relations, 26, 27, 30, 96
Public Relations Society of America, 35*n*
Public Sector, 233–238, 240, 273
Public services, 183, 186, 188; *see also* Services
Public utility regulation, 93
Public works, 189–190
Publishing, 234
Puerto Ricans, 14
Pump-priming, 226
Purchasing power, 112, 130, 148, 149, 152, 154, 158, 161, 194

Quality, 213
Quality of life, 175, 185, 191
Queensbury, Marquis of, 36
Quotas, 9, 160

Race, 188, 215
Radio, 264, 266
Railroads, 20–21, 142, 239, 265
Rapacity, 9
Rationing, 129, 131–144, 148, 152, 154, 160
Raw materials, 147, 149, 155, 195
Razors, electric, 248
Real estate, 102
Real estate taxes, 226
Recall, 39
Recession, 17, 57, 81, 123–124, 188, 212, 218, 226, 228; *see also* Depression
Recession of 1960, 229
Reconstruction Finance Corporation, 4
Recreation, 78, 109, 175, 237, 242

Rees, Albert, 146, 270
Referendum, 39
Refrigerator cars, 142
Refrigerators, electric, 53
Regulation of business, 104
Regulations, 84
Regulatory commissions, 17, 98
Reich, Charles, 58–59
Reinvestment, 222
Relative costs, 99
Relative prices, 135–136, 141, 143
Religion, 5, 26, 32, 40, 78, 85, 109, 188, 263
Renters, 264
Reporter, 272
Reporting, 17, 21
Representative government, 185
Republican Party, 246
Research, 29, 30, 31, 84, 114–115, 198, 200, 201, 207
Resourcefulness, 128
Resources, 23, 78, 79, 90, 107, 108, 112, 115, 116, 119, 121, 137, 163, 189, 198, 221–222, 239, 256
Retail prices, 211
Retirement, 79, 213, 237
Retirement benefits, 19
Retraining, 219
Review of Economic Statistics, 129
Revolution, 184, 266
Revolutionary War, 45, 211, 241
Rhineland, 44, 66
Rifampin, 21
Riker, William H., 26–27, 33–34, 269
Risk, 21, 115, 187, 222
Roads, 115
Robber barons, 89
Robert Morris Associates, 94*n*
Roberts Wesleyan College, 60*n*
Rochester, New York, 103, 275
Rochester *Democrat and Chronicle*, 262*n*
Rochester *Times Union*, 172*n*
Rockefeller Foundation, 234
Rome, 192, 224
Roosevelt, Eleanor, 11
Roosevelt, Franklin Delano, 3–4, 8–10, 225–226

Roucek, Joseph S., 271
Rousseau, Jean-Jacques, 265
Rubber, 129
Rugs, 140
Rule of law, 5, 25, 32–34, 52, 57, 58, 77, 80, 187, 193
Russia, 5, 54, 55–56, 69, 176, 178–179, 182–183, 186, 191, 194–196, 220, 236, 261

Sacrifice, 134, 136
Safety, 17, 69
Salaried workers, 113
Salaries, 116, 118, 119
Sales agreements, 165
Sales tax, 138–144
Sampling error, 216
Samuelson, Paul, 93
Sanitation, 233
Sarajevo, 265
Saturday Review, 272
Saulnier, Raymond J., 270
Savage, Leonard J., 210
Saving, 30, 80, 121, 132, 137, 139, 143, 185, 186, 187, 205, 237, 239, 261
Scandinavia, 245–246
Scarcity, 127, 142, 198
Scarcity economics, 89
Schlesinger, Arthur, Jr., 102
Scholars, 29, 267
Scholarship, 31, 246
Schools, 64, 184, 233–234, 248–250, 253–255
Schoolteachers, 29, 96–97, 234, 255
Schwartz, Anna J., 102, 269
Science, 39, 78, 104, 190, 200, 201, 234, 273
Science, 21
Scientists, 267
Scitovsky, Tibor de, 129
Seasonal unemployment, 126
Seasonal variations, 147, 179, 216
Seat-belts, 69
Second World War, 17, 28, 45, 47, 62, 101, 122–124, 180, 211, 213, 227, 238–239, 242, 244, 269
Secretary of Commerce, 153, 157, 270
Secretary of the Treasury, 120
Securities, 137

Securities and Exchange Commission (SEC), 21, 93, 97
Securities regulation, 24
Security, 185
Selective Service, 47, 50
Self-employed workers, 113
Self-interest, 118
Semifinished products, 155
Senn, Milton J. E., 275
Serbia, 44
Service industries, 114, 116
Services, 135, 143, 177, 179, 183, 201, 227
Seventeenth century, 181, 186, 192, 193, 240
Sewers, 242
Sex, 215
Shafts, 266
Shanas, Ethel, 274
Shipping, 135, 201
Shoes, 160
Shortages, 160
Shultz, George, 30, 167, 270
Sierra Club, 5
Simons, Henry, 3, 30
Sirica, John, 65–66
Sixteenth century, 193
Skills, 114, 129, 185, 240
Slavery, 266
Slums, 234
Smith, Adam, 86
Smith, Alfred E., 4
Snakes, 12
Sobotka, Stephen, 203
Social forces, 182
Social interest, 121
Social justice: *see* Justice
Social philosophy, 60
Social progress: *see* Progress
Social sciences, 38
Social scientists, 89
Social Security, 4–5, 13, 33, 238, 245, 259–261
Social Security Administration, 275
Social Security Bulletin, 273
Social welfare: *see* Welfare
Socialism, 29, 40, 41, 88, 184, 193, 235, 240, 244
Society, 265, 267

Sociologists, 89
Sociology, 64, 95, 96, 209
Solar system, 86
Solomon, Ezra, 269
Solzhenitsyn, Alexander, 5
Sophocles, 275
South America, 8, 15, 50, 69, 170
Southern Regional Council, 275
Space vehicles, 201
Spain, 86
Spanish–American War, 211
Special interest groups, 5, 7, 64, 245
Special privilege, 64
Specialization, 222
Speculation, 81, 121, 188
Speeches, 178
Spiritual values, 26
Spying, 66
St. Augustine, 177
St. Paul, Minnesota, 255
Standard of living, 4, 78, 84, 112, 116,
    119, 132, 141, 187, 194, 218
Standardized average, 215–216
State governments, 220; see also Gov-
    ernment
Statistical biases, 159
Statisticians, 217
Statistics, 180, 209–217, 269
Steamships, 265
Steel, 52–54, 57–59, 160, 195
Stein, Herbert, 167, 270, 271
Stein, Robert, 272
Stereopticons, 177
Stevenson, Adlai, 96
Stigler, George J., 3, 30, 93, 97, 162, 269,
    274
Stock market, 52, 57, 102
Stockholders, 27–28, 103–104
Stone, Harlan F., 5
Strikes, 39, 155
Structure of the economy, 124
Styles, 28
Subsidies, 20–21, 189
Substitution, 142
Suburbs, 254
Suffrage, 244, 266
Sugar, 129, 131, 133, 135–136
Summerfield, Arthur E., 270

Supermarkets, 54–55
Supply, 148
Supreme Court, 57
Surgery, 266
Surreys, 177
Survey of Current Business, 157
Swarthmore College, 93

Tableware, 140
Tail fins, 184
Tariffs, 160, 226
Tastes, 28, 69, 132
Tax(es), 21, 84, 132, 136–144, 149, 163,
    188–189, 195, 207, 224, 256–257
    consumption, 136–138, 142
    cuts, 102–103
    deductions, 263
    economic growth and, 218–223
    excise, 23, 226, 259
    foreign, 263
    income, 5, 13, 58, 62, 137, 138, 144,
        223, 226, 228, 262–264
    laws, 5–6, 17, 263, 264
    rates, 228–229
    real estate, 102
    reduction, 222, 223
    reform, 189, 222–223
    sales, 138–144
    Social Security, 4–5, 13, 33, 238, 245,
        259–261
Tax Foundation, 30–31, 52n
Teachers, 29, 96–97, 234, 255
Teachers' salaries, 184
Technicians, 129
Technology, 4, 20, 78, 81, 98, 116, 119,
    183, 184, 190, 197–208, 239
Telegraph, 266
Telephones, 97–98, 234, 263, 266
Television, 27, 62, 168, 177, 264, 266
Tenants, 246
Textiles, 199
Thant, U, 11
Thermometers, 99
Thomas Jefferson Center for Studies in
    Political Economy, 30–31, 274
Thrift, 119
Timing, 177–180
Tires, 131, 137, 139, 142

Toasters, 137

Tobacco, 69, 72, 104

Tocqueville, Alexis de, 237, 238, 239, 273

Tolerance, 69

Toothbrushes, electric, 248

Torture, 66

Total output, 152

Tourist cabins, 141

Tractors, 178

Trademarks, 24

Traditions, 77

Transfer payments, 16

Transportation, 7, 42, 142, 195, 199, 237

Travel, 154

TraveLodge, 246

Trucks, 142

Truman, Harry S., 57, 62

Trust funds, 260, 261

Tullock, Gordon, 274

Twain, Mark, 11, 272–273

Twentieth century, 36, 39, 125, 170, 183, 209, 265, 266

Typewriters, 131

Unemployment, 12–13, 15, 16, 80, 188, 218, 226, 229, 239
   automation and, 197–208
   inflation and, 12, 13, 165, 166
   seasonal, 126
   statistics, 214–217, 269

Unemployment benefits, 13, 126, 226, 228

Uniformity, 238

Union leaders, 96

Union of Soviet Socialist Republics: see Russia

Unions, 42, 68, 85, 98, 100–101, 124–125, 146, 148, 171

United Nations, 129

United States Customs Service, 19

United States Steel Corporation, 103

United States Treasury, 213, 224, 263, 270

Universal national service, 47

Universities, 30, 64, 68, 85, 235

University of California, 19, 30–31

University of Chicago, 3, 11n, 30, 88, 91–92, 97, 107, 225, 250, 270, 272

University of Miami, 30–31

University of Minnesota, 87n, 91, 93, 252

University of Pennsylvania, 163n

University of Rochester, ix, 13, 21, 22, 26, 29, 30–31, 33, 36, 49, 50, 51, 68n, 71n, 170, 271

University of San Diego, 32n

University of Virginia, 30–31

Unmet social needs, 183–184

Unskilled labor, 98

Urban redevelopment, 184, 228, 242, 245

Urbanization, 4, 42, 220, 243

Utilities regulation, 97–98

Utility, 210

Vacations, 79, 113

Vacuum cleaners, 140

Valuation, 178–179

Value of money, 121

Vegetables, 132, 142

Vermont, 23

Versailles, Treaty of, 45, 66

Vietnam, 45, 50, 68, 157

Viner, Jacob, 30

Vitamins, 251

Voluntarism, 35

Voluntary armed forces, 48–51

von Neumann, John, 210

Voronov, Gennadi I., 56

Vote maximizing, 274

Wage(s), 15, 225
   automation and, 201–204, 207
   contracts, 171
   controls, 14, 19, 57, 59, 93, 145–152, 163–172, 193
   evaluation, 116–117
   guidelines, 59, 145–152
   minimum, 14, 98, 104, 245
   unions and, 124–125

Wald, Abraham, 210

Wall Street Journal, 8–9, 167

Wallace, George, 252

Walras, Leon, 209

Walwyn, Cyril, 275
War, 81, 211–212
War of 1812, 45
War on poverty, 247
Wardell, William, 21
Washington, George, 168
Washington Post, 65
Waste, 26, 133
Wastebaskets, electric, 248
Water, 115, 242, 243, 250, 251
Watergate, 60–67, 68
Waterloo, 44, 265
Waterways, 199
Wealth, 30
Weapons system, 201, 207
Webster's Dictionary, 12
Welfare, 23, 37, 85, 161, 176, 177, 190,
     226, 228, 234, 237, 240, 242–258,
     273
Welfare state, 8–10
Well-being, 26, 114

West, E. G., 253, 274, 276
Wheeler, Raymond, 275
Wholesale prices, 122, 211
Wholesale trade, 100
Willkie, Wendell, 45
Wireless: *see* Radio
Wisconsin, 218n
Witchcraft, 168
Witch-hunting, 125
Women, 17, 19
Women's suffrage, 39
Wood, Kenneth F., 19
Wool, 199
Work week, 181
Working conditions, 177
Working hours, 79
Wrestlers, 72

Yale University, 58
Yellowstone National Park, 234
Youth, 126